Contents

Preface

In the spring of 1984 (as described in the preceding volume of these diaries), James Lees-Milne – a sprightly seventy-five-year-old who thought nothing of walking ten miles in an afternoon and had brought out four books in the previous two years – was found to be suffering from prostate cancer. Two operations followed, and for a time he felt far from well. By the end of the year, however, he had made an excellent recovery; and apart from the usual problems which beset those who have passed their three-quarters century – diminishing eyesight, increasing deafness, and occasional fatigue and depression – he encountered no further serious health difficulties until cancer was again diagnosed early in 1988. The three years covered by this volume may therefore be regarded as a period of remission between his two illnesses, when he was delighted to be alive and did not yet feel that he had embarked on the last lap of life, even if his physical and mental energies were not quite what they had been.

His industry was indeed remarkable. On 1 November 1984, after two years of research, he began writing his biography of the Edwardian *éminence grise* Reginald, 2nd Viscount Esher (1852–1930); the first draft, amounting to some 300,000 words, was finished by 25 April 1985. Two years later, not without misgivings, he embarked on another biography involving extensive research – that of the Whig magnate and art collector, the 6th ('Bachelor') Duke of Devonshire (1790–1858). Between these two ambitious projects, he produced two books on architectural history – one on Venice, the other on Cotswold country houses. During these years he also revised a novel, brought out a fourth volume of diaries (covering 1948 and 1949), contributed to National Trust guidebooks, and wrote numerous articles, obituaries and reviews. At the same time, he kept up his diary; this shows that, apart from his writing (which in fact he mentions little), he continued to travel extensively, maintain a keen interest in art and literature, meet friends old and new – and assess the trends of the times, and human idiosyncrasy (including his own), with his usual sharp and sardonic eye.

When these diaries open in 1985, Jim and his wife Alvilde had been living for almost a decade at Essex House, Badminton, where she had created a garden in the French style. From there, Jim commuted most weekdays to Bath, where he wrote his books in his library (once William Beckford's) at 19 Lansdown Crescent. The events of 1984 had affected their domestic life at Badminton in two notable ways. In February, their irascible landlord, 'Master', 10th Duke of Beaufort, had died aged eighty-three, and their friends David and Caroline Somerset became the new Duke and Duchess. Whereas 'Master' had barely tolerated the Lees-Milnes (he once came near to evicting them after their whippets had chased a vixen), they were now treated as friends of the family and frequently entertained at 'the House'. And their marriage had become closer, as Alvilde cared for him devotedly during his illness; it had often been tempestuous in the past, but they came to cherish and depend on one another in old age.

I remained in close touch with Jim during this period and continued to enjoy his friendship, though he sometimes expressed concern about my mode of life, wondering in his first entry for 1987 whether he had 'done the right thing' in making me his literary executor. I like to think that I have edited this volume much as he would have himself. My thanks are due to those who helped me by commenting on the text, providing information for footnotes, or seeing the work through to publication, including David Burnett, Richard Davenport-Hines, Debo Devonshire, Patric Dickinson, Alexandra Erskine, Fred Grubb, John Harris, Selina Hastings, Bruce Hunter, John Kenworthy-Browne, R. B. McDowell, Grant McIntyre, Hugh Massingberd, Diana Mosley, Gail Pirkis, Stuart Preston, Liz Robinson, Nicholas Robinson, Francis Russell, John Saumarez Smith, Tony Scotland and Caroline Westmore

Michael Bloch
November 2002

. . . as holy and enchanted
As e'er beneath a waning moon was haunted
By woman wailing for her demon-lover . . .

Samuel Taylor Coleridge, *Kubla Khan*

1985

To London for the day to give lunch at Brooks's to Jack Rathbone,[*] recently ill in hospital and not seen for a year. He is not cheerful and has become forgetful, though as gushing as ever. Upstairs in the card room we met Pat Gibson,[†] who joined us. A man I have never got to know, who seems modest, clever without being intellectual, keen as mustard, filled with purpose. He is soon to retire as Chairman of the National Trust on reaching seventy, and told us there were three candidates to succeed him, including Simon Hornby[‡] and Marcus Worsley.[§] I have seen Chairmen come and go, and don't much care who gets it.[¶]

Friday, 11th January

Bruce Hunter[**] writes that Faber's have turned down my novel.[††] I had guessed this, as Charles Orwin[‡‡] never rang me after reading it over Xmas. I am furious, for even if it is not good, I know it is not bad, and better than many novels which are published – and certainly

---

[*] John Francis Warre Rathbone (1909–95); Secretary of National Trust, 1949–68.

[†] Richard Patrick Tallentyre Gibson (b. 1916); director of companies; cr. life peer as Baron Gibson, 1975; Chairman of N.T., 1977–86.

[‡] Chairman W. H. Smith plc, 1982–94 (b. 1934); member of N.T. Executive Committee, 1966–93; kt 1988.

[§] Sir Marcus Worsley, 5th Bt (b. 1925), of Hovingham Hall, Yorks; sometime MP (C) for Chelsea; Chairman of N.T. Properties Committee, 1980–90; Deputy Chairman of N.T., 1986–92.

[¶] There had in fact only been four chairmen since J. L.-M. had joined the N.T. in 1936 – 2nd Marquess of Zetland (1931–45), 28th Earl of Crawford (1945–65), 13th Earl of Antrim (1965–77) and Lord Gibson (1977–86). The new Chairman was to be Dame Jennifer Jenkins (1986–91).

[**] Canadian-born literary agent (b. 1941); joined London firm of David Higham in 1962 and became J.L.-M's agent following death of D.H. in 1979.

[††] Since 1980, J.L.-M. had been writing a novel about a German count, a prisoner in England during the First World War, who seduces first an English schoolboy, then the boy's mother. After it had been rejected by all mainstream publishers, a truncated version was published by J.L.-M's great-nephew Nicholas Robinson in 1990 as *The Fool of Love*.

[‡‡] Publisher (b. 1951) on staff of Faber & Faber, who had recently announced his intention of emigrating to Singapore (see *Holy Dread*, 13 November 1984).

better than the latest volume of my diary which they have lapped up, outbidding Chatto's.* I thought I had Faber's in the palm of my hand. I am now out for revenge, and may not let them have my diaries after all, which will infuriate them, as they rang me last Thursday saying they wanted to publish in October and needed my final corrections immediately. I shall show them. Or shall I?

Tuesday, 22nd January

We have been through ten days of snow and ice, mostly spent cleaning out the Bath flat for a change of tenant, the new one promising to be no better than the last.† On Sunday we struggled to lunch with Tony and Violet [Powell],‡ the Lees Mayalls§ the other guests. Enjoyable little party. Tony is reviewing a biography of Brett,¶ the artist daughter of Regy Esher. He claims that modernism in art began long before the Great War, as did the break-up of moral standards: we are mistaken in thinking that incomprehensible poetry and sculpture and revolting architecture, along with adultery and drug-taking, only arrived in the Twenties. The Symbolists were painting and *avant-garde* poets writing mumbo-jumbo in Edwardian times, while our parents were sleeping with their friends' wives and husbands. He instanced Diana Cooper's** set, the 'Corrupt Coterie'.

Thursday, 24th January

To London to deliver the revised typescript of *Midway on the Waves* to Faber's, my resolution to 'down' them having evaporated with my

---

* The new volume, entitled *Midway on the Waves*, covered the years 1948–49, including J. L.-M's courtship of his wife Alvilde. The previous three volumes had been published by Chatto & Windus, but J. L.-M. no longer felt loyalty to that firm following the recent retirement and death of its formidable chairman, his friend Norah Smallwood (1909–84).
† See entries for 23 May and 17 September 1987.
‡ Anthony Powell (1905–2000), novelist; m. 1934 Lady Violet Pakenham (1912–2002).
§ Sir Alexander Lees Mayall (1915–93); diplomatist; m. (2nd) Hon. Mary Ormsby-Gore, dau of 4th Baron Harlech.
¶ Hon. Dorothy Brett (1883–1977); lived in New Mexico, where she had gone with D. H. Lawrence, 1924.
** Lady Diana Manners (1892–1986); ostensibly dau. of 8th Duke of Rutland (though she believed her father to be Hon. Harry Cust); m. 1919 Alfred Duff Cooper (1890–1954), cr. Viscount Norwich 1953, diplomatist, Conservative politician and writer; mother of writer and broadcaster John Julius Norwich, 2nd Viscount (b. 1929; m. 1st Anne Clifford, 2nd Mary Philipps).

indignation. With A[lvilde]'s help I cut out all the lovey-dovey stuff of our courtship, having previously cut, on the advice of M[ichael Bloch],* what I had written about our differences and my grave doubts about the whole affair. The runt of the diary for 1949 is a poor thing. Bought socks and shirts at Harvie & Hudson sale, then to lunch with Ros[amond Lehmann].† Awful time on the tube, waiting hours for trains and being squashed to a jelly once inside. At Gloucester Road the lifts were not working and I had to walk up a winding stair-case laden with books and purchases, much fagged by the climb.

Ros as alert as ever but wracked with arthritis. She finds Virginia Woolf unreadable – woolly stuff, the characters hazy and unconvinc-ing – but Anita Brookner,‡ who dedicated her novel *Hôtel du Lac* to Ros, inspired. Ros is critical of contemporary novelists for neglecting form. That is why she so admires Brookner, who is an old-fashioned novelist – like me, I thought to myself, Faber's no doubt having rejected me on that score. Ros said to me, 'You are going to get an honour. I am seeing to it. You only missed it this time because there were too many candidates.' I assured her that I didn't want an honour – and I don't. Besides, it would only be an OBE, and what would that mean to me?§ On to tea with M., who was angelic.

Thursday, 31st January

Motored to Oxford, to a gathering of *DNB* contributors. A lecture, quite passable, delivered by a Mr Alan Bell¶ on the history of the *DNB*, founded in 1885 by Smith of Smith Elder, publishers, with Leslie Stephen** first editor, then Sidney Lee.†† As I wandered into the

---

* Friend (b. 1953) of J.L.-M. since 1979, and his designated literary executor; then writing books about Duke and Duchess of Windsor at the behest of their Paris lawyer, Maître Suzanne Blum (1898–1994).

† Rosamond Lehmann (1901–90); novelist, interested in psychical research; m. 1st 1923 (diss. 1928) Walter Runciman (later 2nd Viscount Runciman of Doxford), 2nd 1928 (diss. 1944) Wogan Philipps (later 2nd Baron Milford).

‡ Novelist (b. 1928), whose *Hôtel du Lac* won the Booker Prize in 1984.

§ J.L.-M. refused the CBE he was offered in the New Year's Honours of 1993.

¶ Librarian (b. 1942) of Rhodes House Library, Oxford, later of London Library.

** Sir Leslie Stephen (1832–1904); philsopher, journalist and alpinist; father of Virginia Woolf.

†† Sir Sidney Lee (1859–1926); edited *DNB* from 1891; official biographer of King Edward VII.

packed Sheldonian, I was hailed by Kenneth Rose[*] and Denis Rickett,[†] with whom I sat. I had trouble hearing, but discovered that by cupping my ears with my hands, I hear much better. Everything is amplified. Sat with one ear at a time thus covered till the arm ached, whereupon changed to the other ear. At six we moved to the Divinity School for wine and snacks. Kenneth said, I suppose you will now make a pig of yourself. Certainly, I replied, since I would have no dinner. Most of those present ancient dons, who looked, as I said to K., as if they would soon be in the *DNB* themselves. Dons *en masse* are unattractive, disdainful, too pleased with themselves by half. On leaving I was accosted by Hugo Brunner,[‡] that charming young man from Chatto's. Said he understood my reasons for leaving them, and admitted that he did not much care for his new boss, Ms Callil.[§]

Monday, 4th February

Delightful programme on Radio 4 tonight in praise of Ros, presented by some female critic, name forgotten. She, Anita Brookner, Marghanita Laski[¶] and other eminent women were loud in their praise, expressions like 'genius' and 'best novelist of the century' being bandied about. They said her great quality is an ability to make the ordinary woman share her experiences. Then Ros interjected like a girl of fourteen, modestly deprecating and explaining what her motives were. I felt proud of her.

Wednesday, 6th February

David and Caroline Beaufort[**] dined alone with us last night. I enjoy talking to David, who is a sensitive man underneath. Like John Evelyn,[††] he has days when he skulks along the streets hoping to be unobserved.

---

[*] Journalist and writer (b. 1924); 'Albany' of *Sunday Telegraph*.

[†] Sir Denis Rickett (b. 1907); Fellow of All Souls, Treasury official and banker; member of Brooks's.

[‡] Director (sometime Managing Director and Chairman) of Chatto & Windus, 1967–85 (b. 1935); High Sheriff of Oxfordshire, 1988–9.

[§] Carmen Callil (b. 1938), Australian-born Managing Director of Chatto & Windus.

[¶] Writer (1915–88), broadcaster and Arts Council member.

[**] David Somerset (b. 1928); art dealer; s. cousin, February 1984, as 11th Duke of Beaufort and owner of Badminton estate; m. 1st 1950 Lady Caroline Thynne (1928–1995), dau. of 6th Marquess of Bath, 2nd 2000 Miranda Morley.

[††] Government official and diarist (1620–1706).

He had an awful experience hunting last Saturday. The 'antis' were out in full strength. He had to protect Princess Anne who was out. 'They' made the most disgusting remarks about her, which David could not repeat even to us. He tried to reason with some of the less objectionable 'antis'. One of them said to him, 'You ought not to be riding that horse, it ought to go free.' D. explained that the horse was comfortably stabled, fed twice a day, groomed, and enjoyed hunting even more than he did; that if 'let free', it would be dead in a week. He says that if this concerted group obstruction persists he will have to close down the hunt altogether. They trample the wheat, which the hunters carefully avoid.

Went to London today, staying at Brooks's, so cosy, comfortable and central. Igor,* who is off to Australia, came to tea with me, and was much impressed by the old-fashionedness of the club. The boy is as dotty as ever but has become the squarest of the squares. I fear he will not like Australia and will be back in four months.

Thursday, 7th February

To Chagall Exhibition at Burlington House. Babyish, fanciful, good sense of colour, touching, simple, with messages. Interesting circus themes, violinists squatting on rooftops, the later ones almost Blakean. Early paintings dated 1907, latest ones 1984, so he must be nearly a hundred. Always a relief to escape from these large exhibitions.

Robert Rhodes James,† Rosebery's‡ biographer, lunched with me at Brooks's, after I had been trying to get hold of him for a year. Dry and uncommunicative. I couldn't get to grips with him, apart from the fact that he was difficult to hear with his low, soft voice. Unwilling to talk about Rosebery's homosexuality, and his relations with Drumlanrig who committed suicide.§ I did glean a few things –

---

* J.L.-M's step-grandson Igor Luke (b. 1965); o.s. of Hon. Clarissa (b. 1934; m. 1957 Michael Luke), dau. of A.L.-M. by her 1st marriage to 3rd Viscount Chaplin.
† Robert Vidal Rhodes James (1933–99, kt 1991); writer and MP (C) for Cambridge, 1976–87. His *Rosebery* (1963) was one of several books he wrote about bisexual men which barely mentioned this aspect of their lives, other subjects being Bob Boothby, Chips Channon and Anthony Eden.
‡ Archibald Primrose, 5th Earl of Rosebery (1847–1929); Liberal Prime Minister, 1894–5.
§ Francis Douglas, Viscount Drumlanrig (1868–94), eldest son of 9th Marquess of Queensberry and brother of Lord Alfred Douglas, died in a mysterious shooting accident on 18 October 1894. He had been Rosebery's private secretary, and there were rumours that he had taken his own life in the shadow of a suppressed homosexual scandal in which Rosebery was also implicated.

notably that Sir Robin Mackworth-Young[*] was perfectly maddening, kept R.J. waiting for months reading *Rosebery* and then objecting to the most trivial things. R.J. said Rosebery was disdainful of Esher[†] for snobbish reasons. Barnbougle, the castellated building next to Dalmeny to which Rosebery finally retreated, is crammed with indescribable treasures. Save for a few such as R.J., no one is admitted, for the family don't want it known what they possess. Rosebery was extremely religious. His recently discovered letters to his wife show his devotion to her, and his private diaries are full of religious perplexities while ignoring sex problems. The *Eton Boating Song* was played on his deathbed – a scratchy recording, I imagine, on an old phonograph. What Eton did to these men.

R.J. mentioned two others things. How he loathed James Pope-Hennessy.[‡] I said, 'You would not have loathed him had you known him in his twenties. You would have been bewitched.' And that Philip Ziegler's[§] life of Mountbatten[¶] is a diatribe; hasn't a good word to say of the subject and R.J. wonders what the family will make of it. M. confirms this; says Z. makes Mountbatten out to have been a fraud, a bad sailor, bad Viceroy, a muddle-head, and everything bad except a homosexual.

Sunday, 10th February

Few spectacles are more 'how'[**] than the upturned soles of communicants kneeling at the altar rails. Somehow the soles have a plaintive air, a mournful aspect. Down-at-heel, worn at the toes, they are sad, rather piteous objects not meant to be revealed in this way to the communicant waiting his turn and having a full view. It is taking an unfair advantage over one's neighbour, like seeing him in his bath through a window.

---

[*] Sir Robert ('Robin') Mackworth-Young (1920–2000); Royal Librarian and Assistant Keeper of Queen's Archives, 1958–85.

[†] J.L.-M's current biographical subject Reginald Brett, 2nd Viscount Esher (1852–1930), the shadowy figure who advised monarchs and prime ministers while refusing high office and leading a secret homosexual life. J.L.-M. had been engaged in research since the autumn of 1982, and had started writing the book on 1 November 1984.

[‡] Writer (1916–74); intimate friend of J.L.-M. in 1940s.

[§] Philip Ziegler (b. 1929); publisher and writer.

[¶] Louis, 1st Earl Mountbatten of Burma (1900–79); wartime commander, last Viceroy of India (1947), and *éminence grise* of Royal Family (to which he was connected as a great-grandson of Queen Victoria and uncle of Prince Philip); assassinated by the IRA.

[**] A word from the private language of Harold Nicolson and Vita Sackville-West, meaning pathetic.

I am reading a first-rate biography of Edmund Gosse.* This is the book I wanted to write, until dissuaded by Rupert H[art]-D[avis],† who said a very clever lady was already engaged. Certainly it is a work of scholarship. I could never have done it as well. She quotes from A. J. A. Symons'‡ memoirs: 'The great crime of my life was my marriage.' I felt this remark suited me. Alas, alas. But we are so deeply fond of one another now. Yet I can never make amends. I shall always be haunted by this.

Tuesday, 12th February

At breakfast, A. read from *The Times* an obituary of Peter Fleetwood Hesketh.§ I noticed a few days ago that he was eighty. This surprised me. All that thick, black hair, and yet the funny wizened little face, when he dined with me last year;¶ and I was rather maddened by him; and all those letters about august European families who were his friends; and Billa [Harrod]** saying how absolutely she hated him now. Yet he was my friend, an old friend, and I was happy staying with him at Hale in the old days and motoring with him to look at houses. Oh the hell of these departures, one after the other. Peter Chance†† had his memorial service yesterday, which I did not attend.

Saturday, 16th February

We lunched with the Michael Briggses.‡‡ Dear Isabel on top of the world over the success of the film of her novel *The Shooting Party*.

---

* Sir Edmund Gosse (1849–1928); poet, critic and essayist. The biography was Anne Thwaite's *Edmund Gosse: A Literary Landscape* (Secker & Warburg, 1984).

† Sir Rupert Hart-Davis (1907–99); publisher, editor, writer; Eton contemporary of J.L.-M.

‡ Bibliophile, writer, gastronome and dilletante (1900–41); founder of First Edition Club (1922) and author of *The Quest for Corvo* (1934).

§ Architect, writer and illustrator (1905–85); of the Manor House, Hale, Liverpool; Hon. District Rep. of N.T., 1947–68; m. 1940 Monica Assheton (d. 1982).

¶ See *Holy Dread*, 20 January 1983.

** Wilhelmine Cresswell (b. 1911); Norfolk conservationist; widow of Sir Roy Harrod (1900–79), Oxford economist and biographer of J. M. Keynes.

†† Ivan Oswald Chance (1910–84); Chairman of Christie's International, 1973–6; Chairman of N.T. Properties Committee, 1976–80.

‡‡ Michael Briggs, businessman and aesthete, later Chairman of Bath Preservation Trust, of Midford Castle near Bath; m. 1953 Isabel Colegate; her novel *The Shooting Party* (1980) had also been awarded the W. H. Smith Prize.

Queues a mile long, all the Hooray Harrys and Sloane Rangers pouring in. I asked her how the film came about. She said that the producer, unknown to her, happened to read the novel on a flight from New York to Heathrow or vice versa, and thought it had possibilities. Got in touch with a television company which agreed to go ahead if they could get a merchant bank to back it, which happened. Michael much put out because a large section of the retaining wall in front of Midford [Castle] has collapsed during the great frost and it will cost more than Isabel's earnings to put it back. Since it is part and parcel of the castellar design, put back it must be.

Monday, 17th February

We lunched with Jeremy Fry* at his converted warehouse at Freshford. I wouldn't want to live there myself, but admire Jeremy for not doing what we all do, namely buy olde-worlde houses and fill them with good taste olde-worlde furniture. He has little of the latter and much avant-garde stuff. His bathroom arrangements are superb, wonderful showers with strange sprouts and squirts, and a spare tub set up in the spare bedroom, which is round so that one does not know which end to sit in.

Thursday, 21st February

A. reminded me that all her possessions were destroyed in the war, stored in a warehouse which was totally burnt out. She lost everything she inherited from both her parents† – furniture, pictures, papers, letters, the lot. What she has now came from Princess Winnie‡ or was bought by herself. She has not got a single letter from her father or mother. This must be an unusual state of affairs and is indeed sad.

She also told me that Caroline [Beaufort] has changed since becoming a duchess, becoming sharper, too conscious of her dignity, and less intimate with A. One might expect this from a new duchess not born a lady, but from C. it is odd. I am not sure that the whole business of

---

* Inventor and businessman (b. 1924); m. 1955 (diss. 1967) Camilla Grinling.

† A.L.-M's father, Lieut.-Gen. Sir Tom Bridges, had died in 1939, her mother Janet (*née* Menzies) in 1937.

‡ Winaretta Singer (1865–1943), heiress to sewing machine fortune; m. (2nd) Prince Edmond de Polignac; patroness of artists and composers; close friend during her last years of A.L.-M., then married to the aspiring composer Anthony Chaplin (later 3rd Viscount).

dukes and lords ought not to be abolished. Why, [...]
C. be made President of the Bath Preservation T[...]
tence she knew nothing before receiving this [...]
others – J.L.-M. is one – who have spent their wor[...]
ing, are overlooked?

I rang Billa to ask her whether the Stone Hall [...]
painted. She had lunched there only three days [...] Sybil
Cholmondeley,* but had no idea. She said Peter Hesketh was operated on for prostate and found to be riddled. On his eightieth birthday in hospital he gave a tea party. Three days later he was dead. His
brother Roger lent over to kiss his face and said, 'I shall join you soon'.

Wednesday, 27th February

Looking at fellow passengers in the train to London yesterday, it
occurred to me that most people are caricatures – of themselves, I
suppose. If I were Osbert Lancaster† I could make a caricature of
everyone I passed. The young man with the smooth, unwrinkled face,
pot belly, furled umbrella, waddling when we reached Paddington.
Foxy woman, looking over her shoulder, in fear of the husband who
wasn't there.

Lunched with Charles Monteith‡ of Faber's at Garrick. Nice
learned man, Fellow of All Souls. Charles Orwin invited too. All his
colleagues at Faber's lament his departure for Singapore – even Miss
Goad,§ who asked if I knew his Chinese friend and hoped he would
be good to Charles. She said he would always get a job if he decided
to return for he was extremely well-qualified. At Faber's offices went
through typescript of *Midway on the Waves* to deal with libel queries –
but all those libelled, poor souls, are dead. Charles Monteith chuck-
led as he read out descriptions. Which reassures me that the text is
perhaps not quite so dull and idiotic as I feared.

To Renoir exhibition at the dreadful Hayward Gallery. All Renoir's

---

* Sybil Sassoon (1894–1989); m. 1913 Earl of Rocksavage, later 5th Marquess of
Cholmondeley (d. 1968); châtelaine of Houghton Hall, Norfolk.
† Sir Osbert Lancaster (1908–86); cartoonist, humorist, writer and dandy, of whom J.L.-
M., his Oxford contemporary, wrote a memoir in *Fourteen Friends*.; m. 1967 (as her 2nd
husband) Anne Scott-James (b. 1913), journalist and horticulturist.
‡ Publisher and Fellow of All Souls (1921–95); retired as Chairman of Faber & Faber in
1981, but remained as 'editorial consultant'.
§ J.L.-M's editor at Faber.

n look like sensual variations of his wife, with her sweet,
sant, pudding face and red cheeks. His children most touching,
with beseeching, questing eyes. After walking back across Charing
Cross Bridge I descended to the Embankment. Although it was only
5.30, down-and-outs were already spreading themselves out for the
night on filthy matresses, shabby coats and rugs. A shocking sight to
see in a western capital. Is it necessary?

Stayed the night at Brooks's and gave dinner to M., Richard Shone,*
charmer of all time, and Kenneth Rose. Kenneth was a little drunk.
Said three times to us, 'Were the Messels Jews? Not that I mean it in
a derogatory sense.' I replied, 'I should think not indeed.' M. gave me
an amused look. K. was very depreciatory of Harold [Nicolson]'s *King
George V.*† But he told me (did he invent it?) that Mr Patten,‡ Minister
of Health, whom he had met at the cocktail party he had just been
to, called me 'the best diarist of the century'.

As I came downstairs from my bedroom at Brooks's this morning,
an old boy very slowly descended in front of me, small and fragile, his
braces showing through the thin jacket of his bent back. I am always
revolted by the decrepitude of the old and thought, Oh God, I
suppose he is my age. Sat next to him at breakfast. Discovered he was
Sir James Marshall-Cornwall, aet. 98.§ Sidney, the nice breakfast
waiter, very sweet and kind to him, kept asking if he was all right. I
tackled him about Regy Esher. Rather deaf, but on being addressed
his puckered face became wreathed in smiles. So polite. No, he only
met him once. 'An amiable man. Sort of *éminence grise*, you know.'
One never gets more than this sort of observation. But what a dear
old boy. And nice to meet someone still alive who could be *my* father.

Sunday, 3rd March

Am much enjoying Rupert[Hart-Davis]'s third volume of Siegfried
Sassoon's¶ diaries, which I am reviewing for the *Standard*. I find myself

---

* Art historian (b. 1949); associate editor of *Burlington Magazine* from 1979.

† Kenneth Rose's own acclaimed biography of the King had appeared in 1983.

‡ John Patten, MP (b. 1945); Under-Secretary for Health and Social Security, 1983–85;
cr. life peer as Baron Patten, 1997; a traditionalist on right of Conservative Party.

§ General and military historian (1887–1985).

¶ First World War poet, sportsman, and author of six volumes of autobiography
(1886–1967).

identifying with him. He suffered from *Angst*, and was a romantic queer. Today, lunching at Coote Lygon's,[*] I asked Robert Heber-Percy if he remembered him, for Berners[†] comes into the diaries. Robert said, Yes, he was always complaining. Robert in a pitiable state, moving with a stick with utmost difficulty, helped by two persons. So active as he was. Very dirty, and I suppose has difficulty in washing himself. Nails as long as talons. Luncheon was help-yourself. I sat with Laura Marlborough[‡] who talked of Sir Arthur Bryant,[§] not kindly. Said he had a vile temper which decided her against marrying him, along with the fact that she did not want to become a nurse. I couldn't make out from her how the engagement announcement in the newspapers came about, whether it was a cruel joke on her part. She looks an absolute sight, like a monkey, with coal black eyes and a wizened mask. Wearing corduroy trousers and cap, not becoming. Also talked to Richard Brain[¶] who runs the theological section of *TLS*, being the only person on the staff who is a believer. And Richard Shone said that several people had praised my obituary of John Betjeman[**] in the *Burlington Magazine*.

At a buffet meal, A. always chooses and fetches for me what she knows I like to eat, for she says I am so slow and un-pushing that I am always last. Having produced the meat course she came up to where I was talking, seized the plate and returned with a chocolate mousse. She is away for the night, and I am missing her.

Sunday, 10th March

Derek Hill,[††] painting the Prince of Wales, rings to tell me that the P. feels the mantle of John Betjeman has fallen on his shoulders, and that

---

[*] Lady Dorothy Lygon (1912–2002), yst dau. of 7th Earl Beauchamp; m. 1985 (as his 2nd wife) Robert Heber Percy (1912–87) of Faringdon House, Oxfordshire.

[†] Gerald Tyrwhitt-Wilson, 14th Baron Berners (1883–1950); composer, aesthete and patron of Robert Heber Percy.

[‡] Laura Charteris (1915–1990); m. Jan. 1972 as her 4th husband John Spencer-Churchill, 10th Duke of Marlborough (d. March 1972).

[§] Sir Arthur Bryant (1899–1985), writer; m. 1st 1924–39 Sylvia Shakerley, 2nd 1941–76 Anne Brooke of Sarawak.

[¶] Editor (b. 1928), whom J.L.-M. knew through Harold Nicolson.

[**] Sir John Betjeman (1906–84); poet, broadcaster and writer on architecture; Poet Laureate, 1972–84.

[††] Landscape and portrait artist (1916–2000).

he must now protest against the demolition of worthy landmarks. D.
very full of this 'commission', which Pat Trevor-Roper[*] tells A. is
nothing of the kind. D. got to hear that a portrait he did years ago
was not liked by Prince Charles, and kept badgering him to let him
try and improve it. The P. also lamented to D. that he had not been
able to become proficient at one of the arts, music or painting. Poor
young man, how could he? D. makes a mistake being so touchy about
what people say about or do with his paintings. Would I ask Roddy
Thesiger what he has done with D's portrait of his brother Wilfred,[†]
etc., etc.?

Wednesday, 13th March

Alvilde being away in Amboise, 'doing' Mick Jagger's[‡] garden, I dined
on Sunday with the Beauforts in the Big House. They have not properly moved in and I was their first guest. David kept asking how I liked
what they had done, which is indeed in the best possible taste. He is
rather hypochondriacal, always fearing cancer. I refrained from telling
them what they may already know, that I had cancer last year, for fear
of alarming them. Merely said that I am an authority on the prostate
and when in doubt they should consult me. They are concerned about
their son Eddie,[§] who does not work, and whose child is permanently
dumped on them, which they rather love. I asked what Eddie's interests were. They said, being seen dining in expensive restaurants, like
an Evelyn Waugh[¶] character. While we were dining, the man from
Chubb came through on the telephone, and David greeted him with
his usual excellent manners. Amused me by saying there was nothing
to steal (I thought of the Canalettos and a few other treasures), but he
did not want to be spied on through the windows, etc. David
remarked that a colonel never loses his temper with a general, only
with a major or under. This arose from my mentioning the famous

---

[*] Opthalmic surgeon (b. 1916); co-tenant with Desmond Shawe-Taylor of Long Crichel,
Dorset.
[†] Explorer and travel writer (b. 1910); Eton contemporary of J.L.-M.
[‡] Michael Philip 'Mick' Jagger (b. 1943); singer and songwriter, co-founder of Rolling
Stones, 1962; he had commissioned A.L.-M. to create a garden at his French property
near Amboise, Indre-et-Loire.
[§] Lord Edward Somerset (b. 1958), yr s. of 11th Duke of Beaufort; m. 1982 Hon.
Caroline Davidson.
[¶] Novelist (1903–66).

occasion when Master* lost his temper with us after our dogs chased his vixen† – we being colonel to his general. But I could easily have lost my temper with him, given the chance.

Friday, 24th March

We came back from Rome yesterday.‡

Today we lunched with Woman§ at Caudle Green to meet Diana [Mosley],¶ she looking much better, and beautiful again, and cheerful. We talked of M's books. She said she liked M. immensely, but thought his *Operation Willi* much too long and detailed. I disagreed, saying I thought it a masterly exposition. She asked what he would be tackling after the Windsors. I said a biography of Ribbentrop.** She greatly disapproved of this, and thought she might even write to the widow and sons advising them not to see M. or give him access to papers. This is an example of her ruthless side. She said that when she and O[swald] M[osley] were living in Ireland after the war they had Ribbentrop's young sons to stay, wanting to learn English. They were charming, and suffered dreadfully from the treatment of their father. It was wicked to hang Ribbentrop, who had never been a criminal. The man who deserved hanging was Harold Macmillan†† for sentencing to death all those Poles and Russians who were sent back after the war.

Diana's granddaughter Catherine and husband, the Neidpaths,

---

* Henry Somerset, 10th Duke of Beaufort (1900–84); m. 1923 Lady Mary Cambridge (1897–1987), dau. of 1st Marquess of Cambridge (brother of Queen Mary, consort of King George V); leading figure of the hunting world, known as 'Master' from the age of eight, when he was given his own pack of harriers.

† See *Deep Romantic Chasm*, entry for 21 May 1979.

‡ To stay with A.L.-M's cousin, 2nd Baron Bridges, HM Ambassador in Rome 1983–87 (see entry for 20 August 1985).

§ Hon. Pamela Mitford, 2nd of Mitford sisters (1907–94); m. 1936 (as 2nd of his 6 wives) Professor Derek Jackson (d. 1982).

¶ Hon. Diana Mitford (b. 1910), with whom J.L.-M., a schoolfriend of her brother, had been in love aged eighteen; m. 1st 1928 Hon. Bryan Guinness (1905–92; later 2nd Baron Moyne), 2nd 1936 Sir Oswald Mosley, 6th Bt (1896–1980); resident in France.

** Joachim 'von' Ribbentrop (1893–1946); German importer of wines and spirits, ambassador to London 1936–8, and Foreign Minister 1938–45; hanged at Nuremberg. Michael Bloch's biography was published by Bantam Press in 1992 and reissued by Abacus in 2003.

†† Conservative politician (1894–1986); Prime Minister, 1957–63.

were lunching.* Charming and clever young couple. He wears an
Alfredo-style floppy tie in a bow with falling ends, very idiosyncratic.
Another young man staying with Pam, Justin something,† whom I
met with her a year ago, one of the handsomest boys I have ever seen.
Fair, blue eyes, wonderful brow and eyebrows, straight nose and chin,
an Adonis. Darling Woman beaming and providing delicious Lady
Redesdale food.

Wednesday, 27th March

Walking back to the car from shopping, I was stopped in The Circus
[in Bath] by a lady with a dog on a long lead. She asked, 'Can you tell
me where there is a doctor?' I said I really didn't know. Was it a particular doctor in these parts she wanted, or any doctor? Was it urgent?
'Oh, do come here,' she shouted at the dog, pulling at the lead, adding,
'I don't know what is the matter with her today, I really don't.' 'Is it a
vet you are wanting, Madam?' I asked politely. 'What's a vet?' she
asked. 'A dog's doctor,' I answered. 'No, of course not,' she said. 'A
doctor, mind.' I hesitated, then had a bright idea. 'I would ask, if I
were you, at that door with the large sign if they know of a doctor.
They are sure to. It's a nursing home.' 'A home? I don't want a home,'
she said, looking rather angry. 'Are you suggesting, my man, that I
ought to go into a home? Ha! I suppose you think I ought to go into
a mental home. Well, you can take that back. None of your cheek.' 'I
was only trying to help,' I said plaintively. 'Do you, or do you not,
know where there is a doctor?' she said again. 'I am very sorry,
Madam, I don't.' 'You wouldn't,' she said, and stumped off.

    Audrey‡ rang me up on Tuesday to say that Ted Robinson§ was
found dead in bed on Monday morning. He had been feeling iller and

---

* James Charteris, Lord Neidpath (b. 1948); eldest son and heir of 12th Earl of Wemyss;
owner of Stanway, Gloucestershire (see entry for 23 May 1987); m. 1st 1983 (diss. 1987)
Catherine, dau. of Hon. Jonathan Guinness (later 3rd Baron Moyne), 2nd 1995 Amanda
Feilding.
† This was a distant family connection of the Mitford sisters, whose uncle Rupert Mitford
had married Justin's widowed grandmother; Pamela was devoted to him as 'the son she
never had'.
‡ J.L.-M's sister (1905–90); m. 1st Hon. Matthew Arthur, 2nd Cecil ('Tony') Stevens.
§ Major Edwin Robinson of Moorwood House near Cirencester, husband of Audrey's
daughter Hon. Prudence ('Prue') Arthur (following whose death in 1976 he had remarried).

iller and Richard and Nick* were about to send him to a clinic. It is dreadful that this man who had money, land, nice possessions and three perfect sons should have been so miserable. Drink was the sole cause. Was it the War, I wonder? He was gallant, and won an MC. No fool. But for the past twenty years, impossible. Poor Prue's death of cancer nine years ago was not the cause. He drank while she was alive and drove her almost to distraction.

Saturday, 30th March

Went to Ted Robinson's funeral at Bagendon. The last time I was there was for Prue's. Dear little church packed and people standing in the churchyard. A narrow pew reserved for Audrey, Dale† and me. The three boys not surprised, but sad. We assembled for stand-up refreshments at Moorwood after. Ted's widow there, which surprised me, since she left him after just six months. And Margaret Glenarthur,‡ rather aged, but still handsome and charming, with daughter Victoria. I hope Ted's will contains no horrid surprises. On leaving the churchyard by the lynch-gate, Richard held me in an embrace, which touched me very much. His wife Linda a little darling, simple and sweet.

Wednesday, 3rd April

Derry [Moore]§ came to Bath and wasted my whole day photograph-ing the Library. I fear I was not very nice to him. Not his fault. I don't consider that photographers today can be called artists. He took about fifty snaps of me, one of which may be passable. This is not art. Cecil Beaton¶ used to take one studied photograph with an old Brownie.

---

* Great-nephews of J.L.-M., younger sons of Ted and Pru Robinson. Nicholas (b. 1955), was a publisher; Richard (b. 1957) worked in the City; their elder brother Henry (b. 1953; m. 1984 Susan Faulkner) was a farmer.
† Audrey's daughter by her 2nd marriage, Dale Stevens (b. 1944); m. 1964 James Sutton (b. 1940), mechanical engineer, yr s. of Sir Robert Sutton, 8th Bt.
‡ Margaret Howie, 2nd wife (m. 1939) of Hon. Matthew Arthur (who s. 1942 as 3rd Baron Glenarthur).
§ Dermot, Viscount Moore (b. 1937); photographer, son and heir of 11th Earl of Drogheda; m. (2nd) Alexandra Henderson.
¶ Sir Cecil Beaton (1904–80); artist, stage designer and photographer, whose *DNB* entry had recently been written by J.L.-M.

This evening, to my amazement, the *American Architectural Digest* rang me from Los Angeles to ask me to write yet another article – on Whistler and the Japanese influence, so far as I could gather. A different lady on the telephone. They are never the same. Always scrupulously polite. I hedged and asked for a letter explaining exactly what they want.

Thursday, 4th April

At breakfast this morning A. read from *The Times* that Alec Clifton-Taylor* was dead. A concise obituary, not sufficiently appreciative of his great knowledge of building materials, of the study of which he was a pioneer. I feel sad. Such a nice, good man, a funny, stuffy, moth-eaten creature, always on the crest of a wave. Why has he died after a short illness? Heart I guess, for he was too fat. *The Times* described him as looking like an old-fashioned squire, but he did not sound a gent with his 'heows' and 'neows'. He always liked me and treated me like a naughty schoolboy. Wrote me affectionate letters, yet was prudish and I suspect disapproved of my diaries. He adored Pevsner,† and was hurt when P. was uncivil to him when he made a long and difficult pilgrimage to see P. when dying. I liked him very much, though did not consider him one of my great friends. A decent and happy man, who worked hard and adored his work.

Eardley [Knollys]‡ lunched. Says he is all but cured. Asked how I felt. I said eternally tired. He said he did not feel tired at all.

Peggy§ told us this morning that the village scandal is X having left his wife to live with Y, the village harlot. It must be embarrassing for all concerned, his moving fifty yards to another house in the same street. I find myself a little shocked, yet ashamed of being shocked. I suppose I am a hypocrite, but I believe I would have been shocked with myself had I done the same thing.

---

* Writer and broadcaster on architectural subjects (1907–85).
† Sir Nikolaus Pevsner (1902–83); Professor of Fine Art at Cambridge (1949–55) and Oxford (1968–9); originator of *The Buildings of England* series of county guides.
‡ Painter; formerly on staff of N.T.; friend of J.L.-M. since 1941. Like J.L.-M., he had made a remarkable recovery from cancer in 1984.
§ The L.-Ms' daily help, Peggy Bird.

Saturday, 6th April

In a letter in today's *Times*, the correspondent tells that, shortly before Oscar Wilde's death, his father dreamt of meeting Wilde in the street, who said to him, 'In the whole of life there is nothing more boring than being dead except lunching with a schoolmaster.' Correspondent wants to know whether this is in fact known to have been said by Wilde.

Rushing in to Bath this morning to buy a ball wheel-barrow as an Easter present for A., I tripped in Green Street and fell flat on my face. For a moment I lay still, dazed. A charming middle-aged woman and son of about twenty-five knelt beside me. 'Are you hurt? No, that's good. Now don't get up in a hurry,' they said, pulling me to my feet. I thanked them profusely and proceeded on my way. My right trouser was slightly torn, right knee slightly skinned and my left hand bruised. How angelic people can be. I wish I had thanked them more. I felt foolish and was anxious to move away.

Charlie Morrison and his divine wife Rosalind Ward lunched.* He told me he was chairman of a House of Commons committee concerned with overpopulation. Thank God. I thought the Government didn't care. He says what China is doing is splendid and setting an example to the world. Some African states are deplorable, notably Kenya, which I knew already. Says the population of England is static. I said it would do well to decline. He agreed.

Wednesday, 10th April

Watched an hour-long television programme about Mick Jagger last night. I could not look at the flashbacks of his performances, the deafening row, obscenity of gesture and grimace. But when interviewed he was fascinating. He has beautiful hands with long expressive fingers. His face extremely mobile, eyes and eyebrows speaking as much as that ugly mouth. Most attractive profile. Was wearing a yellow sleeveless pullover, showing off bare, snake-like arms. I can understand the teenage adoration. He was modest about his achievements, but refused to give his views on life and politics. I think he is a sort of genius,

---

* Hon. Sir Charles Morrison (b. 1932), yr s. of 1st Baron Margadale; MP (C) for Devizes, 1964–92; m. (2nd) 1984 Rosalind Elizabeth Lygon (b. 1946), only grandchild of 7th Earl Beauchamp, formerly wife of Gerald Ward.

difficult to define. The vivacity, lack of self, projection of self into any part. When reciting Shakespeare he was excellent. He could have immense power for good, but I suppose *The Times* is right in saying that he is 'insufficiently conscious of his social responsibilities'.

I heard from Bruce today that Sidgwick & Jackson* have turned down my novel, damn them. The third rejection, after Chatto's and Faber's. He is now going to try Weidenfeld. I do not think it is a bad book, and am furious with the three refusers. I shall never do anything to oblige them, if requested, which is unlikely.

Tuesday, 16th April

I think I shall almost certainly die at night, in bed. Lately I have been suffering from nightmares, as I used to do when young. I wake, usually on my back, trying desperately to call out for help. In the dream I am usually in a fearful situation – such as descending a well, looking down upon a terrifying depth – and striving to call for help. Oh, if only Alvilde were there to pull me out, save me. When I finally manage to snap out, my heart is beating like a sledge-hammer. People will say, lucky Jim, he died peacefully in his sleep. Whereas Jim will have fought with a thousand demons and been vanquished. Shall I have an expression of agony on my face, or a deceptive one of angelic peace?

Caroline is in a dreadful state of anxiety about the Queen lunching at the House on Sunday [during the Badminton Three-Day Event]. Can't sleep for worrying. Princess Michael† not invited, as the Queen does not care for her, and was asked instead to the Saturday stand-up luncheon. Princess M. accepted and said, 'No doubt you are expecting me to the luncheon on Sunday too?' 'Oh yes, of course,' said C. When she told David he was furious. He refuses to have her on his left, the Queen being on his right. Is praying that Mary Beaufort‡ will decide to lunch so he can have her on his left, but Mary is unpredictable.

A. has returned from Amboise, where last night she dined with Mick Jagger in a restaurant. The young waitresses were so tongue-tied they could not utter. Jagger looked ghastly, wearing an awful old

---

* Publishers of J.L.-M's forthcoming biography of 2nd Viscount Esher.
† Baroness Marie-Christine von Reibnitz (b. 1945), m. (2nd) 1978 HRH Prince Michael of Kent (b. 1942).
‡ The Dowager Duchess had long been deranged, and was barely aware that her husband had died the previous year.

jersey like a towel. He was impatient that the trees she had planted had not yet grown up. 'You are not a gardener,' she said. Then she said, 'Why don't you, who have such influence upon the young, abandon all this violence in your performances?' He was bewildered. 'Is there violence?'

The cheap press is full of the wicked discovery that Princess Michael's father was a Nazi.* This is unfair, for she was only a child when the war was over, and her mother left her father because of his Nazism. And had Hitler taken control of this country, would not 90 per cent of the population have been Nazis? The recent behaviour of the miners,† their violence and brutality against those who did not join their strike, convinces me that the English are no better than the Germans, only more hypocritical.

Friday, 26th April

At last an obit. of dear old Ralph Dutton‡ who died a week ago. Such a sweet man. I shall always remember his deep-throated laugh of three *her-her-hers*, and much twinkling of those little pig eyes. He was exceptionally ugly, with a large nose. As a youth he must have been singularly unattractive physically, but always redeemed by his niceness and charm. Looked distinguished in old age. But suffered from blindness, had to be read to, could just walk round Eaton Square, wearing a shade over bespectacled eyes and carrying a stick in front of him. Must have suffered from his ugliness. No breath of his ever having had an affair of the heart. Yet he was, not admittedly in words, 'artistic'.§ All his intimate friends were so – Gerry Wellington¶ with whom he travelled, and Geoffrey Houghton-Brown,** with whom I last saw

---

* The press had revealed that Princess Michael's father, Gunther von Reibnitz, who had died in Mozambique in 1983 aged eighty-nine, had served in the SS: it was said he had been responsible for 'liquidating undesirables' in a region of wartime Czechoslovakia.
† The official strike of the National Union of Mineworkers had begun in March 1984 and lasted a year, resulting in victory for the Thatcher Government.
‡ Architectural historian and writer on gardening (1898–1985); squire of Hinton Ampner, Hampshire (see entry for 15 June 1987); s. cousin as 8th Baron Sherborne, 1982.
§ Euphemism for homosexual.
¶ Lord Gerald Wellesley (1885–1972); succeeded nephew 1943 as 7th Duke of Wellington; architect and architectural conservationist; m. 1914 Dorothy Ashton.
** Dilettante and painter (1903–93), in whose house in Thurloe Square, South Kensington J.L.-M. kept a flat from 1946 to 1961.

him when they lunched with us last year at the Grosvenor Hotel.* A correct, patrician sort of man, always full of anecdotes and very cultivated. One of the last Edwardians of that school. A kind of Moley Sargent.†

Today I have written to Lionel Esher‡ telling him I have got my book down on paper, about 600 pages from A to Z. A great deal of work in store, for it still has to be cast into readable prose. Besides, much cutting will be necessary. It is far too long I fear. Still, I have reached a milestone.

Tomorrow I join Eardley for our trip to Ravello.

Tuesday, 7th May

Got back from Ravello on Saturday, parting with Eardley at Victoria. I think he enjoyed it in spite of beastly weather. I think we renewed our old friendship. It has never been broken, or even bruised; but of late has declined. Although we got on very well, something was lacking. Some spark. He is so immersed in his love for Mattei§ that I feel he has little room for others. And I must confess that I too am more indifferent to those of my old friends who survive. I also sense in E. a slight disapproval, even mockery, of me. When he says, 'Who would have thought that *you* would be remembered for your books whereas poor Raymond,¶ that brilliant and erudite critic, will be forgotten', I am not taken in.

On Sunday A. and I motored to Hackwood [Hampshire] for luncheon. The future of this great house, so beautifully run and prettily arranged, a bower of orchids and rare plants, full of good furniture and

---

* See *Holy Dread*, 14 December 1984.
† Sir Orme Sargent (1884–1962); Permanent Under-Secretary for Foreign Affairs, 1946–49; friend of Harold Nicolson.
‡ Lionel Brett, 4th Viscount Esher (b. 1913); architect; m. 1935 Christian Pike. It was at his invitation that J.L.-M. had undertaken the biography of his grandfather, Reginald, 2nd Viscount (1852–1930). His father Oliver, 3rd Viscount (1881–1963), had been Chairman of Historic Buildings Committee of N.T., of which J.L.-M. was Secretary in the 1940s.
§ Mattei Radev (b. 1927), Bulgarian-born picture framer and gilder; close friend of Eardley Knollys since 1950s.
¶ Raymond Mortimer (1895–1980); literary reviewer and sometime lover of Harold Nicolson.

pictures, is in doubt. Seymour Camrose* is clearly not a well man. Drinks heavily, rarely appears before noon. However, on this occasion he was very charming. He is probably the only survivor of that Christ Church set I knew at Oxford, including Randolph,[†] Freddy Furneaux,[‡] Ava,[§] Bill Harcourt,[¶] the rich and well-born. We had a long talk about Randolph, by whose outrageous behaviour he was amused at the time, though it now makes him feel ashamed. Seymour moves with shuffling gait. If he has not had a stroke I guess he is on the verge of it. He took us round the garden after luncheon. Is very proud of the seventeenth-century layout, which he attributes to Le Nôtre,[**] as Le N. was sent by Louis XIV to visit Charles II at Winchester Palace, where the 1st Duke of Bolton who made the garden was in attendance on the English monarch. Remarkable amphitheatrical hemispheres cut in the grass are still discernible. S. wants to fell the huge sequoias planted a hundred years ago. I agreed they obliterate the terrace formation. Formerly there was a lake, which cast reflections as of diamonds twinkling in the morning sun. He does not know what will happen to Hackwood. His nephews don't want it.

Wednesday, 8th May

Since my return, I have refused invitations to give a talk to American undergraduates visiting Bath, to deliver the annual lecture of the National Art Collections Fund, and to deliver an address at a 'meeting' to be convened in memory of Alec Clifton-Taylor. Am surprised that Alec, considering his devotion to churches and cathedrals, was a non-believer. I find these secular memorial ceremonies depressing. Ivy Compton-Burnett's[††] was one such.

---

* John Seymour Berry, 2nd Viscount Camrose (1909–94); newspaper magnate; m. 1986 Hon. Joan Yarde-Buller, dau. of 3rd Baron Churston, formerly wife of Loel Guinness and Prince Aly Khan.

† Journalist and politician (1911–68); only son of Sir Winston Churchill.

‡ Viscount Furneaux was the courtesy title by which Frederick Smith (1907–75) was known before succeeding his father in 1932 as 2nd Earl of Birkenhead.

§ Basil Blackwood, 4th Marquess of Dufferin and Ava; politician and soldier, killed on active service in Burma, 1945; a contemporary of J.L.-M. at prep school, Eton and Oxford.

¶ William, 2nd Viscount Harcourt; banker (1908–79).

** André le Nôtre (1613–1700), landscape gardener to King Louis XIV; also designed gardens in England, including Kensington Gardens and St James's Park.

†† Novelist (1884–1969), about whom J.L.-M. wrote much in his 1940s diaries.

Thursday, 9th May

The blackthorn is still in bloom – very late this year like everything
else, owing to the bitter wind which poisons the sunshine. Strange
how blackthorn grows in straight, sharp, cruel spikes, not languishing
like the may or hawthorn, which are gentle and blowsy and lush. The
very name suggests the black frosts of winter.

Friday, 10th May

Victoria Glendinning and her husband Terence de Vere White* came
to tea on their way to the West. Both absolutely charming and interesting. Intellectuals both, yet modest and willing to put up with
middle-browness. He is the sort of Irishman who doesn't like Ireland.
We spoke of Billy Clonmore,[†] who used to pretend to his wife that
their gardener stole the drink. Billy drank himself to death.

Burnet[‡] to stay weekend. I am feeling well today because I took a
Dalmain pill last night. For a fortnight I have taken it on alternate
nights, feeling ghastly the morning after I haven't taken it. A. asked
me to explain how I feel. I think it is like being in a cement mixer,
going round and round with dizziness and headaches. I sleep for a
couple of hours at most, then doze, with continuous nightmares.

Francis Burne[§] said to A. that, just as good painters usually paint a
few bad pictures, so bad painters usually paint a few good ones. He
put Eardley in the latter category.

Monday, 13th May

The field in front of Lansdown Crescent [in Bath] now golden with
buttercups against fresh, emerald grass. A scattering of fat brown
sheep. Only one cuckoo heard this spring, singing in distant Allen

---

* Hon. Victoria Seebohm (b. 1937), writer and journalist; dau. of Baron Seebohm; m.
1st Professor Nigel Glendinning, 2nd 1982 Terence de Vere White (1912–94), solicitor,
writer and sometime literary editor of *Irish Times*; 3rd Kevin O'Sullivan.
† William Howard, Lord Clonmore (1902–78); pre-war social and literary figure who
converted to Roman Catholicism shortly before J.L.-M. did so in 1934; s. father as 8th
Earl of Wicklow, 1946.
‡ Burnet Pavitt (1908–2002); businessman and music lover, Trustee of Royal Opera
House; friend of J.L.-M. since 1948.
§ Of Wick Manor, Avon; friend of Eardley Knollys.

Grove. It is depressing that we should practically have eliminated this magical bird.

Tuesday, 21st May

My annual excursion with Alex Moulton[*] has come round again. We set off in pouring rain for the Lake District. Stopped at Lancaster, where I wanted to see the music room. We ate sandwiches in the car by the estuary, dismal country and a mess of industrial shacks. On to Brantwood, Coniston Water, where we were met by Olive Watson, my Lees cousin. A splendid situation which Ruskin so loved that he bought the cottage without seeing it, remembering the view. Many relics and drawings, but no Turners left. The mist lifted and the sun almost came out before we left. We stayed at the Farmer's Arms nearby and had Olive and her brother-in-law Derek White, rich bachelor and friend of Alex, to dine.

The next day after luncheon we called at Hawarden Castle [Flintshire] which we muffed last year.[†] Greeted at door by Sir William Gladstone,[‡] charming man of fifty, ex-schoolmaster with smiling clear face and twinkling eyes. Friendly and affable, showed us round. Mr Gladstone's Temple of Peace a large addition, with high, clumsily made bookshelves projecting into the room. Surprising to find a bust of Dizzy[§] facing his writing-table. A pile of axes, one presented by Bulgarians; also a basket of wooden chips. These were presented to worshippers who called at the estate office during his life, like the loaves and fishes. Fine mid-Georgian rooms within the Gothic castellar outside. Surprising.

Then on to Tremadoc over barren mountain passes. At Tan-yr-Allt, where Regy Esher stayed with Ainger his Eton housemaster, we were given tea by Madame Nagy, wife of Hungarian artist, who has lately inherited the house from her father, called Livingstone-Learmonth. Curious woman, Twenties-ish, affected like Pam Chichester used to be. I imagined she was my generation until she let fall she was fifty.

---

[*] Dr Alexander Moulton (b. 1920) of The Hall, Bradford-on-Avon, Wiltshire; engineer and inventor of Moulton bicycle and motor-car suspension; friend of J.L.-M. since 1943.
[†] See *Holy Dread*, 26 May 1984.
[‡] Sir William Gladstone, 7th Bt (b. 1925); great-great-grandson of Prime Minister; Headmaster of Lancing, 1961–69; Chief Scout of UK and Commonwealth, 1972–82.
[§] Benjamin Disraeli (1804–81; cr. Earl of Beaconsfield 1876); Victorian Prime Minister, rival of William Ewart Gladstone (1809–98).

Not a pretty house, but where Shelley imagined he saw an assailant and fired at his reflection in the window. We stayed at Portmeirion, very down-at-heel and scruffy. Is now a Trust and no one seems responsible. Poor Clough [Williams-Ellis]* must be turning in his grave – though he built the place of cardboard and only meant it to last fifty years. I do think the situation the most beautiful in the British Isles. In the morning I walked along the estuary watching the tide come in, and returned to the village by climbing up the cliff face through the woods.

Had a strange dream last night. Met Desmond [Parsons]† wearing a dressing gown loosely around the body, walking along a beach. He looking his most beautiful, but sombre, not teasing. 'Come to bed,' he said, putting his arm around me while we strolled. 'No, I can't,' I replied, and burst into tears. A similar dream to one I had about Tom [Mitford].‡ Something to do with my castration? Signifying absence of love, inability to consummate, or what?

I remarked to Alex that my only criticism of his lovely Rolls-Royce was the cumbersome size of the boot. 'Oh,' he answered, 'in the good old days the boot was much smaller, and the contours finer. You see, people who had a Rolls would have had the luggage sent on ahead.'

Monday, 27th May

M., who has been asked to lay a wreath on the Duke of Windsor's tomb at Frogmore on behalf of the widow,§ asked me what sort of wreath it should be. I suggested a large pincushion of white flowers with perhaps a touch of lilac. Many permissions to be obtained, from Keeper of the Royal Park, Queen's Private Secretary, etc., HM no doubt being consulted herself. I dare say it won't be popular.

---

* Welsh architect and conservationist (1883–1978), who in 1926 began construction of the fantasy village of Portmeirion and founded the Council for the Preservation of Rural England.
† Hon. Desmond Parsons (1910–37), brother of 6th Earl of Rosse, whom J.L.-M. loved at Eton.
‡ Hon. Thomas Mitford (1909–45), only brother of the Mitford sisters; J.L.-M's other Eton love.
§ The ex-King had died thirteen years earlier, on 28 May 1972. The Duchess of Windsor, living in a vegetative state in the Paris mansion where she and the Duke had spent the last twenty years of their married life, was approaching her eighty-ninth birthday (see entry for 1 May 1986).

For Whitsun we had Selina [Hastings]* staying. Adorable. She has finished her biography of Nancy [Mitford]† and sent copies to the four sisters, each of whom has shown the MS to one other person. So Selina is inundated with suggestions. We had long discussions as to which ones she should adopt. Interesting that Nancy in 1934 wrote a childish article in *Vanguard* supporting Fascism, which she mocked the same year in *Wigs on the Green*. Her letters to Palewski‡ are harrowing. Diana [Mosley] writes to me that Selina's book made her cry for days. Paddy Leigh Fermor§ joined us for lunch today, the most entertaining, exuberant man in the world.

Wednesday, 29th May

A. and I motored to Englefield Green [Berkshire] and back for the Droghedas'¶ Golden Wedding party. Not an enjoyable occasion, although many old friends present. Joan in new dress from Hardy Amies, looking very pretty. Garrett white-faced and anxious. We arrived together with Patricia Hambleden and David [Herbert],** the Donaldsons,†† Joan Aly Khan and Seymour Camrose, the latter plastered throughout and talking gibberish. We stood in the sun in the garden for an hour until the Queen Mother arrived, dressed in powder blue from head to toe and wearing an enormous amethyst. Accompanied by Martin Gilliat‡‡ who complained that she never tired and could stand for hours, though sometimes took pity on him. Fabia Drake§§ talked to

---

* Lady Selina Hastings (b. 1945), dau. of 15th Earl of Huntingdon; writer and journalist.
† Eldest of the Mitford sisters (1904–73), who lived in France after 1945; novelist and author of historical works; m. 1933 Hon. Peter Rodd.
‡ Colonel Gaston Palewski (1901–84), principal wartime aide of General de Gaulle; loved by Nancy Mitford; m. 1969 Violette de Talleyrand-Périgord.
§ Writer (b. 1915), living in Greece; m. 1968 Hon. Joan Eyres-Monsell.
¶ Garrett Moore, 11th Earl of Drogheda (1910–89); m. 1935 Joan Carr, pianist (d. 1989).
** Hon. David Herbert (1908–95), yr s. of 15th Earl of Pembroke; his sister Lady Patricia (1904–94; m. 1928 3rd Viscount Hambleden), Lady-in-Waiting to HM Queen Elizabeth the Queen Mother from 1937.
†† J.G.S. ('Jack') Donaldson (1907–98); Eton contemporary of J.L.-M.; cr. life peer as Baron Donaldson of Kingsbridge, 1967; Minister for the Arts, 1976–9; m. 1935 Frances ('Frankie') Lonsdale, writer.
‡‡ Lieut-Col. Sir Martin Gilliat (1913–93), Private Secretary to HM Queen Elizabeth the Queen Mother from 1965.
§§ Stage name of Ethel McGinchy (1904–90), actress known for her portrayal of *grandes dames* in films and television dramas; m. 1938 Judge Maxwell Turner (d. 1960).

me about Dick,* what a saint he had been. Her part in *Jewel in the Crown* has opened all theatrical doors to her; she must be eighty, but is now appearing in *A Room with a View*. I talked to Dadie [Rylands],† who said how anyone could enjoy such a party was beyond his comprehension. He looked very old, red and peeling. A gathering of geriatrics. I must say the Queen Mother looked superb. Planted a tree, or rather shovelled a handful of dry earth, like a pinch onto a coffin, over a cherry tree already planted. When she finally left, Garrett said in his cheeky way, 'Now, Ma'am, just give one of your famous waves.' Obediently she did so and we all sheepishly clapped. I did not have a word with her; was in a small hot room, wedged between Yvonne Hamilton‡ and Alexandra [Moore].

Sunday, 2nd June

Divine weather these past five days. I have been a bit of an intriguer, working on the Vicar§ to get the Grinling Gibbons figures restored to the 1st Duke's monument here, and pushing Simon Verity¶ to do Master's memorial.** The Veritys lunched today. Sweet couple. He is a leprechaun, she a no-nonsense country girl, and intelligent. He puckers his little face and thinks deeply before speaking. She says he sometimes works from five in the morning until nine in the evening, and then collapses for two days. His get-up the same as for last visit – a long, plum-coloured velvet redingote, with brass buttons on the tails, tweed breeches and thick woollen stockings, rather unsuitable for a boiling day. I suppose it is his only smart suit for visiting.

Friday, 7th June

Went to Christopher Gibbs's†† funeral at Lacock. Church quite full. Several old N.T. faces, agents who served under him. Address given

---

* J.L.-M's brother Richard Lees-Milne (1910–84), who had died in Cyprus the year before; m. 1936 Elaine Brigstocke (1911–96).
† George Rylands (1902–99); Shakespearean scholar and Fellow of King's College, Cambridge.
‡ Widow (*née* Pallavicino) of the publisher Hamish ('Jamie') Hamilton.
§ Revd Thomas Gibson (b. 1923); Vicar of Badminton, 1974–93.
¶ Memorial sculptor and letterer (b. 1945); commissioned, on J.L.-M's recommendation, to execute memorials to 6th Earl of Rosse and 10th Duke of Beaufort; m. 1970 Judith Mills.
** See *Holy Dread*, 27 November 1984.
†† Assistant Secretary of N.T., 1935–66.

by John Gaze,* quite well without notes. At the end the priest announced that the family would go to the committal at the cemetery and hoped the congregation would go to Porch House for tea. I did not avail myself of the invitation, for I find these post-obsequy parties an emotional strain. I wrote to poor Peggy Gibbs that I considered Christopher one of the sweetest-natured men I had known – a heart of gold, no rancour, generous, Christian, high standards. I remember when I first joined the N.T. nearly fifty years ago I laughed at his private-schoolmasterish manner, for he had little humour, and was meticulous, unimaginative, and the very opposite of the sophisticated sort of people I then consorted with. Indeed, I rather despised him in my beastly way. But in later years I came to admire him for his goodness and simplicity. I remember staying a night with him in 1936 at his parents' house, Goddards, by Lutyens, half-timber, inglenooks, but compact and well-built. Old father with a beard, retired in study, but smiling; gentle old mother, dowdy, grey scooped hair.

I had just returned to Badminton when the telephone rang. Obituaries editor of *The Times* to say John Sutro[†] was dying and asking if I would write obit. I said I knew nothing of his professional career, if it can be so called, in the film world, and that Harold Acton[‡] was his best friend. Then telephoned Anne Rosse,[§] thinking she would like to know, but she did not seem to take in what I said and produced a maddening gush of sentimentality. I think she must be getting crazed. She said that after Harold, I was her only support. This makes me dread H. dying before me. What a world of disintegration! How depressed I feel, with A. away, Eardley about to go to America for the idiotic exhibition of his boring paintings, and M. in London anxious because the American contract for his Windsor letters is still unsigned.

---

* Chief Agent of N.T., 1976–82, and author of posthumously-published (1988) history of the organisation, *Figures in a Landscape* (1922–87).

† Aesthete, film producer, *bon vivant* and founder of Oxford Railway Club (1916–85).

‡ Sir Harold Acton (1904–94); writer and aesthete; owner of Villa La Pietra, Florence.

§ Anne Messel (1902–92); m. 1st Ronald Armstrong-Jones, 2nd 1935 Michael Parsons, 6th Earl of Rosse.

Saturday, 8th June

David Freeman* took me to Cyfarthfa Castle [Merthyr Tydfil],† the home of the Crawshays. We drove up one of the parallel Welsh valleys, dotted with disused mines, but always the green hills in the background and within walking distance. These miners were never divorced from the open country as Londoners are. A nasty cloud of deadness prevails. David said the community spirit among these people is profound and rather frightening. They do not look beyond their valleys. Cyfarthfa is rather a brute of a building, constructed of that ugly, self-consciously chipped stone, the name of which escapes me. It is not one of Luger's best houses; Glanusk and Maeslough Castle are better. The back of the castle is now an extremely bad secondary school. The front rooms a museum, of everything and anything. An old-fashioned sort of museum, as they used to have before the War – two turnstiles within the entrance hall. Indifferent nineteenth-century paintings and silver presented by the Crawshays who left the place in 1909. No decorative features left; no sign of staircase. We asked to see the curator but were told he had not been there for three months. Great-grandfather Joseph Bailey‡ must have visited frequently. We tried to find Nantyglo where he lived before transferring himself to Glanusk, but failed.

Saturday, 15th June

Lady Glover, with whom Mrs Thatcher stays in Switzerland, and whom A. met on a Dendrologists' tour of the Orleans district last week, says that Mrs T. met her match in the Abbot of Einsiedeln. She was taken there for a meal. On introduction to the Abbot, she said in her bossy way, 'Mr Abbot, you must sit next to me at luncheon.' He replied, 'Madam, my place is at the head of the table with my monks.'

---

* Curator of Tredegar Park, Monmouthshire, 1979–97 (b. 1956).
† Built in 1824 by Richard Luger for William Crawshay II, owner of the Cyfarthfa ironworks, then the largest in Britain, and cousin of J. L.-M's great-grandfather Sir Joseph Bailey. See Margaret Stewart Taylor, *The Crawshays of Cyfarthfa Castle* (1967).
‡ Sir Joseph Bailey, 1st Bt (1783–1858); great-grandfather of J.L.-M. on mother's side; Welsh iron and railways tycoon; MP for Breconshire; cr. baronet 1852.

Sunday, 16th June

A high-spirited luncheon here, with the Nico Hendersons[*] and Patricia Hambleden and David Herbert. Nico a curiously ungainly and untidy man, always with shirt collar too big and overlapping his jacket, but extremely quick and clever. Treated me as an equal, rather nice of him. She a whimsy semi-Bohemian, wearing frilly high shirt-collar, scooped grey hair; likewise plain, with long, ungainly knitted dress, but bright. They talked amusingly of Garrett, but both get him wrong. They say he is arrogant, selfish and difficult. He is difficult, but they do not understand he is a tease, and expects to be teased back. His cheekiness is part of his charm. Patricia admitted that the Queen Mother was not pleased the other day to have her elbow raised by G. with the request that she should 'give her famous wave'. You can't take the slightest liberty with royals, which makes their presence a bore and a blight at social gatherings. They have never forgotten or forgiven G's farewell address from the stage of Covent Garden – we were present in the audience – when he told the Royal Family in their Box that he had put on the lightest music for their benefit and hoped in future they might patronise serious music rather more.[†] Yet the Q.M. says she is frightened of Garrett, fearing his tongue, no doubt. Nico has invented a portmanteau word which applies to people like Garrett and Derek Hill, who are keenly sensitive about their own feelings while treading on the toes of others. It is 'mimophant'. The mimosa is reputed to curl up when touched; the elephant – well!

Thursday, 20th June

Stopping to give the dogs a trot in Oakes Lane on my way to Bath this morning, I thought the fine drops of rain on the bent grass, their fluffy heads almost touching the ground, reminded me of a veil Mama used to wear when I was a child. My Mama wore all sorts of veils. I vividly remember the one she wore when going out hunting. Big spots like squashed flies. I must have been in bed with influenza, for she came into my bedroom wearing it. With her left hand, I think, she would hold up her trailing habit, for she rode side-saddle. Her habit had a

---

[*] Sir Nicholas Henderson, diplomatist (b. 1919); Ambassador to France (1975–9) and USA (1979–82); m. 1951 Mary Barber.
[†] See *Ancient as the Hills*, 19 July 1974.

primrose collar. Top hat on her pretty head and the veil off her face. What a picture of sweetness and romance, and how far away.

Saturday, 22nd June

We motor to lunch with Mary Keen[*] and husband in Berkshire. He nice, old forties, London business. Mary Keen charming, with her young face and greying hair; her grandmother Lady Howe[†] and Aunt Georgie[‡] were both beauties. The Philip Jebbs[§] present. Ate in large kitchen. Sat next to hostess and Margaret FitzHerbert,[¶] favourite daughter of Evelyn Waugh, detached from husband who is Minister in Rome. She already middle-aged, sad, tobacco-stained. Told me that when she submitted her admirable book on her grandfather, Aubrey Herbert,[**] the publishers made her cut it down by half. That is what I shall undoubtedly have to do with Regy. On leaving we followed the Jebbs to their house a mile away. An old house which his grandfather [Hilaire Belloc] lived in, and he inherited, and has altered in a good taste way. Exposed oak beams with proper stops, etc. A most delightful man. David [Beaufort] last night said he was the only saint he knew. We talked about life after death. He believes implicitly in eternal life. I said I was almost as frightened of eternity as of annihilation. 'Oh, but you must understand that the next world will be timeless.' I don't understand, but feel I would get more on this subject from him than from Ros. He and his wife are strict papists. I liked her more this time than last. She was born Hungerford Pollen, very Catholic. Their nice son, young and fair, walked to Rome from England in Belloc's footsteps and wrote articles about it. He said the long, straight

---

[*] Lady Mary Curzon (b. 1940), dau. of 6th Earl Howe; garden writer; m. 1962 Charles Keen (b. 1936), director of Barclays Bank.

[†] Mary Curzon; m. 1907 as 1st of his 3 wives her cousin Francis, Viscount Curzon, later 5th Earl Howe.

[‡] Lady Georgiana Curzon (1910–76), dau. of 5th Earl Howe; m. 1st 1935–43 H. R. A. Kidston, 2nd 1957 Colonel Lewis Starkey.

[§] Architect (1927–95), who restored 40 buildings for the Landmark Trust; m. 1955 Lucy Pollen.

[¶] Margaret Waugh (1942–86); m. 1962 Giles FitzHerbert.

[**] Hon. Aubrey Herbert (1880–1923); 2nd son of 4th Earl of Carnarvon; politician, diplomatist, traveller and secret agent. His daughter Laura m. 1937 Evelyn Waugh. His granddaughter's biography, *The Man who was Greenmantle*, had been published by John Murray in 1983.

motorways in France were a trial. A great accomplishment, almost as grand as Paddy [Leigh Fermor]'s swimming the Hellespont.

Saturday, 29th June

George Dix* staying. A generous friend who brings us each a present. I do the Cherry Orchard walk with dogs. It will soon be too hot. The umbelliferae have turned into the tall, straight, tough kind with large purple heads. No more delicate Queen Anne's lace. In the park each cow pat has a cluster of those brown mahogany flies which when disturbed buzz angrily and settle again. Where do they go when there are no pats? It reminds me of the old song, 'Where do flies go in winter time?' And something about 'Paree'.† I remember dear Chris Bailey‡ singing this song, aged ten, at the top of his voice during the Creed in church and being soundly rebuked by his irate father. This was in Thorpeness, *circa* 1920.

This evening we went to Sally [Westminster]'s§ party for Sue Ryder Homes. Very cold evening, and storm clouds. A sad band in the garden playing old Noel Coward and Cole Porter tunes. A striped marquee in which we ate. I was put between Lady Ryder¶ and Lucinda Prior-Palmer** that was. Latter a very beautiful girl, older version of Princess of Wales, modest and unassuming. I asked if she was ever frightened when confronted by those huge jumps at Badminton Horse Trials. She said she never had time to be frightened for herself, but was fearful of missing a jump and losing prestige. Said she had closest rapport with her horses. Sometimes she and a perfectly nice horse could not get on. Then the only thing to do was to part. Lady Ryder frail, good, dedicated, humourless, possibly a saint. She drank nothing, and ate only a

---

* Friend of J.L.-M. since 1945, at which time he was a US naval officer.
† *Where do Mosquitoes go in the Winter Time?* was written by Joseph McCarthy and Harry Tierney and first performed at the Ziegfeld Follies on Broadway in 1920.
‡ The four Bailey brothers – Dick (1908–69), Anthony (1910–41), Chris (1914–42) and Tim (1918–86) – were cousins of the Mitfords (their mother was Lady Redesdale's sister), living at Stow-in-the-Wold. J.L.-M. saw much of them as a boy (see entry for 26 March 1986); his favourite was Chris, killed in action in North Africa.
§ Sally Perry (1911–91); widow of Gerald Grosvenor, 4th Duke of Westminster.
¶ Founder (b. 1923) of Sue Ryder Foundation for Sick and Disabled; m. 1959 Group-Captain (later Sir) Leonard Cheshire, VC (1917–92); cr. Baroness Ryder of Warsaw, 1978.
** Eventing champion (b. 1953), six times winner of Badminton Three-Day Event; m. David Green.

small plate of strawberries without sugar or cream. Made a short appeal from a microphone. She told me that the godlessness of this country grieved her more than anything. Is horrified that those who know should dismiss the threats around us. The appalling infiltration of the Soviet into every phase of Western life. They say, Oh, the British common sense will never tolerate the worst at the hour of crisis. But she thinks the eleventh hour has already passed.

Monday, 1st July

To London for Alec Clifton-Taylor's memorial, in a panic because I had to give a reading from his book *The Pattern of English Building*. Told to arrive at St John's, Smith Square, at 2.30, when we speakers were made to rehearse our contributions, while piano tuner tuned grand piano and outside road drillers at work. Denis Moriarty,[*] nice fellow, organised the whole show. First speaker Jack Simmons[†] of Leicester University. Made good but dull address. Bad breath, like sardines. He spoke for ten minutes, then applause. Then my turn. Walked up to lectern on platform. Huge congregation. Did not look at faces. Read my piece not as well as I should have done. Then Joseph Cooper[‡] played Brahms. Then two more addresses and two more readings. Did not get away until 6.45. Too long. People came up to me and thanked me. Greatly relieved when it was over. The first hot day this year.

M. dined with me at Brooks's. Very agreeable. Just ourselves. He has finished his book based on the Windsor love letters, and stands to do well out of it. He told me that, at the time of her marriage [in June 1978], Princess Michael wrote to the Duchess of Windsor, saying that but for her 'brave example' she and Prince Michael would never have ventured, etc. The Duchess still just able to take this in at the time, and instructed that Princess M. was to be given some silver and jewellery.

Thursday, 4th July

Drove to Canons Ashby [Northamptonshire]. Took me two hours. Had to take the chair at an Arts Panel meeting after we had spent the

---

[*] BBC Producer of documentaries on art and architecture, including Clifton-Taylor's series.

[†] Professor of History, University of Leicester, 1947–75; author of books on railways (1915–2000).

[‡] Pianist and broadcaster (1912–2001).

morning going round the house commenting on a paper written by Gervase Jackson-Stops.* Questions were so many and staff members so numerous that the meeting became a shambles. Charming though the staff are – I like them all, though only remember the names of about 10 per cent – they somehow have the upper hand, like the trade unions, and turn the Panel into a rubber stamp. They make jokes which I cannot hear, and discuss amongst themselves what ought to be left to the Panel, who remain mute. As I told Dudley Dodd,† I doubt whether the Panel serves any useful purpose at present.

Went on to Weston to tea with dear Sachie Sitwell.‡ He is eighty-seven, and repeats himself. According to the saint Gertrude, who has been with him for sixty years, his children are very impatient and bored with him. It is dreadful to think of.

Sunday, 7th July

Weekend at Chatsworth. Lovely, and as E. Winn§ says, one wonders if each visit will not be the last. I like E. Winn, a brassy rocking-horse with her head held high, showing her scarlet nostrils. A performer like most mimics, but a good one, who can instantly imitate a person's conversation as well as intonation. The other performer was Arthur Marshall,¶ a charming and sympathetic man. Looks very old, though two years younger than me, and shuffles. Lives with schoolmaster friend in Devon. Wears old school tie and is hearty and straightforward. Andrew** looking older but delightful, a generous man with a sense of duty and a large heart. I walked with him in the garden and talked of national affairs. The Philip Jebbs staying. She is quiet and profound – said this was her only visit away this year, she didn't want another.

---

* Architectural historian and adviser to N.T. (1947–95).
† Deputy Historic Buildings Secretary of N.T. (b. 1947).
‡ Sir Sacheverell Sitwell, 6th Bt (1897–1988); poet and writer; m. 1925 Georgia Doble (d. 1980).
§ Dau. of Hon. Reginald Winn and his wife Alice Perkins, sister of Nancy (Tree) Lancaster (whose son Michael m. Lady Anne Cavendish, sister of 11th Duke of Devonshire); professional decorator and renowned mimic.
¶ Humorous writer, playwright, broadcaster and critic (1910–89).
** Andrew Cavendish, 11th Duke of Devonshire (b. 1920); m. 1941 Hon. Deborah Mitford (b. 1920).

Tuesday, 9th July

Have spent two days correcting page proofs of *Midway on the Waves*. Almost lost my nerve. Several offensive entries which I didn't notice in type. Endeavoured to change without altering number of words. Difficult. I have also been asked to write a piece about Lady Berwick for the new Attingham Park guidebook, and one about Baron Ash for the Packwood guidebook.*

Wednesday, 10th July

With A. to London by train, I taking my proofs and she the manuscript contributions for her book.† Then on to Lewes to stay the night with the Julian Fanes‡ in their pretty, slightly twee little house in the town, like an old antique shop. They are a sweet pair and Julian delightful to talk to, if slightly pernickety and bland. Like me he has to write to rule, and wonders what it is all about. But they were angelic to us. Took us to the Box at Glyndebourne to see Britten's *Albert Herring*, which I was not looking forward to. It turned out to be a lovely performance, far beyond my expectations. Splendid sets, and frightfully funny. Music of course rather constipated but if one heard it three times one might detect tunes.

On return, lunched at Brooks's with Martyn Beckett.§ Charming man. We spoke of Regy. I told him about Regy's relations with Maurice,¶ which surprised him. He lamented that Lionel** did not

---

* J.L.-M. had been much involved in the N.T's acquisition of these properties in the 1940s. Attingham Park, Shropshire came by bequest on the death in 1947 of the 8th Lord Berwick, largely owing to the initiative of his remarkable wife (Teresa, *née* Hulton), who continued to live there until 1972. Packwood House, Warwickshire was donated in 1941 by Graham Baron Ash, whose father had bought it in 1905; a sixteenth-century house 'mutilated' by its twentieth-century owners, it would probably have been refused had it been offered after the war, and Ash proved a difficult and interfering donor.

† See entry for 17 September 1986.

‡ Hon. Julian Fane (b. 1927); yr son of 14th Earl of Westmorland (and of J.L.-M's close friend Diana, Countess of W., *née* Lister, d. 1983); writer; m. 1976 Gillian Swire.

§ Sir Martyn Beckett, 2nd Bt (1918–2001); architect; m. 1941 Priscilla, dau. of 3rd Viscount Esher.

¶ As J.L.-M. was to describe in his biography, Reginald Esher had an unusual relationship with his younger son Maurice Brett (1882–1934), whom he bombarded with love letters, and whose marriage (1911) to the actress Zena Dare he personally arranged.

** See note to 26 April 1985.

have his father's humour. His father always lamented that he did not have Lionel's brain.

Monday, 15th July

Ian [McCallum] believes Rory [Cameron] is dying of Aids.* This has been denied; but there is no reason, alas, why it should not be so. M. says many more people than one would suspect have died of this ghastly thing, or will die within the next twelve months. I hope I am immune. But at night, while tucked up in bed, I sometimes feel I am dying from sheer weakness. Always at night, when relaxed, not in the daytime.

At 4.30 today I listened to the first instalment of *Another Self*† on Radio 4, with mixed feelings. The reader, Peter Howell, has a good voice, unbedint,‡ to which one can take no exception – though, as M. remarked, he sometimes puts the emphasis on the wrong word, eliminating irony. He has edited the passages very well. I was nevertheless surprised by certain things which I had forgotten. Each reading lasts twenty minutes, quite a long stretch. I dare say the remaining eight will cause me embarrassment. Before he came on, there was an interesting talk by Fritz Spiegl§ about music. He put on a record of the last of the papal castrati singing from Tosti's *Goodbye* in 1903, warning that it would sound weird. It was indeed haunting and terrifying, like a werewolf.

Tuesday, 16th July

A girl from the BBC, Sandra Jones, came from London to interview me about a new documentary series, *Now the War is Over.* Stayed an hour. Had neither tape recorder nor notebook. Doubt whether she will remember much of our conversation. Wanted to know from me

---

* Ian McCallum (1919–87), curator of American Museum at Claverton near Bath; Roderick Cameron (1914–85), garden designer and travel writer living in South of France. Both men died of Aids.

† J.L.-M's autobiographical novel (often misconstrued as a straightforward book of memoirs), published by Chatto & Windus in 1970 and reissued as a Faber paperback in 1984.

‡ 'Bedint' meant 'common' in the private language of Harold Nicolson and Vita Sackville-West.

§ Austrian-born flautist, composer, music critic and editor (1926–2003).

how the landed gentry reacted to Attlee's government. I told her the South Bank exhibition elevated our spirits – the prettiness, the jollity, the lights. We imagined at the time that contemporary architecture would take a turn for the better. I said a bloodless revolution had taken place in my time. The gentry feared they would be ousted by the barbaric proletariat, without taste or a sense of historical continuity. True in some ways, but not in others, for the barbarians have often proved themselves more enlightened than the philistine, sport-loving gentry. But I stressed the worst things to my mind – the spread of Communism throughout Europe (did our defeat of Hitler bring betterment?), and the ruination of the face of the continent, especially England and Italy, by wires, concrete, bad building development, motorways, etc.

Friday, 19th July

Daphne Moore* asked two nights ago if we knew anyone who would take on Mary Beaufort's parrot, now that Mary was bedridden and would never get downstairs again. She said Mary once told her that her father, Lord Cambridge, owned a parrot which had belonged to King George III, his great-grandfather. So there is someone just alive today who remembers a creature owned by George III.†

We are desperately sad about Rory. Daniele Waterpark,‡ who has just returned from Ménèrbes, rang A. to say there is no question he has got Aids, and is dying. Rory, so fastidious, so clean, scented, dandified, so hating squalor, such a health maniac. It is very tragic. Last night we also learnt some other terrible news, a calamity that has befallen one of A's grandchildren, which she has sworn me not to reveal even to my diary. It makes my blood boil that this child should have to submit to such a thing, that such monsters roam the streets.

Sunday, 21st July

The Times consistently refuses to publish my letters, and then months later I see it has published others along the same lines as my rejected

---

* Eccentric resident of Badminton; protégée of Mary, Duchess of Beaufort.
† This is quite possible: parrots have been known to live for more than eighty years. King George III died in 1820; Prince Adolphus of Teck, later 1st Marquess of Cambridge, was born in 1868; his daughter Mary, future Duchess of Beaufort, was born in 1897.
‡ Daniele Girche; m. 1951 Caryll Cavendish, 7th Baron Waterpark (b. 1926; half-brother of Rory Cameron).

ones. For instance, about six months ago, when the public was urged to send money for famine relief in Ethiopia, I wrote suggesting that every package of food should include a packet of The Pill. This was considered in bad taste. Now I read in several papers, including *The Times*, that food packages are a mere drop in the ocean, and that the only solution to the problem is a reduction of the black population in African countries, where trees are cut down for firewood, nature is despoiled for food, and deserts are increasing with the increase of people. What fools people are, and what damage left-wing sentimentalists are inflicting upon the world.

Tuesday, 23rd July

We dine with the Beits* in The Boltons. Black ties, all very correct and stuffy. Yet nice guests, Lord and Lady Northbourne,[†] Lord and Lady Hood.[‡] Lady Hood a daughter of George Lyttelton so knows Rupert [Hart-Davis] well.[§] Said that many people write to R. thanking him for his Letters, especially mention of worthwhile books to read. Old ladies knit him jerseys. Dear Rupert wonderfully cosseted by June, to whom, Lady H. complained, R. gave no compliment in his valedictory letter to Lyttelton in the last volume. Lord Northbourne told me that his uncle Bobbie James, the great gardener,[¶] always had his own sheets at Brooks's, which he left there and the valet washed for him. He couldn't sleep in sheets other people had bedded in.

Wednesday, 24th July

Delivered to Sheila Birkenhead's** house the little marble bust of Shelley which I bought in 1958 at the Cothelstone House sale of the Esdailes in

---

* Sir Alfred Beit, 2nd Bt (1903–94), art collector and sometime Conservative MP; m. 1939 Clementine Mitford.
† Christopher James, 5th Baron Northbourne (b. 1926); m. 1959 Marie-Synge Claudel.
‡ Alexander, 7th Viscount Hood (1914–99); m. 1957 Diana Lyttelton.
§ Hart-Davis had edited his correspondence with his old Eton housemaster Hon. George Lyttelton (1883–1962), published by John Murray in six volumes, 1978–84.
¶ Hon. Robert James (1873–1960), yr s. of 2nd Baron Northbourne, gardened at St Nicholas, Richmond, Yorkshire with his 2nd wife Lady Serena (*née* Lumley, dau. of 10th Earl of Scarbrough; d. 2000, aged 99).
** Hon. Sheila Berry (1913–92), dau. of 1st Viscount Camrose; m. 1935 Frederick Smith, 2nd Earl of Birkenhead (1907–75); Chairman of Keats–Shelley Association from 1977.

Somerset, on the death of Will Esdaile, Shelley's great-grandson. I am rather sorry to get rid of it but promised that it should go to Keats's House in Rome. Could it possibly have belonged to Shelley's daughter Ianthe? Or her son, who was a friend of Dowden,[*] S's biographer? Certainly not acquired by Will Esdaile, who hated Shelley.[†]

Then to visit poor Rory Cameron in St Mary's Hospital, Paddington. In an extremely bad way. Unable to move hand or foot. Lying on back, propped by pillows, bare, wasted arms over the sheets, pallid white hands. Face razor thin, hollow temples, and that taut, stretched muscle of the neck that betrays a dying man. Eyes staring ahead, expressionless and unnaturally brilliant. Talks in a whisper. Says he likes visitors, but shows no interest or emotion. Dreadful visit for I could not communicate. He does not read, has no radio, just gazes into space. No appetite. I give him about a month. Went on to see M. and talked to him about this appalling scourge.

The librarian of Brooks's, Piers Dixon,[‡] nice fellow, said I was the Club's favourite author. My books are borrowed more often than any others taken out by members.

Saturday, 27th July

Motored A. to Heathrow whence she flew to Morocco to stay with David Herbert, for sun and bathing and a holiday from me. I was unable to leave the car, and had such a 'how' little back view of her pulling her heavy suitcase by herself towards the ramp and out of sight. I wondered, as I always do when we part nowadays, whether I would ever see her again, and if I did not, whether this fleeting vision would reduce me to tears for the rest of my days.

Monday, 29th July

Drove to lunch with darling Pam [Jackson]. Never do I remember the lane from Tetbury to Caudle Green more beautiful. Verges massed

---

[*] Edward Dowden, *The Life of Percy Bysshe Shelley* (1886).

[†] J.L.-M. had visited Will Esdaile at Cothelstone in June 1953, when he succeeded in persuading him to allow the copying of a notebook containing unpublished poems by Shelley (see *A Mingled Measure*). He told J.L.-M.: 'You must understand that until the last few years Shelley's name has never been mentioned in my family. He treated my great-grandmother abominably.'

[‡] MP (C) for Truro, 1970–4 (b. 1928).

with purple fireweed, blue geranium, evening primroses in intoxicating profusion. The Ian Curteises* said it was owing to Mrs Thatcher starving the county councils of funds, so that they have neither poisoned them with weedkiller nor cut them with machines. Hurrah for Mrs T. Curteis middle-aged and bearded, works for BBC. Is writing script for a film about Cecil Rhodes. Very flattering about my writing. Brought *Ancestral Voices* for me to sign. Says my Harold [Nicolson] the best biography ever written.

Then continued to Winchcombe to see that strange Noel Saunders, who is leaving the Evesham firm of solicitors founded by his father, still alive at ninety-three. I decided to seek another solicitor in Bath, finding none of his ex-partners sympathetic. So I shall write to tell them that I shall no longer be their client, reminding them, for Noel's sake, that my father, brother and I have patronised them for some seventy years. Noel has been so kind, and his advice has always been good, and his sympathy and understanding most valuable.

A tiresome consequence of my becoming a eunuch last year† is that all my trousers have become too short in the leg, owing to my unfortunate obesity. Also the pubic hair under my arms has diminished, which I don't mind. No change in the pitch of my voice that I am aware of. In all other respects a marked improvement. Total disinterest in sex, and enhanced detachment; and where I do love, viz. A. and M., I do so with greater purity of motive and enhanced intensity.

Saturday, 3rd August

Colin McMordie‡ is dead. Am haunted by the thought of that beautiful Adonis, so full of the joys of life, and so exquisite, lying like the figure of Shelley by Onslow in University College, Oxford. Poor Colin.

Lunched today with Angela Yorke§ at Forthampton. She lives in a

---

* Dramatist and scriptwriter, on staff of BBC (b. 1935); m. (2nd) 1985 the novelist Joanna Trollope.

† As described in *Holy Dread*, J.L.-M's testicles were removed in April 1984 in connection with the prostate cancer from which he had been found to be suffering.

‡ Expert on early nineteenth-century painting, living in Paris (1948–85); friend of J.L.-M. since 1973, at which time he was an Oxford postgraduate student.

§ Angela Duncan (d. 1988); m. 1937 Gerald Yorke (1901–83) of Forthampton Court, Gloucestershire, er bro. of J.L.-M's friend Henry Yorke (1905–73), who wrote novels as Henry Green.

small wing, the Webb part of the house, her son Johnnie* and wife now inhabiting the greater part of the Court. An enjoyable gathering, rather to my surprise. Deric Holland-Martin's widow Rosamund,[†] charming, and Lady Kleinwort,[‡] late of Sezincote, nice old woman who looks frail and seems to be losing her memory. I saw she had difficulty keeping up with her neighbour on the other side, Cecil Gould,[§] late of National Gallery. He, once so good-looking in the way footmen are handsome, now portly and plain. Very pleased with himself, and full of malice about other museum directors, K. Clark[¶] and John Pope-Hennessy.[**] The other male, Francis Egerton,[††] looks like a blind newt. The moment one thinks one is being a success at a party, one should beware. It usually means that one is being a bore or a show-off, or making a fool of oneself.

Sunday, 4th August

Lunched today with the Lloyd Georges[‡‡] in a posh sort of house which the grandfather would not have liked. Owen L.G. must be rich. Works in the City, I think. She I hazarded to be bedint until she told me how well-born she was. Friendly woman. When I asked him about the extraordinary fact of his grandfather sleeping with his secretary during his premiership and the bloodiest war in history, he said that those who knew of it at the time never spoke of it. When L.G. married Frances Stevenson, someone mentioned that he was 'glad the old man was making an honest woman of her at last'. Owen, aged nineteen, didn't have a clue what he meant. He said that, notwith-

---

* John Yorke (b. 1938); m. 1st 1967 Jean Reynolds, 2nd 1992 Julia Allen.
† Rosamund Hornby (b. 1914); m. 1951 Admiral Sir Deric (Douglas Eric) Holland-Martin (d. 1977); DBE, 1983.
‡ Elisabeth Forde; m. 1933 Sir Cyril Kleinwort, banker (1905–80).
§ Deputy Director of National Gallery, 1973–78 (1918–94).
¶ Kenneth Clark (1903–83), art historian; Surveyor of the King's Pictures, 1934–44; m. 1st 1927 Elizabeth ('Jane') Martin, 2nd 1977 Comtesse Nolwen de Janzé (1925–90); KCB 1938; cr. life peer as Baron Clark, 1969.
** Sir John Pope-Hennessy (1913–95); Chairman of Department of Modern European Paintings, Metropolitan Museum, New York, 1977–86; elder brother of James P.-H.
†† Chairman of Mallett & Sons, antique dealers (1917–2001).
‡‡ Owen, 3rd Earl Lloyd George of Dwyfor (b. 1924); m. (2nd) 1982 Josephine Gordon Cumming.

standing the liaison, the death of Dame Margaret caused his break-up.[*]
Huge table, about fifteen assembled, including Kenneth Rose, who
served in the Welsh Guards with our host. I liked Owen. Intelligent,
shrewd, unassuming, with a merry eye. My father would turn in his
grave if he knew that his elder son had taken a meal from a descendant of L.G., the man most hated by the squirearchy.

Alex Moulton, with whom I dined last Thursday, mentioned that
his factory was not going well. In fact he is closing much of it down
and selling the site. Admitted that people did not want to buy his
bicycle, in spite of its excellence and superiority to others on the
market, for bicyclists were very conservative. I felt sad for him. In the
lamplight from the door he looked much older and worn.

Monday, 5th August

Am reading Hugo Vickers'[†] life of Cecil Beaton, somewhat hooked.
To begin with I thought Cecil the most lamentable sucker-up and
social climber. He made me feel sick. But underneath that sophistication there is a little boy, bewildered by where his charm has got him.
He was vulnerable as well as tough, gentle as well as vitriolic when his
professional work was assailed.

Saturday, 10th August

A. came to my room this morning while I was writing letters to say
that Mrs Wrightsman[‡] (Jayne now to me) had arrived by helicopter
to stay at the big house for the weekend; that this afternoon she was
flying David and Caroline to Cornwall and there was room for one
extra. A. nobly insisted on my going, for last year she joined the party
when it flew to Burghley.

We start at 2.15, from the lawn on the east front. A most celestial
experience. David sits in front next to the pilot, a smooth-faced young
man in his twenties with smart shirt and epaulettes. Caroline, Mrs W.

---

[*] In 1943, David Lloyd George, later 1st Earl (1863–1945), dismayed his four children by
his 1st wife Dame Margaret (d. 1942) by marrying his long-standing secretary and mistress Frances Stevenson (d. 1972).

[†] Writer (b. 1951).

[‡] Jayne Larkin; m. as his 2nd wife Charles Wrightsman, President Standard Oil 1932–53,
art collector, Trustee of Metropolitan Museum, New York.

and I in the three seats behind. The cabin is like a sedan chair, or old-fashioned landaulette. The great propellor rotates above, the doors shut like car doors – no safety catches, one could throw oneself out. Little glass sliding windows which open for air. Glass in front down to the pilot's feet. After a little revving we gently rise from the ground. It is The Ascension. One has no feeling of vertigo – just straight, gentle rising. A beautiful day, cloudy and sunny. I just see our house, like a pimple beside the big house. We fly over Lyegrove and Tormarton, leaving Bath on our left. We rise to a thousand feet at most, flying at about 100 m.p.h. Fields swarming with sheep like slugs. Motor-cars like toys, yellow, blue, red, crawling down motorways. Many pylons. I don't always know where we are, but recognise landmarks – the Wellington Monument, Bradleigh Court, Saltram. The country incredibly green after all the rain. Fields show straight paths of the corn-cutting. Many ugly quarries, that at Chipping Sodbury huge and deep like a canyon. Rather noisy and difficult to talk. No feeling of unease or sickness. Gentle swaying. Without the noise it would be like a magic carpet. Within an hour we reach Plymouth, Mount Edgcumbe visible. Distressing how built-up England is, we are never far from a straggling town. Only over Dartmoor is there nothing as far as the eye can see towards the northern horizon. Eerie too. Pilot does not change altitude and we almost graze the hill tops.

Then Antony comes in sight – on a peninsula two miles from Plymouth. We circle the garden and land in forecourt. David jumps out. I duck the revolving blades. Mrs W. does not get out until they have stopped. Fears for her hair? Sir John Carew-Pole's son Richard* now lives in the house. Great charmer. Takes us into house. He and his wife want the mid-Victorian portico demolished. I deprecate this for it is not bad-looking, and serves a useful purpose in such a draughty place. Look round the beautiful dark house with its portraits of regicides on panelled walls. One of Sir Kenelm Digby before a sunflower, indicating his being a King's man. Good portrait of Charles I at his trial. Sir John, who lives in the grounds, joins us. Charming old man. He and Caroline hug and flirt. Son says, there is someone you know here. Takes me to a pitch dark chamber, where a figure behind an easel with his back to the window turns out to be Edmund

* Richard Carew-Pole (b. 1938); e.s. of Sir John, 12th Bt (1902–93), who donated Antony, where his family had lived for more than 500 years, to N.T.; m. (2nd) 1974 Mary Dawnay.

Fairfax-Lucy,* painting a series of the rooms. Nice boy with dishev-
elled hair. We talk of Alice,† who he says is better. We are given tea
in the kitchen. I ask Richard C.-P. and Edmund, son and grandson of
donors, whether they are pleased that their ancestral homes have been
given to the N.T. Richard says it is always nicer to own your own
house, but for the house's sake it is a good thing. Should a descendant
live at Antony who doesn't like it, he can never break it up. Edmund
says that Charlecote would no longer be standing had it not been
taken over – or would at best be a hotel for Statford-on-Avon.

We say goodbye, get back into our seats, and within four minutes
have crossed the water and landed at Ince Castle (seventeen miles by
road). A funny-looking old man in a pyjama suit greets us, with grey
hair scooped back and tied in a knot. It is Patsy Boyd.‡ She too gives
us tea, which we are unable to eat. A nostalgic visit for David, whose
father lived at Ince in the Thirties. Attractive four-cornered, turreted
house of brick, almost rebuilt inside. Waiting-room taste, Harrods
Hepplewhite furniture. Long passage dominated by large bronze bust
of Alan [Lennox-Boyd]. I wonder if Alan took against me after the
publication of my first diaries, for I never heard from him again.§
More indiscretions about him forthcoming in *Midway*, I fear.¶ We
leave after an hour, Caroline saying we must return as her father
coming to stay. With the wind behind us we are back by 6.30. Once
we see a rainbow ahead. Amazingly, we catch it up. What's more, for
several minutes it seems to fly with us, as if we are at the centre of a
multi-coloured revolving wheel. Extraordinary experience, during
which Caroline writes letters and dozes. How blasé the rich are.
Dining with the Beauforts, I ask David how much the jaunt cost Mrs
Wrightsman. About two thousand pounds, he thinks. I suppose her

---

* Sir Edmund Fairfax-Lucy, 6th Bt (b. 1945); artist; life tenant of Charlecote Park,
Warwickshire, bequeathed by his grandfather to N.T.; m. 1st 1974 Sylvia Ogden, 2nd
1986 Lady Lucinda Lambton.
† Hon. Alice Buchan (1908–93), dau. of 1st Baron Tweedsmuir (the novelist John
Buchan); m. 1933 Brian Cameron-Ramsay-Fairfax-Lucy, later 5th Bt (1898–1974);
mother of Sir Edmund.
‡ Lady Patricia Guinness (b. 1918), dau. of 2nd Earl of Iveagh; m. 1938 Alan Lennox-
Boyd (1904–83), Conservative politician, cr. Viscount Boyd of Merton, 1960 (see *Holy
Dread*, 20 March 1983).
§ J.L.-M's wartime diaries describe the unrequited passion of Lennox-Boyd (then a junior
minister in the coalition government) for the American soldier Stuart Preston.
¶ See entry for 29 September 1985 and note.

journey from London and back costs her the same again. Anyway, I loved my trip.

Wednesday, 14th August

Dear Dick's birthday. I have typed out the first two chapters of Regy, which of course turn out to be longer than the raw text. A. remarked after reading Chapter 1, 'Must we have all this lineage?' But what she calls lineage and the childhood only take fourteen pages. Eton and Cambridge are much longer.

Monday, 19th August

Dear Midi [Gascoigne]'s* eightieth birthday party. Dinner given by Bamber and Christina† in house in Richmond, on the river. They have created a smart little Japanese-style back garden, with rocks down which water gushes when a tap is turned on. About forty, mostly O'Neill and Gascoigne relations. I sat on Midi's left, a great honour. Knew few people; rather a trial. Talked to Lady Plowden,‡ a clever woman who chairs Royal Commissions. Told me she was now researching her family's past. This is the usual pastime of the superannuated.

Tuesday, 20th August

Several visitors this week. First Francis Egerton, on his way to look at gardens in Staffordshire with A. Next Martin Drury,§ sympathetic, keen, capable, perfect for his job. Then, on the 18th, Tom and Rachel Bridges¶ for a night. They told us about the Waleses' visit to Italy, having been in attendance throughout. Liked her, though she has no

---

* Hon. Mary O'Neill (1905–91); m. 1934 Frederick ('Derick') Gascoigne (d. 1974); friend of J.L.-M. since 1920s.

† Arthur Bamber Gascoigne (b. 1935); writer, broadcaster and publisher, son of 'Midi' Gascoigne; m. 1965 Christina Ditchburn.

‡ Bridget Richmond (d. 2000); educationist; m. 1933 Edwin Noel Plowden (cr. life peer 1959); DBE, 1972.

§ Historic Buildings Secretary (1981–95), subsequently Director-General, of N.T. (b. 1938).

¶ 2nd Baron Bridges (b. 1927); diplomatist; HM Ambassador to Rome, 1983–7; m. 1953 Rachel Bunbury. His father Edward Bridges (1892–1969), Cabinet Secretary and Permanent Secretary to the Treasury, ennobled on retirement, was only son of Robert Bridges the Poet Laureate, and A.L.-M's second cousin.

grey matter whatever. Him they found unhappy, complaining that he is not free enough to espouse causes near his heart or become expert in any subject. Unworthy entourage, too cautious, which turned down imaginative suggestions, *e.g.* that they should endear themselves to the Italians by throwing a coin in the Trevi Fountain on the eve of their departure. As it was, they were very popular. The visit to Harold Acton a great success. They thought Harold the strangest mortal they had ever encountered, but loved his company in the museums as he explained pictures to them in an interesting way.

Wednesday, 21st August

Professor Varma* of Canada, an Indian who is an authority on Gothick tales, came to tea, having invited himself months ago. Brought with him a lady whom I made put her name down on paper – Aurelia Duvanel-Hepkema. They wished to 'pay their respects'. A maddening interruption to a difficult passage of my book. They told me two things of interest. In America, people with incurable cancer can have their bodies frozen and kept in deep freezes, to be extracted when a cure for their sort of cancer has been discovered. Then they are to be thawed back into life. Apparently they do not experience the dottiness which is the usual consequence of coma. Next, they told me that Tita, Byron's beloved *gondolier*,† attended Shelley's funeral pyre. Was present at Byron's death, and held the poet in his arms. Then became the servant of Monk Lewis who also died in his arms, of yellow fever while crossing the Atlantic. He then married Disraeli's housemaid, and Dizzy too died in his arms. Tita, who was illiterate despite associating with so many distinguished literary persons, was given a pension by Queen Victoria.‡ I told them that Tita's grandson, a canon of the English Church, sold the ring which Byron gave Tita on his deathbed, which had been given to Byron by his Cambridge boy love John Edlestone. Jock Murray bought it, and now wears it.§

---

* Devendra P. Varma (b. 1923); author of *The Gothic Flame* (1966).
† The strapping Tita (Giovanni Battista Falcieri) entered Byron's service in 1818 and remained devoted to him until the poet's death. He was more bodyguard than catamite.
‡ These details are rather muddled. Lewis (1775–1818) predeceased Byron. It was Dizzy's father who died in Tita's arms, and Tita's widow who received the pension.
§ John Murray VI (1909–93), head of publishing firm; Eton contemporary (later publisher) of J.L.-M. The sale of the ring is described in *A Mingled Measure*, December 1971.

Monday, 26th August

Lunched with Brigid Salmond and husband* at their house in Didmarton, filled with the remnants of the Desborough collection. I sat next to Brigid and her old mother, who comes from Powerscourt [Co. Wicklow] which her silly brother sold. She remembers that during the Troubles her father, who had returned from the trenches, learnt that a mob was advancing to burn down the house. As they approached, he brandished a hand grenade and threatened to blow them all to smithereens. They retreated, shouting 'God bless your lardship'. She asked me if I ever went to Ireland. I said never now, can't bring myself to set foot in the island. Her son,† having frittered away his fortune, applied for the post of butler to the Cavendishes at Holker [Hall, Lancashire], and got it. They are very nice to him, call him by his Christian name, give him £5,000 a year and a cottage, afternoons off, etc. He is very happy, only slightly embarrassed when his friends and relations come to stay.

Tuesday, 27th August

Spoke to M. this morning, off to stay in France with Maître Blum for a week. He told me about his hopeless love for a young actor; knows it is absurd, but can't help thinking of him from dawn till night, and can hardly work for desperation.

Wednesday, 28th August

Met Eardley at Hungerford, The Bear, at eleven this morning. We walked down the canal to Kintbury where we drank ginger ale and ate croutons – delicious. Then walked back again. About eight miles in all and I felt weary. Not so Eardley, who was as spry as ever, and would have walked further. From Hungerford we drove to Littlecote, which is to be re-sold next week by the bloody tycoon who bought it lock, stock and barrel from the Wills family last month. It is very dreadful that these mushroom millionaires can speculate in this way

---

* Brigid Wright (b. 1928), dau. of FitzHerbert Wright and Hon. Doreen Julia Wingfield, o. dau. of 8th Viscount Powerscourt; m. 1950 Julian Salmond, o.s. of Marshal of the RAF Sir John Maitland Salmond and Hon. Monica Grenfell, dau. of 1st Baron Desborough.
† Bryan Henry FitzHerbert Wright (b. 1934); uncle of Duchess of York.

with England's heritage. But it is not a nice house, an over-restored rich-man-of-the-Twenties house. Best things are the armour and buff jerkins from Cromwellian times that belonged to the Popham family. Interesting Cromwellian chapel, with pulpil but no altar, and original pews, screen and gallery. Great Hall, with shuffle table of inordinate length.* Pretty library, with nice black Wedgwood plaster cast busts over the bookcases, which I coveted. Long Gallery, with restored ceiling. No, not a satisfactory or an endearing house.

E. is in extremely good form and quite recovered from last year's severe illness. He said he wished someone would write Eddy [Sackville-West]'s† biography. He thinks Eddy's haemophilia gave him a grudge against life, though he persuaded himself that he was iller than he really was. Got on well with women and enjoyed being pampered by them. A good person underneath, though selfish. The pity is that Eddy destroyed his diaries, keeping only a short account of his conversion to Catholicism.

The tranquillity and isolation of canals. We passed along distant stretches of water between a thick drama of trees, poplar, grey willow, birch. Sometimes a rosy red brick bridge, constructed on a curve, with knapped flint – superb engineering of Regency times. The long towpath flanked by the brown canal and a hedge of pinkish willow-herb. A world of its own, disturbed by the occasional flight of a moorhen.

Sunday, 1st September

Yesterday was Audrey's eightieth birthday. How can I reconcile the Audrey I knew and played with at Ribbesford and Wickhamford‡ with this sweet little octogenarian, with snow-white hair and a pretty face, surrounded by hefty grandchildren? Party at Moorwood, a sort of *Cherry Orchard* occasion for the house is to be let. Dreary collection of friends and relations – really, the boredom of conversation with such as Alice Witts.§ Are you writing a book now? Well, just finishing

---

* The table, some thirty feet long, is marked out for playing shuffleboard (or shovelboard), akin to the old pub game shove-ha'penny.
† Hon. Edward Sackville-West (1901–65), writer and music critic; s. father as 5th Baron Sackville, 1962. A biography would shortly be undertaken – see entry for 27 April 1987.
‡ Their paternal grandmother lived at Ribbesford Hall near Bewdley, their parents at Wickhamford Manor near Evesham (both in Worcestershire).
§ Second cousin (*née* Wrigley) of J.L.-M: see entry for 30 August 1987.

something. May I ask what it is about? I fear the subject would mean little to you. Oh do tell, I'm sure it must be most interesting. It's about someone I dare say you've never heard of, few people have. Who? Lord Esher. Who is that? A. says I am foolish to say I am writing at all. So today at the Hollands',* if asked, I shall say that, being now senile, I have given up for good.

Ghastly how the West have betrayed South Africa. The country is about to go under. Black revolution, chaos and bloodshed will be the result. It is entirely our fault. Our fault too that Persia kicked out the Shah, who may not have been the sort of friend *one* would choose, but a hundred times less ghastly than Khomeini. When shall we learn?

Tuesday, 3rd September

I am feeling tired and unwell. Yesterday morning, sitting at my table typing out the fair copy of Regy, I had twinges in the bladder, and wondered whether it might be the dreaded return of cancer. As the day wore on, it passed. Indeed, as the day goes on I always feel better. I just hope I may finish Regy. I doubt whether I shall have the energy or enthusiasm to start another book.

Cecil Beaton had a shock looking at himself in the glass to find that his upper lip had become strangely long. This has happened to me. I used to wonder at Aunt Dorothy's† upper lip, and then John Fowler's,‡ thinking how ugly they were, making them both look like the Ugly [Red] Duchess in Lewis Carroll.

Wednesday, 4th September

Motored to London for the day. Tiring. To Rosamond for lunch. Ate sandwiches and drank white wine sitting in the depths of her uncomfortable armchair in full view of her knickers. She has collapsed like a big pudding. Is also unhappy. Eyesight going, reading a strain for her,

---

* Sir Guy Holland (1918–2002); farmer and art dealer, who held an annual concert in aid of the National Art Collections Fund; m. 1945 Joan Street.
† Dorothy, *née* Heathcote-Edwards (d. 1968), widow of J.L.-M's uncle Alec Milne Lees-Milne (d. 1931). Her sister was the mother of Sir Oswald Mosley, and she was an ardent Fascist in the 1930s. In her later years, she lived with another woman, grew a moustache and smoked a pipe.
‡ Interior decorator (1906–77), partner of Colefax & Fowler, who did much work in N.T. houses, and was the subject of an affectionate essay by J.L.-M. in *Fourteen Friends*.

and she has had to abandon her car. In telling me how good the Heywood Hills* were to her, she wept a little – always a sign of weakness in the old, especially those who, like Ros, are of forceful personality. But I love her dearly, and we talked for hours. At four I took part in an absurd publicity stunt for Gervase [Jackson-Stops]'s new book *Writers at Home* when we were photographed together, he holding a copy, I taking votes out of Bernard Shaw's hat. Then to Misha† for an hour, he much recovered from his love depression, and perky. Then drove across Serpentine and down Cromwell Road to Brook Green to visit Brian Masters,‡ getting hopelessly lost looking for his road. A nightmare as I peered to see in the rain and falling light while traffic piled up behind me. Finally found his nice Victorian house. He took me to dine at a nearby Italian restaurant, and was charming. He talked of his review of my new diaries for *Books and Bookmen*, and it became clear that he had written this from proofs and quoted at least two passages which I deleted before publication. What is the point of proofs if reviewers are to read one's unamended prose and damaging statements? He is a very clever fellow, and makes me feel slightly ashamed of not being born a cockney. When he talked of the 'posh' way of speaking, I asked him what he meant. He said the Mitford sisters say 'gawn' for 'gone'. I said I thought I did too. Tried it out, and found that I did. 'Oh, but you do not *emphasise* it in the way they do,' he said, trying to make amends.

Alec Clifton-Taylor has left over a million pounds – most of which he earned after his seventieth birthday and had little time to enjoy, poor man.

Saturday, 7th September

A lovely, cloudless, golden day. A. went out to a luncheon party and I went for a long walk with Folly [the whippet] down the Gloucester–Sharpness canal, two hours from Slimbridge to Frampton. Dragonflies with brown striped bodies, and peacock butterflies. A wind ruffling

---

* G. Heywood Hill (d. 1986), bookseller in Curzon Street; m. 1938 Lady Anne Gathorne-Hardy (b. 1911), o. dau. of 3rd Earl of Cranbrook, who had been engaged to J.L.-M. in 1935.
† Michael Bloch.
‡ Writer (b. 1939), becoming celebrated for his psychological studies of mass murderers (see *Deep Romantic Chasm*, 30 November 1981).

the water. A few boats passing when the bridges are wound, not up but round. Talked to a middle-aged couple with largish boat moored. They said you could get to Manchester by canal and the River Severn, and then to Leeds by another canal. Felt pleased with myself, happy that I can still walk six miles.

I wish A. were not so keen on social events. Always inviting people who mean nothing to me and are a great distraction, so that I find it difficult to read or work during weekends at Badminton. I suggested to her this morning that she had no friends and preferred acquaintances. She admitted this was true, that even Freda Berkeley* had ceased to be an intimate.

Sunday, 15th September

Death is the end of expectation; that is all. So long as one can look forward one is still living. Total lack of sex, as in my case, does not matter. On the contrary, life is fuller without it.

This morning A. and I are off to France, she to Jagger's garden, I to stay with Diana Mosley for two nights. Joan Aly Khan has just telephoned that Seymour Camrose is delighted for me and Derry to do an article on Hackwood for the *Architectural Digest*. Maître Blum has asked me to edit the Duke of Windsor's *My Hanoverian Ancestors*.† The *Spectator* has asked me to review Selina Hastings' biography of Nancy. I want to finish typing out Regy before we leave for America on 30 October. Shall I manage it? Without interruption it normally takes me three days to type out a chapter – and I'm now on the seventh of twelve.

Drama in the village. Poor Daphers – Daphne Moore – took 90 sleeping tablets and walked into the pond. But she did it in the morning when there were workmen about. When she was fished out and taken into the House, the butler said 'Mind my clean floor.' She has now more or less recovered in hospital, but has told the Vicar she intends to repeat the performance. David Beaufort said he hoped she would be more successful next time. Poor woman, her shame and misery are not assumed.

---

* Freda Bernstein (b. 1923); m. 1946 Sir Lennox Berkeley, composer (1903–90).

† It was eventually decided not to publish this interesting work of historical anecdote, in view of the uncertainty as to how far it had been written by the ex-King himself, how far by the journalist who assisted him, Kenneth Young.

Wednesday, 18th September

On Sunday afternoon I accompanied A. to Paris by air. There we were met by Mlinaric* and a young colleague – difficult to know whether boy or girl – who dropped me at Temple de la Gloire, Orsay. I had the whole evening and following day alone with Diana [Mosley]. Very rewarding. She is extremely clever and well-read. Sitting with her elegant legs crossed before me, I was reminded of the photograph I took of her at Asthall when she was sixteen. Certainly beautiful, though her skin much creased. We talked of everything – her parents, her sisters, Tom, and of course Nancy. She gave me a proof copy of Selina's biography to read. Too much about early life, much of it silly and shaming. Whenever Nancy ventures upon an opinion it is childish, whereas Diana's views are always reasoned. More interesting when N. marries the lamentable Prod [Peter Rodd]. But oh, her love for the pock-marked Colonel is sad. D. talked to me of Hitler. I said I regarded him as a mountebank, with his Charlie Chaplin moustache and swagger. She said he was not vulgar, but tender and understanding. His ability to charm and to lead was superhuman – like that other cad, Napoleon. On the second night we were joined for dinner by Ali and Cha,† and A. arrived from Amboise, dog-tired.

Thursday, 19th September

Wasn't this day George Lloyd's‡ birthday? Last night after dinner David Hicks§ telephoned to say Rory had died at 7.30. A. pretended she knew already – so odd of her. She adored Rory and cherished the knowledge that she had known him years before David and other grand and rich friends. This morning, poor Gilbert¶ telephoned from Ménèrbes, saying that he had spent the whole night with Rory on his bed, unable to believe he was dead.

---

* David Mlinaric, interior decorator (b. 1939), then engaged at Mick Jagger's property at Amboise where A.L.-M. was creating the garden.
† Alexander Mosley (b. 1938); Paris publisher, er s. of Hon. Diana Mitford by her 2nd marriage to Sir Oswald Mosley; m. 1975 Charlotte Marten.
‡ George, 1st Baron Lloyd (1879–1941); proconsul and politician, whom J.L.-M. had served as private secretary, 1931–5.
§ Interior decorator (1929–98); m. 1960 Lady Pamela, yr dau. of 1st Earl Mountbatten of Burma.
¶ Rory Cameron's French lover.

Wednesday, 25 September

My appreciation of Rory appeared in *The Times* this morning.

Yesterday I went to London for the day. Bruce Hunter lunched with me at Brooks's. So nice, gentle and quizzical. Takes knowing. How I now wish I had gone to him with every book. As it is he is going to take over all my books retrospectively, as it were, with paperback reissues in mind. Bruce asked if I would consider doing an 'album' – the fashion these days – on Tony Powell's *Dance to the Music of Time*, describing all the books and paintings mentioned therein. Extraordinary idea. I explained that I liked Tony immensely but his novels left me cold.

It was M's birthday so I went to tea with him on the way to Paddington and gave him my Parian bust of the Apollo Belvedere, by which he seemed pleased. He told me that, when he arrived at Heathrow on return from Amsterdam, two burly customs officials took him into a room and with icy politeness searched him for drugs. Made him strip and examined every crevice.

Saturday, 28th September

Season of mists and mellow fruitfulness. Beautiful Indian summer. The sun takes hours to force its way through, but it is then very hot, and the dogs pant when I take them blackberrying in Westonbirt. Poor little Honey is in decline, suffering from heart murmur. The other darling unaffected as yet, in fine fettle. Last night A. and I leant out of my bedroom window and heard one owl talking to another, somewhere in the garden of the big house. The moon was full, percolating through the cedar trees. We thought it moving to hear an owl hoot – to such a pass have things come, with the elimination of natural creatures.

Sunday, 29th September

Caroline [Beaufort] and Fred Whitsey[*] dined, latter a nice little man, intelligent and gentle. Caroline had seen Lord Lambton,[†] who has

---

[*] Garden writer (b. 1919).

[†] Antony Lambton (b. 1922); s. father as 6th Earl of Durham, 1970 and disclaimed peerages but continued to use courtesy title Viscount Lambton; MP (C) Berwick-on-Tweed 1951–73, resigning seat and office in Conservative Government following involvement in the 'call girl affair' of 1973; m. 1942 Belinda ('Bindy') Blew-Jones (1921–2003).

been reading my new diaries and told her that I ought not to have left in references to the homosexuality of Alan Lennox-Boyd and David Bowes-Lyon,[*] as both widows are alive as well as children. He begged her not to pass this on to me, which she has done. Doubtless he also mentioned the matter to Diana M., who never passed it on. Diana is always the soul of tact to one's face, and does not tell one what others have said behind one's back.

Tuesday, 15th October

Lunching at Brooks's today I sat next to Alan Clark.[†] Couldn't remember his Christian name at first, but mercifully did so in time to insert it into a sentence. He said he was bored to tears with his work. I said he could always chuck being an MP. He said it wasn't quite as easy as all that. I asked whether he was a Minister. He said, 'Yes, I am, and I can't just up-sticks. What I would like is to go to the Foreign Office.' I suggested he ask Mrs Thatcher. He said, 'You don't know her, evidently.' We talked about Philip Sassoon,[‡] as I recently read K's description of staying with him at Port Lympne. Alan remembers him well. He was sweet to children. Had a smooth face, looked incredibly young, walked on the tips of his toes and impressed one as being a person of importance. He was adored by Alan's mother Jane, who learnt the social graces from him, having been without them at the time of her marriage. Strange thing for a son to say. On getting home and reading *The Times* I saw Alan was in the news, disagreeing with the latest edict enjoining firms to employ more blacks. Alan quite rightly argues that businesses to flourish must employ the best staff irrespective of ethnic considerations.

Main object of visit to London to attend the party given for Selina's *Nancy* by the publisher, Hamish Hamilton, in Marie Antoinette Room at the Ritz. Howling mob and stifling heat. Full of geriatrics

---

[*] In *Midway on the Waves*, J.L.-M. reports a conversation in which A.L.-B. spoke of the 'tiresome necessity' of dissimulation for a married homosexual (20 April 1948), and another in which Hon. D.B.-L. (1902–61; bro. of HM Queen Elizabeth) declared the male form to be 'more aesthetic' than the female, and asked J.L.-M. whether he liked wearing shorts (17 June 1948).
[†] Hon. Alan Clark (1931–99), e.s. of Kenneth, Baron Clark; writer and politician, then Under-Secretary for Employment; he later achieved celebrity as a diarist, declaring J.L.-M. to be his favourite exponent of that art.
[‡] Sir Philip Sassoon, 3rd Bt (1888–1939); politician and aesthete.

– Helen Dashwood[*] who can't walk, Heywood Hill who cannot make himself heard. Gladwyn and Cynthia[†] dined afterwards at Brooks's. Numerous people appear to have read *Midway* whereas I have yet to see the book, the parcel of twelve sent to Bath not yet having arrived.

Saturday, 19th October

Motored to luncheon at Hackwood. Only Seymour and Joan there. Even so, three sideboards groaning with delicious food. Dressed crab, cold asparagus, salads galore on one; roast chicken on another; on a third, enormous bowls overflowing with wild strawberries (picked at Hackwood), raspberries and blackberries. I partook of a small plateful of each. The others ate little. I wondered what would happen to the surplus food. Joan sweet; Seymour benign and sober, though rather lame. Both walked me round all afternoon, he snubbing Joan who never answered back. It is a beautiful house, and has some fine things which belonged to the Dukes of Bolton – splendid gilt mirrors, a pair of torchères with palm-leaf tops, some Chippendale chairs of high quality. Two portraits of Winston Churchill, one of him playing cards which Mrs C. did not like and gave Randolph who promptly sold it to Seymour for £100, and an oil by McEvoy done during the First World War, looking proud but disillusioned while in disgrace after the Dardanelles. Saloon painted in different shades of grey by Joan, and much gold, so the grey looks pink in places. Very pretty. Took a few notes and left notebook behind.

On return I took the dogs for a walk at six. The setting sun shed golden horizontal light. In Vicarage Field, where was a low mist spread like a carpet waist-high from the ground, thin and gauzy. As I moved I was encircled by a sort of halo which moved with me. Indeed I felt saint-like, so moved by the beauty of this autumn evening – and I'm as pure as snow now, without one lecherous thought. The darling dogs ran on ahead, their little ears occasionally pricking through the carpet as they leapt after imaginary squirrels.

---

[*] Widow of Sir John Dashwood, 10th Bt (1896–1966) of West Wycombe Park, Buckinghamshire, wartime headquarters of N.T., whose foibles J.L.-M. had (to her indignation) described in his wartime diaries (she d. 1989).

[†] Gladwyn Jebb, 1st Baron Gladwyn (1900–97), diplomatist; m. 1929 Cynthia Noble (she d. 1990).

Wednesday, 23rd October

Have finished Regy. That is to say, I have produced a readable draft, 650 pages in all. Far too long of course.

Thursday, 24th October

After sunset this evening I look at the moon with and without my spectacles. With them, the moon is three-quarters full, and clear. Without spectacles, there are four moons interlocking. Covering my right eye and seeing only with my left, the moon is ovoid and divided into sections, as though it were a heart with veins; much larger than life; nothing else visible in the gloaming. In the distance I could hear the stags roaring during the rut, a sound more melancholy than expectant of pleasure, more *post* than *ante coitum*.

Friday, 25th October

To London for the day. I deposit typescript of Regy and copy of *Midway* with M., who is still in his pyjamas. I walk across Park to Grosvenor Chapel to practise reading lesson for Rory's memorial service. I ascend to the lectern and declaim, 'Blessed is the man who trusteth in God Almighty.' I look up. A man, hitherto invisible to me at back of the church, looks at me as if I am a lunatic and walks out.

Espie Dod* lunches at Brooks's. Joined by M., who because of my ticking-off is wearing a suit, quite tidy, except tie loose in unbuttoned collar. Espie beautifully dressed in tailored black suit, very chic indeed. A trifle older than I remembered, must be about forty, but very handsome still, and more mature. Charming too, and no trace of Australian accent. He and M. got on well and discovered mutual friends from the stage.

Saturday, 26th October

This evening after dark telephone rings. I leave it to A. to answer upstairs. She calls down, 'Michael wants to speak to you about your book.' Unusual for M. to ring me here. He says he stayed up all last night reading Regy. Full of praise. Says it is splendid, and not too long.

---

* Australian architect; protégé of J.L.-M's kinsman, the horticultural writer Peter Coats.

Amazed at my assumed knowledge of politics, war, etc. Likes the humour, and the intermingling of public and private lives. So sweet of him, I am pleased and relieved. A. sweet about it too.

Thursday, 21st November

From 30 October to 15 November we were in the USA. I kept a few disjointed notes.* It was not much of an adventure. On reflection I enjoyed it, but while I was there I counted the days till we could return. Too much movement. In Washington we stayed at the Hilton and were entertained at the opening of the Treasures of British Country Houses exhibition,† the best loan exhibition I have ever seen. Then a bus tour with some sixty of the lenders to Virginia country houses, Williamsburg, Monticello, etc. Beautiful country, deep, vivid autumn colours. Three nights in Philadelphia with Henry McIlhenny‡ in his sumptuous triple house crammed with art treasures. Then New York for four days. I liked Washington, a beautiful city, but did not care for NY apart from the 'scrapers. The canyon effect of the streets. Went up the World Trade Center.§ Good architecture, of straight perpendicular, close lines and ogival tops to panels. Only lacking a spire to alleviate flat skyline. Became immersed in picture galleries – National Gallery in Washington, Philadelphia (where most exhibits given by Henry), Metropolitan and Frick in

---

* This was J.L.-M's only visit to America; his 'disjointed notes' are reproduced as an appendix to this volume.
† The exhibition *Treasure Houses of Britain: Five Hundred Years of Private Patronage and Art Collecting* took place at the National Gallery in Washington from November 1985 to March 1986. It was conceived and organised by Gervase Jackson-Stops (who took leave from his job at the N.T.) and the Gallery's Director, J. Carter Brown (1934–2002). It received the patronage of the Prince of Wales, and the financial sponsorship of the Ford Motor Company. Some seven hundred objects were lent by some two hundred private owners, and organised in four sections: From Castle to Country House, 1485–1714; The Grand Tour, 1714–80; the Gentleman Collector, 1780–1830; the Romantic Vision, 1830–1985. The lenders, along with a host of distinguished guests including the J.L.-Ms, were fêted at the glittering opening ceremonies, which included a dinner at the Gallery, official receptions at the White House and Capitol, and a tour of Virginia country houses (see Appendix).
‡ Henry P. McIlhenny (1910–86); art collector, philanthropist and *bon vivant*; Curator of Philadelphia Museum of Art, 1935–64; owner of Glenveagh Castle, Co. Donegal (see Appendix).
§ Destroyed by terrorist action on 11 September 2001.

New York. Weather pretty bad throughout visit. Social events most tedious. Americans uniformly kind and welcoming, but *gushing*. Oh the gush, wore me out. Dined one night in NY with John Pope-Hennessy, who I hoped had not read *Midway* where I criticise his mother.* Stiff occasion. But lovely to see Kay Hallé[†] in Georgetown, who is eighty but looks hardly changed. Johnnie [Churchill][‡] staying with her, a silent pudding for she will not let him drink in her house. On leaving I felt a pang for I do not think I shall see either of these beloved old friends again.

We had special VIP treatment on return journey, which was not tiring. Nevertheless it took several days to adjust sleep. Came back to find reviews of *Midway* appearing, but could not bring myself to read them. On Tuesday attended poor Rory's memorial service in Grosvenor Chapel at which I read a lesson – chosen for me – from Revelation. Spent some time with dear M., our relations on the happiest plane. We confide in each other entirely. Am concerned about his debauches, which divert him from work. The most cheering news is from Bruce Hunter who thinks Anthony Blond[§] is interested in my novel – possibly thanks to the good offices of Desmond Briggs[¶] to whom I mentioned it. After seven rejections out-of-hand, this is encouraging. Have told Bruce that, if Blond reject, we had better give up.

Friday, 22nd November

Stayed the night with the Eshers in their Tower. Received with open arms. With intervals for tea and dinner, I went through the Regy typescript with Lionel. He was full of praise, but had several minor but helpful corrections, and a few major objections to what he called

---

* On 18 June 1948, J.L.-M. motored Dame Una Pope-Hennessy (1876–1949) to Petersham and had 'a down on her' as she spoke of nothing but her own literary success. When J.L.-M. modestly remarked that his own recent book on Robert Adam 'made no pretensions to being a contribution to literature', she snorted in reply, 'Of course it isn't!'
† Pre-war American friend of J.L.-M. who wrote books on Churchill family (d. 1992).
‡ J. G. Spencer-Churchill (1909–92), nephew of Sir Winston; artist; friend of J.L.-M. since they had crammed together for Oxford in 1927.
§ Of Blond & Briggs, publishers; m. (2nd) Laura Hesketh, niece of J.L.-M's recently deceased friend Peter Fleetwood-Hesketh.
¶ Former partner of Blond & Briggs (1931–2002); novelist (as Rosamond Fitzroy); a JP for Wiltshire. He and his partner Ian Dixon became great friends of J.L.-M's later years.

'smut' – notably references to Regy's vicarious enjoyment of his son's affairs at Eton. I remonstrated, but feebly, that we must be careful not to overlook his homosexuality, for without reference to it readers would find him a stuffed shirt. Finally I gave way. He called up Christian and read the offending passages to her and she (who never contradicts him) agreed. I understand his objections, for Regy was his grandfather, though all the passages he made me remove had already been used by Oliver in his unpublished book. I now have a week's worth of rewriting, and long to get rid of Regy.

In the morning motored to Oxford. Attended memorial service to Colin McMordie in Oriel Chapel. This beautiful building lit by candlelight was filled with young friends of Colin. John Martin Robinson* read an address – very good, what I could hear. We were invited to go to the Common Room afterwards but I sloped off. I didn't want to meet Colin's father and see what the beautiful Colin might have become.

Drove to Iffley and found John Sparrow† pruning roses outside the front door of the house which All Souls has lent him. Sweet, but very forgetful and repetitive. A boring man with black beard and an oriental wife called, wishing to meet me. When they had gone, we went to the nearby hotel for sandwiches and coffee. Poor John is just two years older than me, yet quite senile. And he was one of the cleverest, sharpest and best-educated of men, whom Harold [Nicolson] held in high esteem for his intellect.

Wednesday, 27th November

A. being at Amboise I dined with Alex at Bradford. During dinner in his kitchen he kept jumping up like a jack-in-a-box, not merely between courses but between mouthfuls, to turn the cooker higher or wash up some fork or plate. Made me feel quite giddy. He is worried about his latest bicycle which has not turned out a success, though an object of great ingenuity. He showed me one in his office.

---

* Librarian to Duke of Norfolk, and writer and consultant on architectural and genealogical subjects; Fitzalan Pursuivant of Arms (later Maltravers Herald of Arms) Extraordinary, and Vice-Chairman of Georgian Group (b. 1948).
† Warden of All Souls' College, Oxford, 1952–77 (1906–92).

Wednesday, 4th December

To London, staying with Eardley for the first time in two years. Tonight went to huge dinner party given by Alfred Beit for Clementine's seventieth birthday, she a mere chicken. The Subscription Room at Brooks's, arranged with high table and four long tables, looked like the Waterloo Banquet at Apsley House. I sat next to Marian Brudenell,* whom I like, but is rather affected and absurd, and Lady Egremont, whom I liked immensely.† Max [Egremont], in passing to his seat near A's, said 'good luck'. She v. intelligent. Seemed surprised when I told her that, were I to be left on my own, I would try to enter a monastery in order to pray for the world. 'But do you really suppose that would do any good?' She said her late husband John Wyndham, whom I never liked, a rude, drunken man, totally neglected Max when a child. And Max is as charming as could possibly be. Clem made a good speech, witty and to the point. Heat appalling and I did not dare drink anything but water.

Thursday, 5th December

Had Anthony Blond to lunch. He brought with him his Indian apprentice Sanjay, who went through my novel with me after luncheon. A touching little person, like a tiny brown flea, with whom I was much impressed; extremely gentle and clever. He told me what alterations he advised. He thinks the book a potential prize-winner, superior to Anita Brookner's *Hôtel du Lac*. Acceptance depends on another firm taking it in paperback after its first appearance in hardback. Blond have written recommending the book to three such firms and are hopeful one will take it. How I pray.

This evening Eardley, M., and Betty the Lampshade Queen‡ dined at Brooks's. Very expensive: these two indifferent meals cost me over £100. No opportunity for a word with M. alone.

---

* Hon. Marian Manningham-Buller (b. 1934), e. dau. of 1st Viscount Dilhorne; m. 1955 Edmund Brudenell of Deene Park, Northamptonshire (b. 1928).
† Pamela Quin (b. 1925); m. 1947 John Wyndham, later 1st Baron Egremont and 6th Baron Leconfield (1920–72), who was succeeded as 2nd and 7th Baron by their son Max Wyndham (b. 1948), farmer and writer.
‡ Miss E. C. Hanley (1915–2002), American-born owner of a business in Westminster which held a royal warrant as suppliers of lamps and lampshades.

Friday, 6th December

At Euston, joined Dudley Dodd, Bobby Gore[*] and Brinsley Ford[†] and trained to Bangor, North Wales. They produced delicious pheasant sandwiches and wine, which we consumed at a table for four. Much merriment. They stay at Beaumaris Hotel, I with the Douglas-Pennants.[‡] Talk over tea a strain owing to Lady Janet's extreme shyness. Yet she is a nice woman. We drove to Penrhyn Castle for great dinner given to the Douglas-Pennants to thank for all they have done for the National Trust. It was 1951 when I first stayed with them, and I am flattered that they should have asked for me to be included in the celebration. Penrhyn much improved by hanging of some excellent pictures, notably of superb Rembrandt over fireplace in the breakfast room. I sat between Lady Williams-Bulkeley[§] and Lady Anglesey.[¶] Latter fascinating and beautiful. Spoke frankly about the Nicolsons, saying there was never any likelihood of her marrying Nigel.[**] She thinks he will never write a great book, good writer though he be. He will be remembered for the faultless editor he is. Lord A. came up in a very noisy, jolly manner, laughing too loud for ease, in a subtly patronising way which I don't like. Extreme friendliness amounts to condescension. He was patronising about the Douglas-Pennant boy, yet well informed about his family. Talking and gesticulating with Brinsley, the tiny boy looked to me like a figure in a Thomas Patch conversation piece.

---

[*] Francis St John Gore (b. 1921); adviser on pictures to N.T., 1956–86; Historic Buildings Secretary, 1973–81.

[†] Sir Brinsley Ford (1908–99); sometime Trustee of National Gallery, Chairman of National Art Collections Fund, and Hon. Adviser on Paintings to N.T.; kt 1984; Eton contemporary of J.L.-M.

[‡] Hon. Edward Gordon Douglas (1800–86), yr bro. of 18th Earl of Morton, m. 1833 Juliana Pennant, co-heiress to Welsh slate fortune and neo-Norman fantasy castle at Penrhyn. He assumed name of Douglas-Pennant and was cr. Baron Penrhyn, 1866. His grandson Frank (1865–1967) succeeded as 5th Baron in 1949 and donated castle to N.T.

[§] Renée Neave; m. 1938 Richard Williams-Bulkeley, later 13th Bt.

[¶] George Paget, 7th Marquess of Anglesey (1922–2001); military historian; m. 1948 Shirley, dau. of the novelist Charles Morgan, sometime head of Women's Institute.

[**] Soldier, politician, writer and journalist (b. 1917), yr son of Harold Nicolson (1886–1968) and Vita Sackville-West (1892–1962), who had invited J.L.-M. to write his father's biography in 1976; resident at Sissinghurst Castle, Kent, which he had donated to N.T. in 1968.

Saturday, 14th December

A frightful photograph has been sent me by the Fellow of All Souls who 'snapped' me with John Sparrow. We both look too hideous and ancient for words – John like a veteran pugilist with no teeth, I grinning like an Irish zany, quite bald with tufts of white hair and my mouth open. Oh what a terrible thing to be photographed in old age. How I hate it. John Sparrow told me on this occasion of his one meeting with Mrs Thatcher. Was invited to luncheon. When he got there he found half a dozen other guests. In presenting him to the last, Mrs Thatcher said, without embarrassment but with some hesitation, 'And you know Mr John Sparrow I dare say – Mr, er, John Sparrow.' It soon became apparent that the other John Sparrow was known to Mrs T., he not at all. It had been a ghastly mistake on the part of her secretary. I asked him who his namesake was. John said, 'I have no idea, but he was very dim – dimmer, if I may say so, than myself.'

It is curious how the simple mind gets satisfaction in ticking items off a list of things to buy and do: toothpaste, a bicycle bag for Gerald,* a cleaned cardigan, some stamps. There is dissatisfaction when an item cannot be erased. I wanted to buy an instrument for boring a hole into which to put a hook. The little shop in Bath tried to sell me a bradawl. I told them I had a bradawl already, and wanted a gimlet. The surly man said such an instrument no longer existed. I protested that all carpenters must have them. No longer, he insisted crossly.

Today motored to Stourhead to meet Audrey at The Spreadeagle, where we lunched off soup, toasted sandwiches and coffee. Poor A., her last King Charles died yesterday. She was brave and showed no sign of distress, whereas I would have been in tears. On parting I said, so as not to let her suppose that I did not sympathise deeply, how sorry I felt for her. Without a tremor, she replied, 'Yes, when one lives absolutely alone and sometimes sees no one to talk to for a week, one does miss one's constant companion.' She hates her cottage in Penselwood, wishes she had taken a flat in Cirencester to be near other old fogies, and thought she might still take one, though this seems unlikely at eighty. She said she felt fairly well, but had so little to look forward to. Poor little Audrey, she has always wrung my heart-strings.

---

* Gerald Bird, husband of the L.-Ms' daily help Peggy.

Tuesday, 17th December

Jamie Fergusson[*] came to lunch in Bath where he was shopping around old book stalls. He is a clever and civilised young man, more so than any of my family, all of whom, save Nick, are utter barbarians and bore me stiff. Then I went to London. Stayed with J[ohn] K[enworthy]-B[rowne][†] who kindly met me at Paddington, and the following morning motored me to Brooks's. Very sweet and solicitous he was. Still working on Paxton. I have never heard of any scholar taking so much trouble over detail as he.

Wednesday, 18th December

Carried my Regy typescript to Sidgwick & Jackson, having telephoned last week to forewarn Mr Robert Smith, my new editor. Hateful dealing with new people who know not my ways, probably not my name even. I reached the door, on which a notice directed me to another entrance in Museum Street. I suppose I was looking around while walking, for I stumbled on the pavement and fell headlong into the gutter. Lay there a few seconds, assessing situation. Decided I was not badly hurt, and picked myself up. Contents of my pockets were strewn in the gutter, but not so my typescript, which remained in its cardboard box. Arrived shaken, hands cut, clothes torn, face dirty. Surprised lady directed me to lavatory. No concern. When I indicated the typescript, she said coolly, 'Just put it down there, will you.' After four years' intensive labour, the precious thing was accepted as though it might be an unwelcome Christmas card. God knows if it will even reach Mr Smith. How I hate Regy. Fed up with him. And the more I revise, the more corrections I find to make. I hope to spend the next month without hearing of him. But when I do, no doubt it will be to be asked to cut the book down by a third.

I then went, sent by Bruce Hunter, to Waterstone's, a new bookshop and publishing enterprise run by young persons. Very laudable. Was delighted to hear they intend to open a shop in Bath. They asked if I

---

[*] Antiquarian bookseller (b. 1953) and founding obituaries editor of the *Independent*, whose father was a second cousin of J.L.-M.
[†] Expert on neo-classical sculpture, formerly on staff of N.T. and Christie's (b. 1931); close friend of J.L.-M. since 1958.

would like to write a biography for them of Robert Byron,* Guy Burgess,† Brian Howard‡ or E. F. Benson.§ I said 'No' to all these people, as I liked none of them except Robert, and him not much. They then asked whom I *would* like to write about. I said a romantic figure such as Byron, Beckford,¶ or Ludwig II of Bavaria, on all of whom there are too many books already. Or Gustav III of Sweden,** who is insufficiently well-known and would involve me in language difficulties. Then (put up to it by Bruce, no doubt) they talked of reprinting *Roman Mornings*†† and getting me to do a sequel, *Venetian Evenings*. Could I write the Venice book in nine months? Impossible, I said, for though I know Venice well, much reading would be necessary. But I promised to think about it. The truth is I feel worn out mentally, without a spark left inside me. Yet I don't wish to have no work to do.

Lunched with Geoffrey Houghton-Brown in South Kensington. He much aged, lined and grey, and resigned to nothingness. Very sweet, but without purpose. After leaving Geoffrey, went to see Emily and Dolly.‡‡ A rude shock. Emily broke her leg ten months ago and is now a bent, lop-sided, tiny old lady leaning heavily on a stick. Pitiable in their horrid little cabin on fifth floor of Sutton Estate. Still waiting for modernised flat on ground floor. I left them with dreadful feelings of guilt and sadness. Called on M. on way to Paddington. Hardly had we begun talking when his father entered. A tall, broad, distinguished man, but with a certain vacant look in the eye. Not interested in any subject raised. Something very wrong. M. is worried. On train I felt sad – over

---

* Travel writer, Byzantinist, and early Secretary of Georgian Group (1905–41); his biography was soon afterwards undertaken by James Knox.
† Diplomatist and traitor (1910–63), whom J.L.-M. had known through Harold Nicolson; a biography was eventually undertaken by Andrew Lownie.
‡ Aesthete (1905–58), the model for Anthony Blanche in *Brideshead Revisited*, already the subject of an enormous biography by Marie-Jacqueline Lancaster, *Portrait of a Failure* (1968).
§ Novelist and archaeologist (1867–1940), whose 'Tilling' novels had recently been successfully adapted for television; a biography by Brian Masters appeared in 1991.
¶ William Beckford, writer, traveller and collector (1759–1844), about whom J.L.-M., who occupied his library at Lansdown Crescent, had already produced a slim but acclaimed volume in 1976.
** Like Ludwig of Bavaria (1845–86), Gustavus III of Sweden (1746–92) was known for his unconventional private life and passion for the arts.
†† Published in 1956, when it won the Heinemann Award.
‡‡ 'Miss Emily' had been housekeeper at Geoffrey Houghton-Brown's house in Thurloe Square, South Kensington, where J.L.-M. had his London base from 1945 to 1961; he made an annual pre-Christmas visit to her and her sister Dolly.

the wrecks I had seen today, over my own disintegration in body and mind, and the fact that I am a bore to M. His sweetness never relaxes, but I am a lame dog to him.

Sunday, 29th December

Christmas not yet over. I went to Bath to work on Friday, but all shops shut, and that feeling of emptiness in the city. Until New Year festivities are over things won't be normal.

Coming out of church at Acton Turville this morning, I fell on a sheet of concealed black ice over concrete. Tom [Gibson] full of solicitude and rushed to my assistance. But I was all right, except for some stiffness in right arm; returned home, and took the dogs for a walk on The Slates. I seem unable to keep upright these days, and may soon break a limb.

Clarissa* stayed with us for Christmas, without husband, whom she has at last discarded, and without children. A dear goose. Could not remember the name of her mother-in-law. She told me that her father once said to her husband that his vision of Clarissa was clothed in white, wearing black patent-leather shoes, a wide beaming smile on her face, and standing in a cowpat. At the time Michael was cross with this estimate, but the other day he told C. that he thought his father-in-law had not been far wrong.

On Christmas Day we lunched at the House. I sat between Caroline Beaufort and little Fred, the cousin they are kind to and find a bore. Mrs Fred is one of the three female cousins who are claimants to the Botetourt barony. Apparently the women cannot agree among themselves and until they do so the barony will remain dormant, unless one claimant survives and the other lines die out. It was in abeyance for 250 years before being revived in the eighteenth century. I begged them to see to it that someone assumes this title, which dates from the early fourteenth century and must be a rarity.[†]

On Boxing Day the Henry Robinsons brought their five-week-old

---

* J.L.-M's stepdaughter Hon. Clarissa Luke (see note to 6 February 1985).
† The barony was created in 1305 by the summons to Parliament of John de Botetourt, a military commander of Edward I, and went into abeyence with the death of his great-granddaughter in 1406; it was briefly revived in the eighteenth century, and again in 1803 in favour of the 5th Duke of Beaufort. With the death of the 10th Duke ('Master') in 1984, the succession rights to the barony passed not with the dukedom to his cousin David but to the descendants of his sister Blanche (1897–1968).

son. I was bidden to admire the little creature, resembling a baby piglet. It was lain on my bed upstairs. After luncheon I held it while we were photographed. The children think it astonishing to have a great-great-uncle and -nephew immortalised together. I think it is revolting.

Tuesday, 31st December

It is odd to think that typescripts of two of my books (Regy and novel) are with two different publishers, while the synopsis of another book (Venice) is with a third. I feel drained and incapable of writing anything again. My fall last Sunday has given me much pain in left leg and right arm. I am perpetually tired. Would like to hibernate and not leave my bed until the spring comes.

1986

David Cecil's* obituary in *The Times*. A. gave a cry at breakfast. We knew of his frailty but not that he had been ill. He had charm and traded on it. Difficult to pin down. Would accept invitations with alacrity and feigned enthusiasm, then chuck at the last minute. We were to have lunched with him last summer and he excused himself the day before. His frail and porcelain appearance and somewhat faun-like looks (see portrait by Augustus John) led some to mistake him for a homosexual in his youth, which he never was. Rachel a darling. He wrote delicious biographies in beautiful prose which appealed to society folks as well as highbrows, though I suspect the pedants considered him a lightweight. I liked his *Melbourne* and *The Stricken Deer* enormously when they came out. A. used to see him with Puffin[†] and the Asquiths at The Wharf. I once made a fool of myself as an Oxford undergraduate when, sitting next to him and at a loss for what to say, I asked him whether he had written *The Stricken Deer* all by himself, an idiotic remark to which he found a suitably cutting reply. Nerves will make the young say the most extraordinary things.

Today Tony Mitchell[‡] motored me to Dorchester where we spent hours in the County Records Office. He is writing the guide book to Kingston Lacy. I had a cursory look at some of the W. J. Bankes papers.[§] Read through bundles of letters he wrote to his grandmother when he was a Cambridge undergraduate, including a fascinating

---

* Lord David Cecil (1902–86), yr son of 4th Marquess of Salisbury; writer and historian; Goldsmiths' Professor of English Literature, Oxford, 1948–69; m. 1932 Rachel MacCarthy.

† Hon. Anthony Asquith (1902–68); film director; son of H. H. Asquith (Prime Minister, later 1st Earl) and his 2nd wife Margot Tennant.

‡ Anthony Mitchell (b. 1931); N.T. Historic Buildings Representative 1956–96 (for Wessex Region 1981–96); m. 1972 Brigitte de Soye.

§ William John Bankes (d. 1855); friend of Byron, MP, and traveller in the East; owner of Kingston Lacy, Dorset, bequeathed by his successor to the N.T. in 1981 with its contents and estate; obliged to live abroad for much of his life owing to homosexual scandal. Before embarking on the life of 2nd Viscount Esher in 1982, J.L.-M. had thought of writing his biography.

account of how, in 1811, he broke into Fonthill Abbey's guarded pre-
cincts by exchanging clothes with a workman. He just missed
Beckford, who was returning from a drive round the estate just as
Bankes was leaving, and would probably have been attracted by the
rich and handsome youth of twenty-one. I believe I would be able to
write a short biography out of this material, for he was a strong and
positive character, and a sad one too.

Came home to find Igor [Luke] staying. We can get nothing out of
him about Australia where he spent ten months. He is now thinking
of going into the Brigade of Guards – ranks of course, for he has no
qualifications for a commission. A. is sending him to see a neighbour
of ours, Colonel Parker Bowles* of the Blues. I advised Igor to call
him 'Sir' if he is interviewed in the barracks by the Colonel in
uniform, and asked him what he knew of the history of the British
army, about which he was bound to be asked some questions. 'What
sort of questions, Jim?' 'Well, he might ask who you considered the
greater soldier, the Duke of Marlborough or the Duke of Wellington.'
He had not heard of either, nor of the Battle of Waterloo. Disclosed
that he thought a sergeant-major of higher rank than a colonel. I give
him up.

Then I wrote M. a reprimand about his pursuit of low life and
wastage of his talents. I am becoming a dreadful disapprover, shocked
by everything. Was shocked this morning on returning from church
to hear a *battue* going on in Allen Grove, and thought of those hopeless Somerset boys[†] slaughtering pheasants too weakened by the cold
to rise. I am too censorious, instead of smiling blandly upon the world
and keeping my mouth shut.

Wednesday, 8th January

Eardley writes that he is smitten by Stephen Spender's[‡] diaries and
writing to him to congratulate. I don't admire Spender any more than
I did Christopher Isherwood[§] who has just died. Their communist
side did much harm intellectually in the 1930s, and many of their ideas

---

* Andrew Parker Bowles (b. 1939); m. 1973 Camilla Shand (diss. 1994, in which year he
retired from army with rank of Brigadier).
† The three sons of 11th Duke of Beaufort.
‡ Sir Stephen Spender, poet (1909–95); m. (2nd) 1941 Natasha Litvin.
§ English novelist, dramatist and scriptwriter (1906–86), who lived in USA from 1939.

have always struck me as drivel. Nevertheless, Ros once passed on to me a message from Isherwood that he liked my diaries for their candour.

Saturday, 11th January

Went to Charlecote for wedding party of Edmund Fairfax-Lucy to Lucy Lambton, Harrod that was.* She is a very positive and determined girl and I wonder if she won't bulldoze that nice, vague little Edmund, who is a painter first and foremost. About two hundred people there. Never seen such a scrum. I went for old times' sake, A. because she likes any party. A hundred old faces, N.T. and non-N.T. Billa[†] present. Alice F.-L. looking perfectly well, and affirming that she was so in spite of her appalling accident, but wearing a hat and dark glasses. She has always been neurotic, hiding behind protection. Lady Lambton,[‡] the bride's mother, tried to dress like Henry VIII and succeeded, for she has a large florid face. Wore a dress that looked like ermine, and a hat such as the monarch wore in the Holbein portrait, pulled down one side of her head, and gloves of dark blue velvet given to her by David Somerset. I said how generous David was. 'Yes, but I too give expensive presents,' she said. She was sitting on a piano stool in the library, and to hear her I had to kneel on the ground. 'Is this a proposal?' she asked. Amusing woman, whom I had not met before; she and John Wilton[§] were inseparable years ago.

Wednesday, 15th January

I asked Helen Dashwood to lunch with me at Claridge's yesterday, after Freda Berkeley told me how crippled she was. She was rather pathetic, the old fire subdued. Conversation not easy because she was inattentive, though not gaga. She is very immobile, shuffles with two sticks. Occasional sparks in that she is still beastly to porters and taxi drivers. I had to smile and joke with them to placate. When I took

---

* Lady Lucinda Lambton (b. 1943); dau. of Viscount Lambton (see 29 September 1985); photographer, writer and broadcaster; m. 1st 1965 Henry Harrod, 2nd 1986 Sir Edmund Fairfax-Lucy, 6th Bt, 3rd 1991 Sir Peregrine Worsthorne.
† Billa Harrod was the bride's former mother-in-law.
‡ The flamboyant 'Bindy' Lambton had lived apart from her husband since the 1970s.
§ John Egerton, 4th Earl of Wilton (1921–99); m. 1962 Diana Galway.

her back to her flat afterwards, she said she had enjoyed herself, kissed me, and said, 'Now we are chums again, aren't we?' Poor, dear Helen. She is convinced that there is an after-life and she will be reunited with her loved ones. But won't the loved ones take flight, in flocks?

For dinner I had Selina alone at Brooks's. Conversation never flagged. Her *Nancy Mitford* is doing well. Hamish Hamilton have now asked her to write a biography of Evelyn Waugh and offered an advance of £80,000 which she can't refuse, having no money of her own, she says. I thought there were enough books about Evelyn, but she says there is no straightforward biography, only literary assessments and memoirs by Frankie Donaldson and Christopher Sykes.*

Helen told me that King Edward VIII went to pieces when he discovered that Freda Dudley Ward had taken another lover, Michael Herbert. He was never the same again.†

Saturday, 18th January

Sanjay, that clever and sensitive assistant of Anthony Blond, telephoned, not with the hoped-for news that a paperback publisher had accepted my novel, but to say that he has had an offer of a better job and leaves his present employment on 1 February. I am delighted for him. So strange that I can communicate with this youth, an Indian and fifty-five years younger than myself, as if we are contemporaries. I can't think of anyone else over so wide a gap with whom I can do this.

Sunday, 19th January

A. stricken with bad cold, I dine with the Loewensteins.‡ The Michael Briggses and Camilla Fairbairn§ present, latter looking extremely hand-

---

* Writer, journalist and broadcaster (1907–86); his *Evelyn Waugh: A Biography* appeared in 1975.

† In 1918 Edward, Prince of Wales met Freda Dudley Ward, wife of a Liberal MP and niece of Reginald, 2nd Viscount Esher. He began an intense love affair with her which lasted six years. Almost from the start he was jealous of Michael Herbert, yr bro. of 15th Earl of Pembroke and a rival for her affections. On 6 March 1920, he wrote to her: 'I loathe Michael with a hatred that passeth all understanding' (Rupert Godfrey [ed.], *Letters from a Prince* [1998]).

‡ Prince Rupert zu Loewenstein (b. 1930), financial adviser, of Biddestone Manor, Gloucestershire; m. 1957 Josephine Lowry-Corry.

§ Camilla Grinling; m. 1st Jeremy Fry (inventor and Bath resident), 2nd John Fairbairn.

needed. He said my *Last Stuarts*, which he favourably reviewed when it came out, was a first-rate book which had not received justice. I sat next to his daughter, aged seventeen and about to go to Worcester College, Oxford to read history, specialising in the eighteenth century.[*] On being told by her father that I was an expert on the period, the child talked *at* me about Dr Johnson and Wilkes, her chosen subject, impressively but too earnestly. On Caroline's other side was Peter Saunders,[†] now living alone in a flat in Charlton,[‡] looking old, collapsed and forlorn and seeming nicer in consequence. After dinner I listened fascinated in the Library while he, clad in a rather preposterous Indian jacket with spangles, talked of his past history, how he came to England in the 1930s with (he claimed) Prince Philip under the wing of Kurt Hahn,[§] the founder of Gordonstoun School, who was the cleverest and wisest person Peter ever knew and meant more to him than his own father. Who the father was one could not quite make out. But much talk of his millionaire maternal grandfather who died in 1916, leaving a huge house in Munich and a grand collection of art objects. As a married man in his fifties he fell in love with a beautiful girl of nineteen he met in the English Gardens and made his mistress, this being Peter's grandmother. I imagine he was Jewish, and Peter also.

Monday, 27th January

A film on TV of Molly Keane's[¶] *Time after Time* which I read last year. About a terrible Irish family of three sisters and one brother living in a *délabrée* Victorian house. Haunting story of decadence, genteel poverty, meanness, stealthy little squalors, oh so well told. How I hate the Irish. Must write to congratulate John Gielgud,[**] who played the brother.

---

[*] Petronella Wyatt (b. 1969); journalist; daughter of Sir Woodrow by his 4th marriage.

[†] Clothes designer.

[‡] Charlton Park near Malmesbury, a 17th century 'prodigy' house converted into flats *c.* 1975.

[§] German educationist (1886–1974).

[¶] Mary Nesta Skrine (1905–96); playwright and novelist, who successfully resumed her writing career in the 1980s after an interval of more than twenty years; m. 1938 Robert Keane.

[**] Actor (1904–2000), with whom J.L.-M. had 'a short-lived affair' around 1930 (see *Deep Romantic Chasm*, 13 January and 7 March 1981).

Tuesday, 28th January

Saw on TV piles of porcelain retrieved mysteriously from a sunken eighteenth-century Dutch sailing ship bound for England.[*] Astonishing how, when divers broke open the wooden crates in which these commodities were beautifully packed, the wood dissolved revealing the china blue and white plates, tea services, tea pots etc. all in pristine condition. To be sold at Christie's. I think the heirs of the original owners ought to be recompensed, not the pirates who have dredged them from the bottom of the sea.

Cotters[†] and an old friend, a dealer in rare books, came to tea in Bath. Much talk about books and the bargains they have found in their time. Cotters still works for Booth's shop in Hay-on-Wye.[‡] He brought me *The Quest for Corvo* in paperback, saying what a grand writer Corvo[§] was, whereas I have always considered him a horrid man who bit every hand that fed him.

Saturday, 1st February

Managed to get to London on Thursday despite deep snow here, with blocked roads, telephone wires down, etc. No snow in London but a bitter east wind. Stayed in a room on top floor of Brooks's, and dined with Eardley and Richard Shone, E. looking well after latest operation and cooking delicious dinner. Much laughter. On Friday I saw Agnews' exhibition of nineteenth-century watercolours, including some Edward Lears; Wildenstein's exhibition of splendid French Impressionist paintings from the collection of the foundress of *Reader's Digest*; then Reynolds at Burlington House. Reynolds knew everyone and was full of culture and erudition but is not a good painter. His portrait of the future Duke of Hamilton who married Beckford's daughter Susan was captioned, 'Commissioned by William Beckford, millionaire homosexual snob'. Must complain about this to Secretary of Royal Academy.

---

[*] Known as the Nanking Cargo.

[†] Michael W. F. Cottrill (b. 1948), antiquarian book expert; protégé of Penelope, Lady Betjeman (see *Through Wood and Dale*, 3 September 1976).

[‡] Richard Booth had bought the castle at Hay-on-Wye, Breconshire, in the 1970s, and transformed that sleepy town into an international centre of the second-hand book trade.

[§] Baron Corvo was the alias of the novelist Frederick Rolfe (1860–1913), whose elusive life was the subject of A. J. A. Symons's famous study *The Quest for Corvo* (1934) (see notes to 10 February 1985).

At 11.30 I went to see Robert Smith of Sidgwick & Jackson, a nice, decent bald-head of forty, lacking enthusiasm or emotion. Said he had enjoyed my typescript, but admitted he had not yet finished it and was worried about its length. I begged Smith to show it to Frank Longford* who had got me to write it in the first place. Smith did say however that they were determined to publish it this year. We discussed the title. He does not like *Viscount Esher with Humble Duty* and suggested *The Power behind the Throne*, which made John Saumarez Smith[†] squirm when I told him.

We dined with Nan Bernays[‡] to meet that extraordinary lady Kay Elliot,[§] the youngest child of Sir Charles Tennant who was born in 1823.[¶] She told us of the party given by Mrs Thatcher to celebrate the two-hundredth anniversary of Downing Street as the residence of the Prime Minister. Queen invited. Kay was there, having lived in the house as a girl with her half-sister Margot Asquith. Has highest opinion of Mrs Thatcher and thinks it inconceivable that she could tell a lie, as she is alleged to have done over the Westland business.[**]

Sunday, 2nd February

Dined with Sally Westminster to meet Molly Keane, delightful lady of over eighty though looking sixty. Full of humour and diffidence.

---

[*] Francis Aungier Pakenham, 7th Earl of Longford (1905–2001); politician, humanitarian campaigner, writer and publisher, who as Chairman of Sidgwick & Jackson in 1981 had originally suggested that J.L.-M. write life of 2nd Viscount Esher; m. 1931 Elizabeth Harman, writer.

[†] Managing Director of G. Heywood Hill Ltd, booksellers in Curzon Street.

[‡] Nancy Britton (d. 1987: see entry for 22 March 1987); m. 1942 Robert Bernays, MP, who was killed in action, 1945.

[§] Katharine Tennant (1903–94); m. 1934 as his 2nd wife Walter Elliot (d. 1958); created life peeress (among first batch, 1958) as Baroness Elliot of Harwood.

[¶] Sir Charles Tennant (1823–1906), Scottish industrialist and politician; m. 1st 1849 Emma Winsloe, by whom his many children included Edward (cr. Baron Glenconner) and Margot (m. H. H. Asquith, Prime Minister); m. 2nd 1898 Marguerite Miles, mother of Lady Elliot.

[**] The most serious domestic political crisis faced by Mrs Thatcher during her premiership arose as a result of differences between herself and the Industry Secretary Leon Brittan on the one hand, and the Defence Secretary Michael Heseltine on the other, as to how the problems of the Westland helicopter firm should be resolved: the PM and Brittan (along with the firm's board) favoured a takeover by the American Sikorsky Corporation, while Heseltine supported a 'European' solution. On 9 January 1986 Heseltine sensationally resigned from the Government, complaining of Mrs Thatcher's autocratic behaviour; Brittan's resignation followed on the 24th, and the PM came under much pressure.

Said Chatto's had turned down both *Good Behaviour* and *Time after Time*, silly idiots. She had enjoyed the film, though thought the Jewish cousin overplayed her part. The producer barely asked her advice. A nice, sharp, jolly, Irish country lady, not outstandingly intellectual. Feels deeply about Ireland and hates the Ulstermen, holding them and not the English responsible for Ireland's ills during the past century. She has a good-looking, dumpling face like dear Billa. Must have been very pretty, and is great fun.

Saturday, 8th February

In the bath I listened on the wireless to Charles Tomlinson[*] being interviewed at his home, a mile west of Alderley[†] up the valley. The stream that flows beside their Gothic cottage formed an audible back-drop to the talk. Between questions and answers he read from his poems in a monotonous voice. Charles's poetry has feeling but lacks spontaneity. He considers his geographical position, on a tributary of the Severn, reflects his position in the world – living a secluded life of asceticism and abstemiousness away from the hum of men, yet almost within sight of Bristol into which he makes weekly forays to teach lit-erature to the young. Something a little musty and cockney (in the sense applied by Byron to the Leigh Hunts) about this Wordsworthian poet from Stoke-on-Trent and his blue-stocking wife.

Yesterday M. came from London to spend the day with me in Bath. Extremely cold and bitter out-of-doors. A. joined us for a filthy lunch-eon in the snackery of the Lansdown Hotel which used to be so good. M. told me he had been visited by a strange man calling himself Prince Paul of Romania.[‡] He is King Carol's grandson by a brief early marriage to a dancer called Zizi Lambrino, and is looking for someone to help him write a biography of his grandfather. M. and I sat over cups of tea in the library, chatting happily. What is the secret of his attraction for me? His cleverness, his lack of inhibition, his good nature, his affection.

---

[*] Poet (b. 1927); m. 1948 Brenda Raybould.
[†] Alderley Grange, Georgian country house at Wotton-under-Edge, Gloucestershire, where the L.-Ms lived from 1961 to 1974. Their neighbours included the Tomlinsons, the Derick Gascoignes, and the Bruce Chatwins.
[‡] Paul Lambrino (b. 1948); photographer; known officially as Prince Paul of Romania from 1955, when a French court accepted the claim of his father, Carol Lambrino, to be a legitimate son of King Carol II (d. 1953). His biography of his grandfather appeared in 1988 and acknowledges editorial help.

I had been meaning to lend him Mrs Villa-Gilbert's[*] novel *Mrs Galbraith's Air*, but this morning A., who had already read it, suddenly demanded it back, as if she had a premonition that I meant it for M. So strange. Also in the new collection of V.-G's short stories I have found one with undoubted resemblances to my novel. Norah Smallwood, to whose memory the book is dedicated, lent me two of the stories some time ago thinking they might give me inspiration for my novel. Did she, I wonder, proceed to submit my novel to V.-G. who, though turning it down on Chatto's behalf, was subconsciously inspired by *it*? V.-G. has now turned from romantic evil creatures to squalid, amoral punks.

Sunday, 9th February

Dined last night at the House. Only the Christopher Thynnes staying.[†] I sat next to Antonia, an alarming girl, shrewd, sharp, semi-educated, worldly. They boasted of a nasty trick they played on Brian Masters. Christopher rang pretending to be the editor of an American magazine offering him an huge fee to write a piece on the dinner party he would give for the most socially brilliant of his contemporaries. Suspecting nothing, Brian went into raptures about 'Lord and Lady Christopher Thynne, a young couple of the height of sophistication, my great friend the Marquess of Londonderry,'[‡] and other celebrities. The Thynnes secretly tape-recorded the conversation and replay it when they want to amuse themselves and their friends. Oh lord, not my sort. To my surprise, C. embraced me on leaving. Our heads knocked together, emitting a hollow sound.

There is a horrible move among Tory malcontents, led by that shit Heseltine,[§] to oust Mrs Thatcher. That splendid woman is showing signs of giving in, and I suspect may be on the verge of a breakdown. That would be terrible, for her victories over the Unions herald the salvation of this benighted country. But Charlie Morrison with whom

---

[*] Mariana Villa-Gilbert, novelist. Norah Smallwood, who published them both at Chatto & Windus, had recommended her fiction to J.L.-M., considering it similar to his own – they both wrote horror stories, in country-house settings, about the destructive influence of narcissistic characters.

[†] Lord Christopher Thynne (b. 1934), yr s. of 6th Marquess of Bath (and brother of Caroline, Duchess of Beaufort); m. 1968 Antonia Palmer.

[‡] 'Alistair' Vane-Tempest-Stewart, 9th Marquess of Londonderry (b. 1937).

[§] Conservative politician (b. 1933), whose resignation as Secretary of State for Defence in January 1986 had precipitated the Westland crisis (see notes to 1 February 1986).

we lunched today believes Mrs T. must go if the Conservatives are to win the next election, though he would rather she were succeeded by Walker* than Heseltine. Despite his saying this I rather liked Charlie today, quite human and easy to talk to for an MP and not the stuffed shirt I had supposed.

On return I walked the dogs through the Dog Leg and Slates and witnessed sun and snow together. A deep purple pall approached over the Park, releasing soft flakes which dissolved on landing. The sun ahead remained stationary, a fiery ball of gold issuing flanges like wisps of wild hair.

Am appalled by the latest snapshots showing me with the children at Christmas. I appear as a very old man, with mouth open; the look of a zany; slack neck and throat muscles. But worst of all, thin wisps of grey hair, and skin the colour and texture of a ripe, shiny plum, as though I may have a stroke tomorrow. Begged A. to destroy them. She says the dreadful colour is the printing, and doesn't represent me. Yet the children look of good, real, young colour.

Saturday, 15th February

Am reading Proust's *Albertine Disparue*, which in Scott-Moncrieff's translation has the absurd title *The Sweet Cheat Gone*, because of the section on Venice. At times I think it the most boring rubbish I have ever read. I must have read it once before, for I read the whole of Proust at a sitting, so to speak, when I was in the Hospital for Infectious Diseases in the 1930s, Harold [Nicolson] having sent me the lot. Found I had then marked with a pencil certain passages I would mark today. I dare say it is the case that Proust meant boys when he wrote of the girls of 'the little band'. The names he chose – Gilberte, Albertine, Andrée – are boys' names adapted to the feminine, just as an English writer might call his loved ones Frances, Alexandra, etc., in disguise for Francis and Alexander.

Richard Wood,† who dined with us last night, told me that he was once present when Master interviewed a gardener. He told the man that his three conditions for engaging him were that he must be a supporter of fox-hunting, a Conservative and a member of the Church of England.

---

* Rt Hon. Peter Walker, MP(C) for Worcester (b. 1932); Sec. of State for Energy, 1983–7.
† Land agent of Badminton estate.

Sunday, 16th February

A delicious day at Moorwood. The christening of my great-great-nephew Alexander James Winwood Robinson at Bagendon church by Mr Woodhouse, the old parson retired and great friend of the family. Perishing cold day and east wind. Moving little service. We all clustered round the font, a party of young friends of Henry and Suzy, and a few oldies like us, Audrey, and old Willy, who is eighty-five and told us he had known and served five generations of Robinsons. The child behaved perfectly when a mug of ice-cold water from the stream (all taps frozen) was poured over him. Never cried or showed any disapproval of this barbaric treatment. Mr Woodhouse said the child must feel he belongs to this place, *his* place, for he would be the next squire.

Luncheon at Farm Cottage. Sat next to niece Dale and new wife of Terry Faulkner, Suzy's brother. Terry an amusing and attractive fellow. I brought a pair of silver hair-brushes engraved with initials, which A. thought an unsuitable present for these days; and I left a long letter to be given to Alexander on his twenty-first birthday, telling him what I remember about our upbringing and our forebears – matters which the young are not interested in until they cease to be young and there is no old member of the family left alive to consult. Listening to the gaiety, fun and laughter of this luncheon I thought how lucky Henry and Nick are to be parentless and well-off, with a nice house and property and all the responsibility which they assume so happily. If only I had had some money and independence when I was in my late twenties.

Saturday, 22nd February

Have spent the last two days feverishly going through three chapters of Regy returned to me with corrections by Sidgwick's reader Mrs Jagger. On the whole she has not cut out much that I mind about; but in her pedantic way she has made the syntax too staccato, and not *me*. But I can hardly be bothered to question her abbreviations.

A week ago we lunched with Desmond Briggs. I motored Daphne Fielding* there and back. She seemed anxious and on return begged

---

* Hon. Daphne Vivian (1904–97); novelist, mother of Caroline, Duchess of Beaufort; m. 1st 1926 Henry Thynne, later 6th Marquess of Bath, 2nd 1953 Xan Fielding, war hero and writer.

me to accompany her into her house, though it was still daylight. On opening the door we heard the sound of rushing water – a burst pipe. I soothed her and she said she would telephone someone on the estate to deal with it. Thought no more. Then yesterday Caroline told A. that Daphne had gone off her head, accused her maid of trying to poison her, asserted that her telephone line was tapped. C. took her to the Chesterfield Home in Bristol where the psychiatrist told her that her mother was seriously deranged. D. became violent when asked to take certain pills. A pretty kettle of fish. She cannot live alone and is now staying at the House. David returned from Nassau to find the place a lunatic asylum, with Mary Beaufort, Daphne Moore, and now his mother-in-law, all round the bend.

Sunday, 23rd February

We lunched with the Lloyd Georges at Freshfield. Conventional party of elderly married couples (goodness knows who they all were), plus the egregious Francis Burne, kissing every woman left and right. After luncheon I asked to go to the WC in order to have another glimpse of the framed *Punch* cartoons on the back staircase. So good they are – L.G. in all the crises of his career. I think they may be by Owen John,* father of my Eton friend Hoel Llewellyn, who once took me motoring with his pretty, faded wife, a nice, tubby, mustachioed man in an open touring car. In the WC itself, over the seat, are signed photographs of Hitler and Mussolini, with affable and complimentary dedications to the great man. Owen Lloyd George is charming, with twinkling brown eyes and the kindest face. Strange how he has become 'county' within two generations – married to a Gordon Cumming and as right-wing as is decent, with a large house in the country. He has since sent me three interesting letters written by Regy to his grandfather, showing more intimacy between the two than I suspected. I don't think L.G. thought much of Regy, whom he considered a busybody, and Regy certainly held the other to be a bounder and twister.

Monday, 24th February

Dear Nick lunched with me at Brooks's. I noticed in the shaft of pale sun through a window that he already has a few silver hairs in his

---

* J.L.-M. probably had in mind the Welsh sporting cartoonist Dai Gwilym John.

otherwise raven head. The hair of the old is seldom silver, rather grey or white, but the odd turned hair in a young head is bright, burnished silver. Nick so sympathetic. Has finally given up smoking, and is eating less in order to keep his figure.

Sunday, 2nd March

I telephoned Dadie Rylands at King's College, Cambridge. His voice that of a man of forty, strong, clear and precise. Sentences interlarded with 'dear boy', which I find characteristic of his generation, and endearing – no young man now would call another by this term. He speaks highly of his nephew living in Venice and wife, who will welcome me there in April.

Tuesday, 4th March

Strange how, driving in fog, one can see more clearly through the back window (by means of looking-glass) than through the windscreen. Fog and rain today, breaking a terrible freezing February, the worst since 1947.

Thursday, 13th to Tuesday, 18th March

In Galicia [north-western Spain] with A., accompanying her on the International Dendrological Society's gardens tour. Two nights spent in Santiago, which I last visited in 1934. I had retained vivid memories of the beauty of this city, uniformly built of dazzling granite, and was not disappointed. City centre completely unspoilt and surely one of the most beautiful in Europe. Environs hideous of course with modern buildings. Indeed, whole of Galicia ruined by straggling development along roads, joining up towns, and the worst litter I have seen in any country, every lay-by a dump of trash, rusting cars, disused washing machines, etc. However, nothing exceeds the beauty of the Romanesque cathedral, so severe and austere within, yet relieved by gilded Baroque accessories and the illuminated figure of St James, dominating with quizzical medieval stare the body of the church. As for the Baroque elevation, El Obradoiro, nothing I know excels it for loveliness and grandeur. The granite sparkles when the sun shines (it rains here inordinately) like candy sugar. The gold is enhanced by streaks and splashes of moss-gold lichen. Have described in notebook the wonderful experience of the *botafumeiro* swinging.

[*This is the descripton to which J.L.-M. refers:*

16-18 March: Staying in Santiago at Hospicio de los Reyes Catolicos in Playa de Obradoiro. On Monday we attended mass given for senior citizens of Galicia. Bishop in full canonicals and attendant priests and acolytes. We in south transept. When mass over, the six attendants in long plum-coloured capes carried on a pole into transept the silver *botafumeiro* (the previous day we saw 2 in the Treasury). They attached it to long rope suspended from a metal cage of pulleys in centre of the crossing. The six in perfect drill pulled, like bell-ringers, each at a separate rope, and swung the thing from side to side. With great violence they made it swing the entire length of the crossing, rising higher and higher, until it practically reached the vaulting, descending with a roar like wind and clearing the pavement by a mere 4 feet, belching flames and clouds of incense. A most exciting, mysterious and somehow violent experience. Spaniards do not do things by halves.]

Thursday, 20th March

A. and I motor to London to attend farewell dinner to Pat Gibson in Spencer House. This setting sounds very well but is at present totally empty of furniture, curtains and carpets, so that the din was appalling. For an hour we stood shouting at one another, with result that next day I developed a sore throat. Walls and ceilings over-decorated, too much gold introduced. I visited this house once years ago with Jack Spencer,* when it was much battered by the war, windows blown out and boarded up. A lovely house.

After dinner Angus Stirling[†] delivered a panegyric of Gibson. He did it well, though it sounded a bit hollow to me, as Stirling has worked with Pat for two years at most. When I recall the chairmen under whom I worked – Lord Zetland, David Crawford, Oliver Esher – Gibson is a minor figure, though decent and efficient. He lacks the gravitas of the others, as did [his predecessor] Ran Antrim.[‡]

---

* Albert Edward John Spencer, 7th Earl (1892–1975).
† Director-General of N.T., 1983–95 (Deputy Director, 1979–83); (b. 1933, kt 1994).
‡ See notes to 8 January 1985.

Wednesday, 26th March

There is the faintest touch of spring in the air after one of the worst winters I remember. February was continuously below freezing, although lacking snow. Not a leaf yet in bud. Blackthorn not even out. Snowdrops out, but many weeks late. Awful winter for colds, and I do not really feel well. Saddened too by *dégringolade* of poor little Honey whose execution we have made dates for and stayed. She is still with us but will have to go soon.

I am correcting the corrected typescript of Esher. The distinguished lady editor's corrections make me feel what a poor writer I am. Some of her cuts are well-chosen, but she has excised many of my anecdotes, with the result that the book is not *me*. I am bored to tears with the whole thing, and there is more work to come. Once I have finished this reading, I will have the Royal Librarian's blue-pencilling, then the galleys, then the index and preface and footnotes, then the page-proofs. Meanwhile I have embarked on my book about Venice, where I go next month. J.K.-B. wants to accompany me. I am torn between the desire for his company and protection, and the need to be absolutely alone in order to soak myself in the visits to monuments and note-taking, and drafting of text in my hotel bedroom.

Went to Tim Bailey's funeral at Broadwell Church near Stow-on-the-Wold.* Met dear Woman in Stow and we lunched together at Deborah's Kitchen, started all those years ago by Bunny Denning. Dead long ago, I suggested? Not at all, Pam said, she still lingers. We spoke of the dreaded Bailey Week when we were children, of tennis and cricket matches which the Mitfords and I all hated. All four Bailey brothers are now dead. Tim the youngest – a mere 67. I went because of the old days and the kindness of the Baileys to me, for I did not love them, except for Chris. 'Same here,' Pam said. At the sad little service I was not the least moved, even when I watched Richard Bailey, Dick's boy, carrying the bedint little brown tin casket of Tim's ashes under my nose to the churchyard, just as I witnessed Tim carrying his mother's in 1971. Debo there, having come from Chatsworth. She told me to go and see the Colonel's† gravestone with the words 'He loved England', which always moves her to tears.

---

* For the Bailey brothers (first cousins of the Mitford sisters), see notes to 29 June 1985.
† Percy Bailey (1875–1947), Colonel 12th Lancers; m. 1907 Dorothy ('Weenie') Bowles (1885–1971); Bunny Denning was a friend of 'Aunt Weenie'.

Thursday, 27th March

Maundy Thursday, and a day of mourning indeed. I telephoned Riley the vet who suggested I bring Honey at 6.30. What with Easter on our heels, A. agreed I should take her today – better than further delay and the agony of watching her decline. Riley a saintly man, who bore with my bitter tears which I could not control. I sat in the waiting room with Honey, stroking her neck and ears without daring to look at her. For her it was no worse a visit than many previous ones. Riley came in with syringe in hand and instantly gave her a prick which she did not even feel. In five minutes she was asleep, having lain herself on the floor. I apologised for my emotion. He said it was normal and right and he felt the same over his own dogs' demise. When it was clear she was unconscious, he said, 'You may go now. Just give her a pat.' I did so and kissed her little head, and bolted. This was pre-arranged, for then he would despatch her. A. had gone to Communion in my absence; when she returned, we both shamelessly wept. I said the piteous thing about dogs was their innocence. She said it was their implicit trust in us. Whatever it be, they wring the heart. I felt remorseful over my occasional irritation with Honey, who did have some tiresome habits – not coming in when put out last thing, and other sillinesses. Remorseful about the times I was angry with her and smacked her. *Eheu*, I grieve and am miserable. She was good, good, good, devoid of malice and spite. My companion for over a decade who, until she became incontinent, slept on my bed at nights. The hell of it all.

Wednesday, 2nd April

Pickwoad, the National Trust book expert, called to examine my library. Within three-quarters of an hour he had assessed the lot and thought little of my books, except for the Beckford ones and the silver-mounted prayer books, and one seventeenth-century binding left me by Ted Lister.* Lunching with me at the Lansdown Hotel, he said librarians and scholars were the worst book vandals. For example, the priceless volumes from Chatsworth which were given to the

---

* Edward Graham Lister (1873–1956) of Westwood Manor, Wiltshire (which he bequeathed to N.T.); diplomatist, furniture restorer, needleworker and harpist; friend and admirer of J.L.-M. until the latter's marriage in 1951.

Government in the 1950s in lieu of death duties are now stored in the bowels of the British Library, where they have deteriorated through neglect.*

Thursday, 3rd April

Hugh Massingberd† lunched at Brooks's. He is worried about his weight, which has increased from twelve to sixteen stone. Always modest and self-deprecating, yet a delightful man, with humour. Extremely prolific. Writes regular articles on small squires' houses, reviews for every journal, and does pot-boilers, including one on Kingston Lacy which he wanted to talk to me about. I asked after his uncle, Peter Montgomery. Alas a cabbage now, and does not recognise him. Told me how bigoted the Irish still were about divorce. He stayed for a week with his friend Mark Bence-Jones,‡ whose mother, who lives in the house and has known Hugh all her life, would not address a word to him on account of his divorce and remarriage.

Heard on the wireless that Peter Pears§ has died. Nice man but flat, reedy voice. I remember meeting him and Britten at Ursula Nettleship's house at Cheyne Walk at the very beginning of the war. They were sitting on the floor drinking tea, and their earnestness struck me as pathological. He once stayed with us at Alderley when he was singing at the Bath Festival, and had to borrow my father's old tailcoat which I then used for weddings, and he could hardly get into. Britten always struck me as touchy and humourless, and envious whenever Lennox [Berkeley] received acclaim. He and Pears were both certainly wrong-headed about Russia, where they were acclaimed as VIPs, and seemed completely taken in.

---

* Nicholas Pickwoad points out that this represents a misunderstanding on J.L.-M's part. He had in fact told J.L.-M. 'that I had always found it ironic that books from houses like Chatsworth were said to have been "saved for the nation" when they were removed from lightly-used collections in clean country air to heavily used collections, such as the British Library, in polluted city centres'. He intended no criticism of the British Library.
† Hugh Montgomery-Massingberd (b. 1946); writer, journalist, publisher, genealogist, and future author (2002) of a play – *Ancestral Voices* – based on the diaries of J.L.-M.
‡ Mark Bence-Jones (b. 1930), writer, of Glenville Park, Co. Cork; o.s. of Colonel Philip B.-J. and Victoria *née* Thomas; ed. Ampleforth.
§ Tenor and organist (1910–86); partner from 1937 of the composer Benjamin Britten (1913–76), with whom he lived at Aldeburgh and was involved in the Aldeburgh Festival.

Saturday, 5th April

We motored to Kingham [Oxfordshire] to lunch with Ian Lowe* and wife Mary. We imagined the latter, whom we had not met before but had heard to be obsessed with whippets and dog shows, to be *farouche*, but on the contrary she is sympathetic, pretty and distinguished. They produced a puppy of nine months, already baptised Missy after one of Louis XV's dogs. A darling, already rather big, with the same colouring as Honey except for white markings. More bullish, not so pretty, shorter nose. A. offers her to me as a present. We have to make up our minds within a few days.

On return we stopped at Northleach and had a delicious cream tea in the little square. Then to Barnsley, and while A. visited Rosemary Verey,[†] I walked to the church. Remarkable for scalloped piers of nave like exaggerated fluted columns of the Parthenon. A curious and rather ugly east window, the bottom rather obscured by chancel added later. Window covers whole width of nave and seen from the outside on approach looks as though the mullions lean inwards. An oil painting in north aisle, signed Ribera, subject Domine Quo Vadis. I wonder if genuine. Presume not or it would long ago have been sold to an itinerant dealer. Brasses on floor. One of a donor to the church, rather worn, date 1458 with Latin inscription to effect that nothing is worth doing unless it be for the love of God. Back home I find from notes that I visited this church years ago, and made the same observations as I have written above.

Sunday, 6th April

After motoring A. to Heathrow I lunched with the Droghedas. Lady Poole[‡] and Mrs Peter Cazalet[§] staying. At first Joan had no idea who I was, but towards the end of luncheon she kept looking across at me and smiling whenever Garrett said anything outrageous, as she always used

---

* Art historian (b. 1935); curator at Ashmolean Museum, Oxford, 1962–87; later briefly Director of American Museum at Claverton; m. Mary Howard.
† Rosemary Sandilands (1918–2001); m. 1939 David Verey (1913–84), architectural historian, of Barnsley House near Cirencester; garden designer; compiled a series of books with A.L.-M.
‡ Daphne Bowles; m. 1st Brig. Algernon Heber-Percy, 2nd 1952–65 Oliver Poole, sometime Chairman of Conservative Party (cr. 1st Baron Poole, 1958).
§ Zara Mainwaring; m. 2nd Peter Cazalet (1907–73), racehorse trainer.

to do, as though we were in collusion in laughing at dear G. Drove home in a dense snowstorm. Still bitterly cold.

Tuesday, 15th April

Am in blackest depression. Confided in A. last night on way to dine with the Thomas Messels* who had William Rosse and his charming young son Patrick staying.† Earlier I had been to Lacock where William was opening an exhibition of photographs by his great-grandmother Mary Rosse,‡ she being an early pioneer, somewhere between Fox Talbot and Mrs Cameron.§ I stayed only half an hour, and was so overwhelmed by claustrophobia and unknown people talking to me that I fled before the ceremony. A. says it is the relentless appalling weather we have been having, and indeed, there is still a scattering of snow on the fields as I drive to Bath. But it is not that. There is no reason for it.

Billa telephoned yesterday to say that Penelope Betjeman¶ had died in India, as she was getting off her pony on the Himalaya foothills. Just as she would have wished – but oh, the sadness. This morning, Max Hastings,** editor of *Daily Telegraph*, rang to ask if I could write a thousand words on her by tomorrow. I was filled with dismay, and telephoned Billa for help. She clearly wanted to do it herself so I rang Hastings back and told him so. Thank God I have got out of that task.

Then Freda Berkeley telephoned to say Heywood Hill had died in his sleep of pneumonia, having become skin and bones. Lord, is there an end to it? Never was there a happier couple than H. and Anne.

---

* Of Bradley Court, Wotton-under-Edge, Gloucestershire (b. 1951); designer and furniture maker; nephew of Anne, Countess of Rosse, and first cousin of 7th Earl of Rosse; m. 1981 Penelope Barratt.
† William Brendan Parsons (known in England as William and in Ireland as Brendan), 7th Earl of Rosse (b. 1936); his e.s. and heir Patrick, Lord Oxmantown (b. 1969).
‡ Mary Field (d. 1885); m. 1836 William Parsons, 3rd Earl of Rosse (1800–67), scientist involved in the development of the telescope.
§ Lacock Abbey, Gloucestershire, had been the residence of the photographer William Fox Talbot (1800–77); his granddaughter donated the property (1944) to the N.T., which established a Museum of Photography there.
¶ Hon. Penelope Chetwode (1910–86); m. 1933 John Betjeman (1906–84; kt 1969), later Poet Laureate.
** Journalist and military historian (b. 1945); editor *Daily Telegraph*, 1986–95, *Evening Standard*, 1995–2002; stepson of J.L.-M's friend Sir Osbert Lancaster; kt 2002.

Both these deaths may be called mercies. Penelope was not happy and hadn't been so for years before John's death. She had just sold her house and was planning to retire to a nunnery, which cannot have been an altogether jolly prospect. And H. suffered cruelly from Parkinson's.

William Rosse is gentle and sweet, but lacking humour. The boy, Patrick Oxmantown, a charmer. I told him Anne [Rosse] adored him and I would write to her with my opinion of him. When goodbyes were said, he asked me earnestly what I was going to tell his grandmother. 'You just wait,' I said.

Reagan's bombing raid of Tripoli[*] is a disastrous mistake. It will exacerbate Arab anger and incite endless reprisals. Instead the western nations should have imposed stringent sanctions on Libya, expelled all Libyans living in their countries and severed air links. I am all for terrorists being shot on sight, but it is a mistake for one state to bomb another, killing civilians. This action may provoke a third world war, and indeed Gaddafi has threatened as much.

Sunday, 20th April

Everyone says Penelope would have wished it. But would she? I think of the pretty, pouting, determined little face when we met in the woods at Witham Abbey on a hot June day, all of us naked but for a few bracken branches. That must have been in 1930, when Johnnie [Churchill] had the mouth of a Botticelli angel.[†]

On the 16th, Selina and her mother[‡] lunched in Bath. We were called by a grand hired car and taken to the Huntingdon

---

[*] Muammar Gaddafi (b. 1942), who assumed power in Libya after the overthrow of the monarchy in 1969, outraged the West through his sponsorship of terrorism and invasion of Chad. The United States severed relations with his regime at the beginning of 1986, and in April carried out an air raid on his capital from British bases, of which he was the intended target: some hundred people were killed, including members of his family, but the dictator himself escaped.

[†] On this occasion, John Churchill and Penelope Chetwode, then in love with each other, went through a mock pagan marriage ceremony, at which J.L.-M. 'officiated' (Witham Woods belonged to J.C's grandmother, Lady Abingdon). The romance was terminated by P.C's parents, who disapproved of J.C. and took their daughter to live with them in India for a year.

[‡] Margaret Lane (1907–94); writer; m. (2nd) 1944 as his 2nd wife John Hastings, 15th Earl of Huntingdon (1901–90).

Chapel,* where we waited and waited in an overheated room for the Duchess of Kent.† When she came and we were presented, she said 'Yes' in a daze of non-recognition. That is all we waited for. When her back was turned I saw how thin she was – anorexia – and when she turned round again, how drawn, with *Weltschmerz* in her eyes, an unhappy, tormented woman half in this world and half in her own. She is Isabel Briggs's first cousin, and looks rather like her. Margaret Huntingdon holds Selina on an invisible leash, like a lady her little dog on a pavement – keeps an eye on her and addresses her when she is really speaking to us. Yet Selina is not in awe of her.

On the 17th an utterly charming man came to tea, one David Burnett‡ (stress on -*ett*), like a breeze from the Dorset Downs. Tall, strong, handsome and sensitive. Begs me to write a book for his little publishing company, similar to David Cecil's last,§ on *Some Cotswold Country Houses*. He enthused my flagging spirit and I said I would if I could possibly manage it. Told him of my other commitments, namely Venice (certain) and Bankes (as yet uncertain).

Andrew Devonshire came for the night on Friday, very charming and appreciative. We had a dinner party for him, asking the Michael Briggses and Charlie Morrisons. Andrew held the floor. Towards the middle of dinner the telephone rang. A boy said he was the son of John Poë¶ and was stranded in the Park, having lost his wallet and failed to meet up with friends. Wanted a bed, but A. would not hear of it. I felt very guilty and unchristian, advised him to sleep in his car and come to us for breakfast in the morning. This he did, looking scruffy and not very attractive. Anyway he was polite, and I gave him money. Andrew agreed with A. not to let him in during dinner, having an aversion to inarticulate teenagers; but Isabel (a generation younger than the rest of us) would have let him come.

---

* In the eighteenth century, Selina, wife of 9th Earl of Huntingdon, founded a nonconformist sect known as the Countess of Huntingdon's Connexion, designed to bring religion to the upper classes, and established several chapels, one in Bath. The Bath chapel, out of use and derelict for some years, had just been restored by the Bath Preservation Trust, and is now the Museum of the Building of Bath.
† Katharine Worsley (b. 1933; sister of Sir Marcus Worsley, 5th Bt – see notes to 8 January 1985); m. 1961 HRH Prince Edward, Duke of Kent (b. 1935).
‡ David Burnett (b. 1946); novelist and publisher, owner of Dovecote Press.
§ *Some Dorset Country Houses* (1985).
¶ Army officer who was a second cousin of J. L.-M.; m. Emma Batten (see entry for 3 December 1987).

In church this morning, Psalm 110 with the line, 'The dew of thy birth is of the womb of the morning'. What words could be more poetic?

Andrew said he asked Lord Hailsham[*] the other day in what particulars he thought he might achieve immortality. H. replied that it would not be through any of his actions or speeches, nor his diaries or memoirs (as he had written none), but perhaps through one of the half-dozen portraits which had been painted of him. 'Which one is that?' Andrew asked. 'By an artist called Derek Hill. Do you know him?' I have passed this on to Derek.

We watched Horowitz's[†] concert from Moscow, televised live. An extraordinary experience. He left Russia in 1925, vowing never to return; lost all his family in the Revolution, and hated everything the Soviets did and represented. And yet there he is, back after sixty years. Wonderful playing, every note distinguishable. Rather crablike hands, fingers turned up at the ends and kept flat against the keyboard. Jolly and eccentric, stuck out his tongue at the camera. Russian audience looked far better dressed than when we were there. Before the concert we saw him and his wife, daughter of Toscanini, visiting Scriabin's house, where he met S's daughter, distinguished old lady with vacant look and female keeper, and played on S's piano, a baby grand.

Tuesday, 22nd April to Thursday, 1st May

In Venice, entirely on my own, staying at Pensione Seguso on the Zattere. Weather disappointing – April is not a safe month in Italy. Little sun, much rain, blustering wind, dull skies. I worked extremely hard, off at 8.30 every morning, returning from churches to snooze on my bed and read guide books. Room full of outdated furniture, heavy, comfortable mid nineteenth-century hanging cupboard and pretty (but bogus) Venetian-glass-framed mirrors. Bathroom to myself. All this time I saw hardly a soul to speak to. Lunched and dined alone. Made acquaintance of nice American couple at next table,

---

[*] Quintin Hogg (1907–2001); MP (C) Oxford, 1938–50; s. father as 2nd Viscount Hailsham 1950 but disclaimed title, 1963, becoming MP for St Marylebone; cr. life peer, 1970, as Baron Hailsham of St Marylebone; Lord Chancellor, 1970–74 and 1979–87; Eton contemporary of J.L.-M.

[†] Vladimir Horowitz, Russian-born pianist (1903–89).

David and Patricia Cleveland, educated and enthusiastic sight-seers. He works for Voice of America, she economist.

I have now selected my monuments for *Venetian Evenings*, studied them with care and made notes. Yet am I inspired to write a second *Roman Mornings*? No, I am not. My love affair with Venice ended years ago. The terrible scourge in Italy today is the schoolchildren and undisciplined teenagers who swarm like locusts, making shrines disgusting with their litter, their transistors, their rudeness, their mere presence.

The Duchess of Windsor died while I was away. M. attended the funeral service at St George's Chapel, which was eerie. No sign of official mourning, and never once was the name of the deceased uttered. The Queen however was seen to be in tears at the graveside, touched perhaps by the sadness of those wretched lives. Meanwhile the *Daily Mail* is publishing extracts from the Windsors' love letters, which will bring M. as their editor notoriety and I hope some money. He is fed up with being congratulated for what is none of his writing and refuses to sign copies of the book,* which Weidenfeld are bringing out on the 15th, showing that publishers can produce a book within weeks if they want to.

Friday, 2nd May

I go to Bath to see the ladies who are cleaning my books. A very good job they have done of them. I hope they will be finished by Monday, when I wish to return to work. They have discovered a pair of early Georgian silver sauce boats, the only silver I have with the Lees crest, in a small box behind *Grove's Dictionary of Music and Musicians*. I must have tucked them away a dozen years ago when we moved from Alderley. From time to time I have said to A., 'Where can they be? They must have been stolen.' Nothing is rasher than putting valuable objects away in safe places.

Monday, 5th May

The ladies haven't quite finished, but they have gone, which is a relief. Curious how strangers always break one's things – my front door lock,

---

* *Wallis & Edward, Letters 1931–1937: The Intimate Correspondence of the Duke and Duchess of Windsor* (Weidenfeld & Nicolson).

the lamp in the library, and the Isfahan carpet badly creased. But I mustn't grumble, for they have done me a kind service, free of charge. Next Sunday we are having the lot to tea at Badminton.

Saturday, 10th May

Missy, the new puppy to replace poor Honey, has been with us a week. A darling, very good and very pretty, but nervous. Backs away when called. A terrible thing happened while we were out walking, she on lead, Folly free and trotting ahead. F. went under a wire. Missy touched it and gave blood-curdling yells, slipped her collar and ran off. Took me an hour to cajole her back to the village where kind Mrs Foster cornered her in her front garden. Result is that Missy regards me as a cruel torturer and avoids me like the plague.

Today motored to Swinbrook. Lunched with Diana [Mosley] in Pam [Jackson]'s cottage which she has rented for two months, on the River Windrush, opposite The Swan. Debo staying, and Micky Mosley* spending the day. A very jolly luncheon, with hoots of laughter. Debo addressed Diana as Mosley, the way her parents and mine addressed the parlourmaid. I asked M. Mosley how his aunt Baba Metcalfe† was. Fine, he said. She is eighty-four; has a cottage at Hazeley where she has to 'do' for herself at weekends. Telephones M.M. for advice. 'What am I to do with old tea bags?' She once asked him how to heat up a dish bought at Marks & Sparks. 'Put it in the oven for half an hour, Aunt Baba.' She rings up again. 'I left it in the oven for half an hour and it is still stone cold.' 'Did you turn the oven on?' 'Oh dear, does one have to do that?' M.M. a charming fellow, a loner who does good works in the East End apparently. Lives in a house in Chelsea and is well-off.

M. is having a swimgloat and being very modest about it. Repels congratulations over the Duchess of Windsor's letters, which although not officially out till Thursday are on sale at Hatchards who have taken 2,000 copies. He has sent me one, nicely produced with a pretty jacket. His introductory remarks, linking passages and footnotes are good. He stands to do well out of this, but I warn him to heed the

---

* Hon. Michael Mosley (b. 1932), yr s. of Sir Oswald Mosley by his 1st wife Lady Cynthia Curzon.

† Lady Alexandra Curzon (1904–95); dau. of Marquess Curzon of Kedleston; m. 1925 Major E. D. 'Fruity' Metcalfe.

cautionary tale of how Harold [Nicolson] and Jamesey [Pope-Hennessy] squandered the proceeds of their best-sellers about King George V and Queen Mary.

This past week I have begun my Venetian book, roughing out the first chapter, about Torcello. I hope I may finish it by the autumn.

Monday, 12th May

Audrey remarked breezily on Sunday, 'Of course, Uncle Robert [Bailey]* was a friend of T. E. Lawrence.'† 'Really?' I said. 'How did you know that?' 'Oh, Mama always said so.' I wonder if this can be true.

Thursday, 15th May

To London for day. By taxi to Pat [Trevor-Roper] for examination of eyes, both of which have deteriorated during past year. Pat took infinite pains with his examination, and assured me that nothing was seriously wrong, though I am more short-sighted than ever. Both my almost blind eye and the relatively good one can be helped with stronger lenses. Signs of cataract, but not worth operating. He gave me drops which put me in such a daze that for the rest of the day I hardly knew where I was. However, I walked to London Library, and on to Brooks's, where M. had left a message that he would be late. Tiresome, as I had come for the day only and had plenty to do. He arrived wearing garish blazer with stripes, and a little distrait. Said the publicity over the Windsor letters is driving him to lead a hermit's life. Confided that he has a girlfriend whom he is taking to Paris for the weekend. I warned him that this could mean only one thing, and he must be prepared. He is extraordinarily naïve, just like Jamesey Pope-Hennessy.

At four attended a meeting of reps at Sidgwick & Jackson. Was met by managing director Armstrong,‡ my editor Robert Smith, and

---

* Robert Bailey (1882–1917); only brother of J.L.-M's mother; ed. Eton and Magdalen College, Oxford; a clerk to the House of Commons; killed in action. A great hero to J.L.-M.
† Soldier, writer and archaeologist (1888–1935): 'Lawrence of Arabia'.
‡ William O'Malley Armstrong (b. 1938); managing director of Sidgwick & Jackson, 1971–96.

chairman William Rees-Mogg,* and marched into a long, stuffy room. Spoke from notes for a quarter of an hour, and think I acquitted myself quite well. Rees-Mogg tells me that Ston Easton [Park],[†] now a hotel, is haunted by an eighteenth-century ghost who was recently encountered by a guest. I asked if the guest experienced an icy feeling. No, he said, it was like a mild electric shock.

Thursday, 22nd May

To London for the night, invited for first time to the Royal Academy Banquet, poor A. not included. I fancied I might be the only guest not in white tie with decorations, but the majority, like myself, were in black tie with no gongs. On arrival was handed a beautiful card with my name in impeccable script, containing guest list and seating plan, an arrow pointing to my name. My neighbours two elderly men, one President of Scottish Academy, the other I did not discover. Mary Fedden opposite me, charming, stout, beaming lady with pretty face, distinguished painter and cousin of Robin.[‡] Princess Anne the principal guest and speaker. Spoke well and confidently about the art of horses, trotting out technical terms to show that it wasn't only painters who employed the expert's jargon. I was sitting quite close, and surprised by her beauty. Full face, long nose and expessive eyes, splendid fair hair and that flawless royal complexion. Next came the Foreign Secretary, Geoffrey Howe.[§] He told funny story of once attending a banquet in the Soviet Union, at which the table was covered with marvellous Imperial silver. The bigwig who was presiding noticed his neighbour slipping a silver spoon into his jacket pocket and thought he would do the same, but accidentally struck his spoon against a glass as if to make a speech. Unperturbed, he rose to his feet, offered to do a conjuring trick, showed the spoon, and pulled its twin out of the neighbour's pocket. The third speaker was Gervase Jackson-Stops, who bravely overcame his stammer and delivered a splendid speech about

---

* William Rees-Mogg (b. 1928); editor of *The Times*, 1967–81; chairman of Sidgwick & Jackson, 1985–88; cr. life peer as Baron Rees-Mogg, 1988.
† Palladian house in Mendip Hills with grounds by Repton, formerly residence of Rees-Moggs.
‡ Robin Fedden (1909–77); J.L.-M's successor as Historic Buildings Secretary of N.T., 1951–68.
§ Sir Geoffrey Howe (b. 1926); Foreign Secretary, 1983–9; resigned from Government, contributing to downfall of Mrs Thatcher, 1990; cr. life peer, 1992.

the Washington exhibition. Food good. Whole thing lasted from 7.30 to 11. Wandered for a few minutes, looked at two excellent pictures of interiors by Edmund Fairfax-Lucy, and to Brooks's for the night.

Monday, 2nd June

Here we are, Midsummer nearly reached, and filthy weather. The occasional fitfully sunny day, then greyness and rain again. Twice heard the cuckoo this year. The heron steals our fish, and left one so pitted with bites that it had to be destroyed. A's garden a dream of tulips, and the most beautiful blue clematis on the west, wisteria wall. Green as green, and the bluebells in the long grass under the cedar trees. But no sitting in the garden.

For the weekend we had Pat Trevor-Roper and Selina [Hastings] to stay. Very enjoyable. Only snag that neither A. nor I could hear more than one word in ten from Pat, whose delivery is stumbling and mumbling, with parenthesis after parenthesis. Yet he has much to say worth listening to, if only one could hear. Great arguer and debunker, with no regard for wildlife or conservation which infuriates A. Selina the best value in the world. Very intelligent talker. Mischievous? I suspect so, though it does not make her the less adorable. Pat defines an intellectual as one who is capable of conceptual thought, which rules out both self and A. A. maintained that Mary Dunn[*] who lunched here on Sunday was an intellectual, but the rest of us didn't think so – clever, bright and sophisticated, but no more.

The Johnnie Nuttings[†] who were staying at the House came for a pre-luncheon drink. He a charmer, she public-spirited and clever. She is Chairman of the N.T. Regional Committee, but does not enjoy it. She says the bureaucracy is frustrating, and makes it difficult to get things done.

Thursday, 5th June

On Tuesday I motored to Marske-in-Swaledale, 270 miles, to stay two nights with Rupert and June [Hart-Davis]. The usual wonder-

---

[*] Lady Mary St Clair-Erskine (b. 1912), dau. of 5th Earl of Rosslyn; m. 1933–44 Philip Dunn.
[†] John Grenfell Nutting (b. 1942), barrister; son of Sir Anthony Nutting, 3rd Bt, Conservative politician (to whose baronetcy he succeeded, 1999); m. 1973 Diane, widow of 2nd Earl Beatty.

ful welcome, Rupert assuring me we were the last survivors of our
Eton group. He has changed since my last visit. Much older, though
in splendid form; his legs all over the place, his face longer. Reclined
most of the day in a tilted chair, his feet on a gout stool, getting up
to go through my galleys at a table, breaking when exhausted. Never
takes exercise, of course. ('Never use *of course* in writing,' he says.)
They have not stayed away or gone further than Richmond for five
years. Family come to him. When I remarked that it shocked me now
how our parents had addressed their parlourmaids by their surnames,
June said gently, 'My mother was a parlourmaid, and her mistress
changed our name, which was Bowel, to Bowles because it sounded
better.' June is a slave to R., she adores him and he her. Never says a
stupid thing; very quiet, good and sweet.   R. showed me a first
edition of *Zuleika Dobson* which had belonged to Beerbohm* who
had scribbled illustrations on the margin of every page. He was given
it by Lady Beerbohm's sister for whom he has managed Max's literary estate all these years, out of love. He has been offered £10,000
for it. Speaking of his friend J. B. Morton† ('Beachcomber'), R. said
his inspiration was prodigious. On the spur of the moment he composed such lines as

> Here lies Albrecht Kartoffelspiel
> Best known as Lord Fitzwarren,
> A corner of an English field
> That is forever foreign.

Conversation and anecdotes were non-stop.

Saturday, 7th June

Dining with the Loewensteins we met Mick Jagger, who had unex-
pectedly turned up from Germany for the night. Just the five of us. He
was wearing a thick open-neck jersey of diamond pattern and thin
tweed trousers, tidy but not chic. Hair down to shoulders, tiny body,
gesticulating arms, huge hands, large head, pig eyes (not unlike mine),
mobile features, pugnacious chin, ugly, expressive mouth. Magnetic

---

* Sir Max Beerbohm (1872–1956); writer, caricaturist and critic.
† Humorous journalist (1893–1979), disciple of Hilaire Belloc, who took over the *Daily
Express* 'Beachcomber' column in 1924 and continued it until 1975.

personality. Ready to act a part, but by no means a clown. Entertaining and delicious company. He and A. get on well and tease each other.

Sunday, 8th June

Still a bitter wind. When I remarked on this to Mrs Punter, passing her with the dogs, she replied that when such a wind blows, the Badminton folk say, 'Go to Tormarton and shut the gate.' She did not know the origin of this expression, but presumably in the pre-motor age the grassy lane to Tormarton had gates like so many I remember in Worcestershire in my boyhood, such as the lane from Broadway to Snowshill.

Wednesday, 11th June

Just as I was leaving Badminton to fetch A. from Heathrow, she rang to announce there was a French air strike and she could not return. So I went to London and took J.K.-B. to Anita Brookner's lecture at Royal Society of Literature on Goncourt Brothers. Excellent it was too. Made out a case not for their characters, which were horrid, nor for their diaries, which are recognised for the superb chronicles they are, but for their novels. The extracts she read inspired me to read them. A funny little woman, sharp, delicate features, slight of build, soft-spoken. Hair like a bird's-nest, but tidy. J. and I agreed afterwards how hard it is to concentrate on lectures. How much, he asked, did I remember of hers? She had mentioned three false claims made by the brothers for themselves, but I could only remember one – that they had introduced Japanese taste to the West. But they were compassionate and not wholly acerbic. The Pope-Hennessy brothers were sometimes compared to the Goncourts.

Tuesday, 17th June

Buttercups this year either stunted or leggy, and in great profusion. Likewise cow parsley, but not superabundant as last year. The last two days have been really hot, like the old days. Today a cold wind, rather a relief for I do not like stifling weather, but do like the sun to shine every day.

Overheard by Rupert H.-D. at a Richmond bus stop: 'Emily was feeling poorly, so we opened a tin of crab.'

Thursday, 19th June

To London for the day. Saw Stuart Preston* at Brooks's before luncheon, in good form and full of interesting chat. He is happy in Paris
because he is moving flat, but misses Colin [McMordie] sadly. Lunched
with Bruce Hunter at the Athenaeum, with its wonderful library
running the whole length of the building, shades of Trollope and Mrs
Proudie. We discussed my future writing, if future there be. Bruce
asked if my *Italian Baroque* might be republished. I told him it was out
of date. Then suggested my *English Baroque Houses*. I said it was one of
a series [published by *Country Life*], and could only be repeated if the
volumes by Hussey,[†] Cornforth[‡] and Girouard[§] came out too. At least
I am committed to the Venice book, and keen to do the Cotswold
Houses.

I went to Agnews' exhibition of French drawings and paintings, and
then to the Kyle Gallery where the Hugo Buchanan exhibition was
already over. But the gallery owner, when I told him who I was (who
am I?), was very welcoming and gave me a poster as a present. It was
very hot and, struggling down Bond Street with my bag, I sweated
profusely, as of old. Called on M., back from America, on my way to
Paddington. He was sitting in a daze surrounded by a chaos of books,
papers and half-unpacked clothes, very untidy like so many of my
unmarried friends.

Friday, 20th June

The Royal Librarian Oliver Everett[¶] telephoned this morning to say
that I need make no alterations to the extracts of my Regy manuscript which I sent him, apart from his request that in my footnotes
I put 'RA' for Royal Archives. However, he did say that the Queen
had read them, and was hurt that Lord Esher should have criticised

---

* American bibliophile, resident in Paris (b. 1915); friend of J.L.-M. since 1938.
† Christopher Hussey (1899–1970); architectural adviser to *Country Life* 1930–64 (editor
1933–40); prolific author of books and articles on architectural history; m. 1936 Elizabeth
Kerr-Smiley.
‡ John Cornforth (b. 1937); architectural historian on staff of *Country Life*.
§ Mark Girouard (b. 1931); writer and architectural historian; Slade Professor of Fine Art,
Oxford, 1975–6.
¶ Diplomatist and courtier (b. 1943); Comptroller to Prince and Princess of Wales,
1981–3; Royal Librarian and Assistant Keeper of Queen's Archives from 1985.

her great-grandfather King Edward VII as a man of limited intelligence and no reading. I explained to Everett that these views were not mine but E's. The Queen was also slightly shocked by E's reference to Edward, Prince of Wales having had his first 'amourette' while in France during the Great War. I replied that most young men had their first woman at some time or other. Thirdly, the Queen was rather shocked by Esher writing in his Journal that he was slightly in love with the Prince himself. At this, I thought it best to warn Everett that there were other revelations concerning E's romantic feelings which might dismay the Queen were she to read the book. He said he had guessed as much from a remark contained in the extracts I sent him, referring to E's incestuous attachment to his son. So I said I would be prepared to cut out, even at this late stage, anything that offended the Queen. No, he said, let it all stand. I do hope the book will not cause further offence in royal circles. It amazes me that the Queen should read these extracts herself. Everett asked me to be sure to write the usual dedication in the copy I am to send her, assuring me that she would much like to have it, and will doubtless put it among her collection of books on the royal family in her private sitting room. He said the publicity following the Duchess of Windsor's death had distressed her.

Saturday, 28th June

Stuart [Preston] tells me to read Simon Raven's novels for descriptions of Venice. I buy *The Survivors* in paperback. The first sentence reads: '"Shit!!" cried Captain Detterling.' I wonder if I can persevere.

When we were dining at the House, David [Beaufort] suddenly lost his temper with Derry [Moore], who tried to interrupt him when he was telling a story about one of his partners. David blazed at him, 'Either you are going to tell this story or I am. I hate people who interrupt on subjects of which they are ignorant.' Poor Derry shut up like a clam. Sally [Westminster] sitting next to me noticed nothing and went chirping on to me about poetry. 'I hate godderel,' she said. 'Doggerel?' I suggested. Meanwhile Caroline was telling us how shy she was before she married. She was once invited to Drumlanrig by Molly [Buccleuch]'s[*] children. First evening she was seated between

---

[*] Vreda Esther Mary Lascelles (1900–93); m. 1921 Walter Montagu-Douglas-Scott (1894–1973) who in 1935 s. as 8th Duke of Buccleuch and 10th Duke of Queensberry.

the Duke of Gloucester* and another equally boring man. She could make no headway, thought she had been a dreadful failure, and felt Molly was looking at her with a critical gaze. The next morning the housemaid announced that her bags had been packed and taken to the front door. Appalled, Caroline said goodbye to Molly and thanked her for the visit. 'But I thought you were staying several days?' said Molly. I thought so too, replied C. through tears. Then suddenly M. said, 'Is that your luggage? You silly girl. They should have packed Mrs X's, who will now miss her train, and it's all your fault.' Caroline has never liked Molly since.

This has been a ghastly week of entertainment. Dinner with Dutch people called Fachs, table groaning with silver, course after indifferent course. Westmorlands[†] present, and snobbish, forced conversation. Then last night we dined at American Museum to help entertain American contingent on tour. Talked before dinner to a youngish man with curly hair, very sure of himself. I failed to realise he was Carter Brown[‡] until he made a short speech in reply to Ian [McCallum] at the end of the dinner. It is American gush that I cannot stomach. Tiresome women talking to me about my books which they have not read. And then A. took a party of twenty of them round the garden. Agony for me to find things to say, and when found, dross.

Wednesday, 2nd July

Saw three herons together in Vicarage Fields, noble birds, standing as if in earnest conversation. The dogs and I were quite close to them before they loped off, leisurely. No wonder we have lost all our goldfish of late.

Sunday, 6th July

All this week taken up with correcting page proofs of Regy. Now I have the index to look over, completed by the excellent Douglas

---

* HRH Prince Henry, Duke of Gloucester (1900–74), the notoriously tongue-tied and slow-witted third son of King George V; m. 1935 Lady Alice Scott.
† David Fane, 15th Earl of Westmorland (1924–93); Master of the Horse, 1978–93; m. 1950 Jane Findlay.
‡ J. Carter Brown (1934–2002); Director of National Gallery, Washington, 1969–92 (much involved in organising *Treasure Houses* exhibition there).

Matthews* in a week. He says it is the best book I have written, 'if I may say so'. Such a nice man.

We attended a dinner at the Warrenders'† last night for about twenty people. Didn't enjoy it much. Full of lords and ladies, yet A. and I given *places d'honneur*, I suppose being the oldest present. It is good of them not to observe the absurd formal precedence at meals. On my right was Lord Ampthill,‡ a man in his fifties whom I much liked. I think he must have been the baby in the famous Russell Baby Case,§ whose mother Christabel became a pen-friend of mine to whom I wrote when she was ill in Ireland (addressing my letters to the Cavalry Hospital until she told me it was Calvary). Geoffrey Ampthill is Deputy Speaker of the House of Lords, who sits on the Woolsack when the Lord Chancellor is absent. Says the House is the best club in the world, cherished by all who take their seats there, irrespective of party or whether they arrive by heredity or promotion. He has inaugurated a long table in the dining room at which all peers sit when not entertaining guests. This makes for good feeling, and they all get on well. He said it was wonderful how diplomatically they manage to dispose of mad backwoods peers who try to thrust themselves forward. Among the younger peers, Lord Melchett¶ is considered rather bumptious, whereas Simon Glenarthur** is regarded as perfection. He said peers are discouraged from dying in the House because the Coroner has no jurisdiction. When the former Labour cabinet

---

* Librarian of London Library, 1980–93 (b. 1927).

† Hon. Robin Warrender (b. 1927), yr s. of 1st Baron Bruntisfield; m. 1951 Gillian Rossiter; underwriting member of Lloyds.

‡ Geoffrey Russell, 4th Baron Ampthill (b. 1921); chairman of committees and Deputy Speaker of House of Lords from 1983.

§ In the sensational divorce case of *Russell v. Russell* (1922–4), Hon. John 'Stilts' Russell, future 3rd Baron Ampthill and a transvestite, claimed that the baby Geoffrey Russell was not his but the result of the adultery of his wife Christabel (*née* Hart). Despite medical evidence to the effect that Mrs Russell had been a virgin at the time of the baby's conception, his claim was accepted by the High Court and Court of Appeal. The House of Lords, however, allowed Christabel's appeal by a majority of 3 to 2. After the death of the 3rd Baron in 1974, Geoffrey Russell's claim to succeed him was contested by his younger half-brother, but eventually accepted by the House of Lords after a ruling by its Committee of Privileges.

¶ Peter Mond, 4th Baron Melchett (b. 1948); campaigner on environmental issues.

** Simon Arthur, 4th Baron Glenarthur, son of 3rd Baron by his 2nd wife Margaret (1st wife having been J.L.-M's sister Audrey); Conservative politician, at this time Minister of State at Foreign Office.

minister Gordon-Walker* died in a taxi on the way there, the red-liveried usher failed to persuade the driver to take him to the nearest hospital. As it was a busy moment when he had to attend to the arrival of other peers, he shoved him in a wheelchair into a broom cupboard. Later, Lady Gordon-Walker arrived and asked for her husband, whereupon the usher wheeled the corpse out of the cupboard. Ampthill says there is no need to reform the House of Lords, because the public can see from television that they are harmless.

Monday, 7th July

Lunched with Rosamond [Lehmann], who is very wretched and awaiting a fourth eye operation. Complains that she sees very little and can't go out. Talked about her first marriage, to Runciman. It was a disaster from the first. Although she believes he was not truly homosexual, he affected to be so during their marriage, which was never consummated. At that time Ros had no money of her own, while the Rs were rich industrialists in Newcastle. Then Wogan Philipps arrived up there and they fell in love. R's father-in-law who had seemed fond of her was scandalised when he learnt of the affair. Although Ros explained to him that her husband had never been in the least interested in her, he took his son's part and refused to allow him to be divorced by her. In those days, it was unthinkable for a 'lady' to be divorced by her husband, and Ros had no money with which to run away. So she took up her pen and wrote *Dusty Answer*, inspired by her troubles and unhappiness. The large sales from this book enabled her to run off with Wogan and eventually marry him. 'I've never told anybody this story, darling,' R. said.†

Monday, 14th July

I now have a car radio and listen to it while driving to and from Bath. The news these days is appalling. Nothing but murders, assassinations and bombings in Ireland, Spain, the Near East, India; and the ostracism of South Africa horrifies me. Those bloody Commonwealth

---

* Patrick Gordon-Walker (1907–80); writer and Labour politician; cr. life peer, 1974.
† This account cannot be regarded as wholly reliable (the marriage had certainly been consummated to the point of her becoming pregnant), nor was Rosamond reticent in relating various versions of it.

Games in Edinburgh! I wish we had called them off to cock a snook at those African countries boycotting them. Awful that we, a once great country, have to submit to insults from savages. Mrs Thatcher is absolutely right not to give in to pressure for sanctions.* An article in *The Times* gives abbreviated biographies of all the black rulers clamouring for sanctions, who are all without exception thugs, terrorists and tyrants, motivated by communistic tendencies. At my age I should not read the daily newspapers or listen to the radio, but my curiosity gets the better of me. I can't sit back like an ostrich and bury my head in the sand. Yet I am appalled by the views of the people I hear on the radio, all soppy socialists who are against the police and what they call 'the Establishment'. Bring back the birch and the rope, I say. Actually, not the rope, which is a degrading form of execution; rather a lethal prick, which raises no revulsion among either public or perpetrators and is no doubt a delicious sensation in the victim.

Thursday, 17th July

A. and I went to Diana Cooper's memorial service at St Mary's, Paddington Green, at noon. We had an hour to spare beforehand, and went to the Berkeleys'. Freda in despair over Lennox who is quite gaga, recognising no one. Cannot speak except in broken sentences and wanders round the house after Freda. She almost confesses that she wishes him dead. We walked to the church, lovely sunny morning, Freda guiding Lennox while the others walked ahead. One of the most beautiful services I have ever attended. Lasted an hour. Packed with friends. Began with Gloria from Mozart's *Missa Brevis*, sung by choir in gallery. Then stirring hymn, 'For all the Saints'. Lesson read by Henry Anglesey.[†] Menhuin[‡] played Gavotte and Praeludium of Bach, which sounded rather squawky unaccompanied. Edward Fox[§] read beautifully from *Intimations of Immortality*. Hymn 'He who would valiant be' (which was Diana's attitude to life). Address by Martin Charteris,[¶]

---

* Mrs Thatcher's Government reluctantly imposed limited economic sanctions against South Africa in the autumn of 1986.
† Lord Anglesey's mother, *née* Lady Marjorie Manners, was Diana Cooper's sister.
‡ Violinist (1916–99); cr. life peer, 1993.
§ Actor (b. 1937).
¶ Lord Charteris of Amisfield (1913–99); Private Secretary to HM The Queen, 1972–7; Provost of Eton, 1978–91; his mother, Lady Violet Manners, was another sister of Diana Cooper.

another nephew. Told story of Diana in early 1900s giving sixpenny notebook to Eddie Marsh,[*] who loved her like all his generation. Eddie kept notebook all his life and got 120 famous writers to contribute some piece to it. Martin managed to buy it for Eton College Library for a price rather greater than current equivalent of sixpence. When Diana visited Eton, he showed it to her and she wrote on the last page an affectionate letter to Eddie as if he were alive. Lilian Watson, soprano, then sang Schubert, followed by the choir singing 'God be in my head, and in my understanding'. Finally the congregation gave a rousing rendering of 'Mine eyes have seen the glory of the coming of the Lord'. Most moving ceremony, the sun streaming through the clear windows into this packed and pretty little church. Nigel Ryan[†] added a short appreciation of Diana's help to friends in trouble. All these tributes to Diana made me feel an unworthy person, not so much a worm as like that fragment of broken translucent glass set in the floor.

We lunched with June and Jeremy [Hutchinson][‡] in their garden in Blenheim Terrace, off salmon and white wine. So much fun and laughter, an unforgettable hour and a half with these two dear friends. They have a Spanish woman in the basement who looks after them, called America. 'America, darling, be an angel and bring the sugar.' Jeremy motored A. to Paddington and me to Bedford Square on his way to the House of Lords. I went to Sidgwick by long-standing appointment, only to find that the proofs of index and footnotes had not yet arrived. Bought a Pickering *Horace* at the shop on the corner of Little Russell Street from the little man I bought Pickerings from in years gone by.[§] It cost £50, but a combination of *joie de vivre* and crossness over Sidgwick made me devil-may-care. Anyway, what is £50 these days? I took away the heavy Brett photograph album and left it at Brooks's.

---

[*] Sir Edward Marsh (1872–1953); civil servant, writer and aesthete who befriended young literary men, including Rupert Brooke before the First World War and J.L.-M. in the 1930s.

[†] C. N. J. Ryan (b. 1929); journalist, writer and translator; director (later Chairman) of TV-am.

[‡] Jeremy Hutchinson, QC (b. 1915); m. 1st 1940 Dame Peggy Ashcroft, 2nd 1966 June *née* Capel (daughter of J.L.-M's friend Diana, Countess of Westmorland, and formerly wife of Franz Osborn); cr. life peer (Baron Hutchinson of Lullington) 1978.

[§] J.L.-M. collected the miniature volumes of the classics published by William Pickering (1796–1854).

Then visited Emily and Dolly in their Sutton Estate flat. Greeted
by Dolly instead of Emily and wondered for a moment if E. had died.
She hadn't, but was in an extremely bad way, having broken her leg
in the same place as last year, poor dear. Hobbling on two crutches,
can't get out or manage those terrible stairs, on the fifth floor, no bathroom. Rather deaf, very blind, and wandery. Kept repeating, 'I can't
think why these things have hit us recently. We've always kept well
and been so happy.' Dolly too has been ill, suffering from varicose
veins and ulcers, and is very bent. They have no interest in anything.
Do not read, or listen to the wireless at all; no friends. They told me
how good taxi drivers were to them. For before her latest accident, E.
used to go shopping with D. once a fortnight and came home by taxi,
offering fifty pence to the driver to carry their things while they stag-
gered up behind. Never would the drivers accept the fifty pence, and
sometimes in leaving the shopping they would leave beside it the
money paid for the fare. How kind these people are to those of their
own sort they see to be in distress.

Got to Brooks's to find M. waiting for me. We dined and he took
me to see *A Room with a View* at the Curzon. Enormously enjoyed it.
Beautiful and funny. The Bonham-Carter girl excellent. Noticed that
the interior of Mrs Vyse's London house was Anne Rosse's house at
Stafford Terrace.* M. returned with me to Brooks's where we drank
Drambuie. A lovely day, apart from the sorrow over Emily and Dolly.

Friday, 18th July

Lionel came to Brooks's to collect the Esher album. Would not stay
to breakfast, for which Nick [Robinson] joined me. Looking superb
after his holiday in Turkey, brown, healthy, unscruffy, wearing tidy
white jacket and trousers, so tall and handsome. We talked about publishing, he confirming that Robert Smith of Sidgwick's is nice but not
bright. Ordered shirts at Harvie & Hudson, and went at eleven to
Apsley House, where Joan Wilson, curator, had asked to talk to me
about Gerry Wellington. What lovely rooms are reserved for the Duke
downstairs. I went there but once in Gerry's time. The Douros† live

---

* The carefully preserved 1880s interior of this house (now open to the public) had been
created by Anne Rosse's maternal grandfather, the *Punch* cartoonist Linley Sambourne.
† Arthur Wellesley, Marquess of Douro (b. 1945); son and heir of 8th Duke of
Wellington; MEP for Surrey; m. 1977 Princess Antonia von Preussen.

on the top floor which she says is just as pretty. Delicious Wyatt rooms with smell of well-kept furniture, books and pot-pourri. Complete tranquillity. Talked to her for an hour and a half. Charming woman, but not as well informed as she ought to be.

Igor lunched with me at Brooks's, arriving on foot from Harley Street, having had an operation on his toe. Must have been in agony, for it was very hot. He looked distinguished and Christ-like. Took him to the big table upstairs where we were joined by Nigel Clive,[*] Martin Drury and Dudley Dodd, to all of whom Igor spoke without fear or favour. Full marks for this. Then in the library I talked to him about his future, as A. and Clarissa had enjoined me to do. He admitted he had no interests except for sport. I told him it was ridiculous to expect to start a career in tennis at the age of twenty-one when the world champion was younger. Advised a craft, such as book-binding or picture-framing. I tremble for him and told him he could always get in touch with me the moment he was in a fix.

Back to Sidgwick, where proofs of Regy had at last arrived. Corrected index and footnotes, then thought I would have a quick look at revised proofs of text, which the author never normally sees. Discovered a number of mistakes, and wondered how many others I had no time to find. It is despairing. For better or worse, Regy really is finished now. To cost £15, so no one will buy.

Sunday, 20th July

Lunched with the Garnetts[†] at Cannwood Farm, their new house near Frome. An old red brick farmhouse much added to. Pretty and higgledy-piggledy, crammed with furniture, ornaments and knick-knacks, children falling over each other, maids with babies, muddle, confusion, jollity; a house such as I could never make. Polly much improved, fine eyes, immensely clever and quick. Took us for a walk in a meadow they own which has been scheduled 'not to be disturbed'. As it has never been 'improved' by farmers or treated with pesticides, it is a tapestry of wild flowers, such as one sees in a Cluny panel and indeed one saw every day in one's youth. Scabious, clover, vetch blue and yellow, cornflowers, marguerites and eighty varieties

---

[*] Diplomatist (1917–2001).
[†] Andrew Garnett, entrepreneur; m. Polly Devlin, journalist and writer.

of grass, so Polly says. The field next door, which has been 'improved', utterly dead like a landscape on the moon. To think that A. and I have lived to see this change.

Last night Nico and Mary Henderson, bringing Derry and Alexandra [Moore] and Robert Kee,* came to No. 19 with a picnic supper which we ate uncomfortably. Champagne also, which I dislike. They took us to T. S. Eliot's *The Cocktail Party* in [the Theatre Royal] Bath. I suspect it is mostly spoof, and Nico told us that Eliot himself warned a friend not to 'be taken in by that rubbish'. All words, words. Rachel Kempson† much aged and forgot her lines. Kee charming and as bright as a gold sovereign. A terrible breaker of women's hearts.

Friday, 25th July

We dine at the House to meet the Beits who are staying. Sat next to Clem who says that although Alf makes light of the latest robbery of his pictures,‡ he is very upset and broods. Thinks the IRA are involved. If so, they are robbing Ireland of some of the world's best pictures, for they no longer belong to Alfred, who has left them in trust to that stinking nation. He does not believe they have been acquired by 'gloaters' – i.e., eccentric millionaires in South America who seek to acquire world-famous pictures for their secret collections – but that in a year or so a ransom will be demanded. The alarm went off in the middle of the night; curator awakened; police arrived; nothing found disturbed; police left, and curator retired to bed. But meanwhile one of the gang remained hidden in the house and managed to de-activate the alarm system and admit his accomplices. They cleared out the saloon and were off. Had a long talk with Alfred about Gerry [Wellington], Mrs Wilson having got in touch with him at my suggestion.

---

* Writer and broadcaster (b. 1919).
† Actress (b. 1910); m. 1935 Michael Redgrave.
‡ This was the second of a series of spectacular art robberies from Russborough House, the Beits' seat in County Wicklow. The Provisional IRA was responsible for the first, in 1974; the second turned out to be the work of a professional criminal, Martin Cahill, who was later murdered by the IRA. Most of the pictures stolen were recovered on each occasion.

Monday, 28th July

A. being bogged down with great-grandchildren, I went alone to spend weekend with Billy Whitaker* at Pylewell [Park near Lymington, Hampshire]. Utmost comfort and luxury, tables groaning with silver, butler, old housekeeper and army of unseen housemaids. The first day was one of delicious idling, largely spent in my room where I read or dozed. Loelia Lindsay,[†] Margaret-Anne Stuart,[‡] Tom Parr[§] and Tony Pawson[¶] staying. At first the upper-crust chatter and gossip was fun. After twenty-four hours I had had quite enough. The others left on Sunday afternoon and I spent the last night alone with Billy and sister Penelope.[**] Both sweet but so devitalised that I found tea and dinner heavy going. Billy showed me a school group taken in 1920 at Lockers Park, in which he and Peter Coats[††] are sitting on the ground in front row next to each other. Other recognisable boys are myself, Tom Mitford, Dick Bailey,[‡‡] [Basil] Ava and Matthew Arthur. *Eheu fugaces!*

Returned to Bad. to find A. exhausted from looking after these children. I hate to see her thus, but she will do it. Chloe looking fat in trousers, with enormous bottom. Talking rot about organising an exhibition of pictures in Burlington House for Band Aid, the crusade to help the starving Africans who take everything and give nothing, and want weeding out, not encouraging to multiply. The whole thing makes me sick.

---

* William Whitaker (1910–88); bachelor landowner (sometime High Sheriff of Hampshire), whose ancestors (their fortune deriving from Marsala wine in Sicily) had lived at Pylewell for three generations; contemporary of J.L.-M. at preparatory school and Eton.

† Hon. Loelia Ponsonby (1902–93), dau. of 1st Baron Sysonby; m. 1st (1930–47) 2nd Duke of Westminster ('Bendor'), 2nd 1969 Sir Martin Lindsay of Dowhill, 1st Bt (1905–81).

‡ Margaret Anne Du Cane (niece of Sir John Carew-Pole, 12th Bt: see entry for 10 August 1985); interior decorator; m. 1979 as his 3rd wife David, 2nd Viscount Stuart of Findhorn.

§ Interior decorator (b. 1930), currently Chairman of Colefax & Fowler.

¶ A. J. Pawson (1917–90).

** Penelope Whitaker (b. 1913), unmarried sister of William.

†† Peter Coats (1910–90), kinsman of J.L.-M., who was his contemporary at Lockers Park preparatory school, Hertfordshire; garden designer and horticultural writer; patron of Espie Dod; lifelong friend of Billy Whitaker.

‡‡ Eldest of the four Bailey brothers (1908–69); an exact contemporary of J.L.-M. at Lockers Park and Eton. (See notes to 29 June 1985 and entry for 26 March 1986.)

Tuesday, 29th July

On my way home from Pylewell yesterday I thought I must make an effort to see Osbert [Lancaster], whose birthday is on 4 August, two days before mine. Then heard on wireless this morning that he had died. Another friend gone. He was the ugliest man I ever knew, with his pock-marked complexion. In conversation he had the reputation of being a great raconteur, but his wit was of the undergraduate kind, in imitation of Maurice Bowra,* and I never found it very funny. As a cartoonist he excelled, rivalled only by Max Beerbohm whom he enormously admired and of whose work he had a large collection. His first wife Karen was a dear. So too is Anne. How this beauty ever became mistress and then wife of the monstrous O. I cannot imagine.

At breakfast was told to my horror that Chloe had gone off to take her driving test, parking her two infants on us. A. also told me that Freda [Berkeley] had just telephoned to say that Lennox wandered out of the house yesterday and cannot be found. They have been keeping it dark hoping for his return, but must now release the news to police and press.

Sunday, 3rd August

David and Caroline dined with us in the middle of the week. D. said he could not bear X. because of his dirty clothes, and wondered whether it was wrong to take against people for such trivial reasons. I said that I was apt to judge from first appearances, and although I might subsequently change my opinion, I usually found in the end that my first reaction had been right. Then he asked whether I looked at the faces of the mourners at funerals as they processed out of the church. He does so out of the corner of his eye as it interests him to see which mourners are sad, which mightily relieved, which pleased or displeased by their inheritance, etc. I said I tried not to look as I did not like to see people trying to restrain their tears, and also coffins revolted me for I always wondered what the corpse was looking like within.

The next night, 31st, we dined alone with Charlie and Rosalind Morrison. Charlie spoke critically of Mrs Thatcher, saying that unless she is made to stand down before the next election the Tories stand

---

* Sir Maurice Bowra (1898–1971); Warden of Wadham College, Oxford, 1938–70.

no chance of returning. Also doubted whether there would be another female PM for a hundred years, for she has demonstrated the worst failing of the female mind – obduracy. He said Ian Gilmour* was the most intellectual of the MPs in the House, but impatient with those whose intelligence does not match his own.

Rosamond whom I telephoned was surprised that I had not heard of her motor accident. She said she had been driving in the country at eighty miles an hour when the accelerator jammed and she ran into a concrete lamp-post next to a police station. I questioned these circumstances, but not to her. I asked if she was gravely injured. Just a few bruises, it seems. Anyway, it has persuaded her to give up driving, which is wise. Her memory is prodigious. She said, 'Do you remember when we were dining in a South Ken. restaurant some twenty-five years ago and Osbert [Lancaster] knocked on the window and insisted on joining us?' I don't remember at all.[†]

Monday, 4th August

Quite often at this time of year we find the silver, slimy trail of a snail on either the staircase carpet or the rush matting of the downstairs passage. Where the snail (if it is a snail and not a slug) lives in the house we cannot discover. Peggy has searched for it in vain.

Today the Mitchells motored us to Kingston Lacy. We went over the house before the public arrived at one o'clock. They are coming in droves, seven hundred a day, which is too much. It is to be hoped these numbers will diminish after the first excitement, for it is not an attraction for the ordinary tourist but for the connoisseur. Tony M. has done marvels. Pictures cleaned; every object in the house repaired and refurbished. A superb Rubens of a Genoese bridge rehung, a silvery vision. My interest in W. J. Bankes is reviving. I wrote, perhaps foolishly, to John Cornforth for his advice on whether I should tackle this biography.

We lunched in a loose-box in the stable buildings, joined by the Lees Mayalls and Michael Briggses. Isabel always walking by herself,

---

* Sir Ian Gilmour, 3rd Bt (b. 1926); owner and editor of *Spectator*, 1954–9; Conservative politician, Lord Privy Seal, 1979–81; m. 1951 Lady Caroline Scott, dau. of 8th Duke of Buccleuch.
† He did however mention the episode in his diary: see *Ancient as the Hills*, 11 December 1973.

observing, but answering brightly when addressed. I like her independence. Mary Mayall got quite tipsy on red wine and told us amusing
stories about Arthur Duckworth's* three wives.

American *House and Garden* telephoned me from New York, asking
me to write an article on Kedleston [Hall, Derbyshire] at short notice.
I asked to be given twenty-four hours to reflect. Don't want to do it
in the least, but of course consented. For 2,000 words they offer $3,500
which seems to me immense. They will also send a car from London
to motor me there and back. I have never received such treatment.

Wednesday, 6th August

My [seventy-eighth] birthday. I went to London for the day and had
Hugh Massingberd and M. to lunch at Brooks's, each having expressed
a desire to meet the other. A great success. Hugh asked M. to write
obituaries for the *Daily Telegraph*. M. saw the point of Hugh, a
delightful baby, all harassed and pursued, but brilliant, missing
nothing. Noticed his endearing habit of making asides to himself,
commenting on what he has just said.

Monday, 11th August

Punctual to the minute, a huge Mercedes drew up to the door at 9.30.
A nice youngish driver with excellent manners took me to Kedleston.
Was glad of this, as it was a filthy day. We got there at 12.30, too late
and too early, and went to a pub for lunch. He ate little, and nothing
on return journey except a mug of tea. Though he could not have
been nicer, conversation was uphill. On passing Worcester, I told him
that the hump on the left was where Cromwell stood before the battle
of Worcester, while Charles II was in the Cathedral tower. He knew
nothing of Cromwell or Charles II. On the way back, I explained that
another tump was where the last witch was burned. He asked, 'Was
that before the Great War?'

Kedleston is a truly wonderful house, not outside but in. Paine's
front is stodgy, Adam's south front unfinished. But the inside unpar-
alleled. The alabaster hall could not be more splendid. The pretty
fireplaces seem too elegant for so much Roman robustness; the

---

* Of Orchardleigh Park, Somerset (1901–87); MP (C) for Shrewsbury, 1924–45.

drawing room likewise superb – the inset frames to pictures, the alabaster door-frames and Venetian window, and the view therefrom, over the delicate railing and Adam gates to the lake and the bridge. The dining room has been painted hideously, also the library – mulberry walls and yellow ceiling. Some Lady Scarsdale had no taste at all. I was last here forty years ago.

Tuesday, 19th August

A. being absent in Tangier, Eardley came to stay for four days. I arranged several entertainments to avoid meals at home. First night we dined with G.D., where I hadn't been for ages. Charles Monteith and a couple of queens staying. D. too awful for words, got drunk, kept asking E. whether he had had affairs with various people. Charles M. spoke about All Souls, where they cannot stop John Sparrow, who thinks he is still Warden, dining every evening and boring them all to tears with his drunkenness and senility. On the 13th E. and I motored to Upton to see the Bearsted pictures. My first visit for over thirty years. What a splendid collection it is. There is something of everything – Rembrandt, Rubens, Reynolds; Dutch, French, English and Italian. Dick Bearsted* was away but we were told he had had a stroke. His father and mother such dear people. Dinner with Alex [Moulton] on the 14th was a success. E. much impressed by enthusiasms of Alex, who showed photographs of his inventions and brought in his latest bicycle. On the 17th we lunched with Janet Stone† in Salisbury. She was very sweet and charming, dressed not in her usual Edwardian get-up but sensible cotton skirt and blouse. Is publishing a book of photographs. Is delighted by two paintings by Jones which K. Clark left her. Folly bit her hand when leaving.

Eardley and I got on well but there was not the rapport of old. Few giggles, not much laughter, some reticence and disapproval on his part, some irritation on mine. For some reason the spectacle of him helping himself to spoonful after spoonful of marmalade at breakfast irritated me profoundly. I am getting more irritable than I used to be. I have also been fussing over my article on Kedleston, which I finally

---

* Marcus Richard Samuel, 3rd Viscount Bearsted (1909–86), whose father had donated Upton House, Warwickshire with its garden and picture collection to N.T. in 1946.
† Janet Woods (1912–98); m. 1938 Reynolds Stone (1909–79), designer, wood engraver and artist.

delivered, on my way to pick up Alvilde at Heathrow, to a scruffy little gin-soaked agent outside the Cavalry Club. Felt like Blunt or Burgess handing over secret documents to a KGB agent. Next day, Miss Shelly of *House and Garden* rang me up to say she had received it, and liked it, though she wanted a few more anecdotes. I thought I would write something about Lord Curzon's unhappy childhood there, as described in Kenneth Rose's biography,* but could not find my copy of this. She said she would get one for me. Sure enough, the following day the agent motored down with it to Badminton!

Saturday, 23rd August

Motored Brigid Salmond to see Sally Westminster in Frenchay Hospital, Sally having had a serious motor accident. Very bruised, and had lost her false teeth which smashed, a thing I dread. She is full of courage. Brigid told me that a young relative of hers, a boy at Eton aged fifteen, was bribed £5,000 by the press to tell them how much he understood his cousin Sarah Ferguson to be in love with Prince Andrew.†

Michael Rennison‡ brought Barbara Leigh-Hunt§ and Doda Conrad¶ to lunch from London, to talk of Princess Winnie [de Polignac]. Barbara Hunt a charming woman and good actress.

Sunday, 24th August

We motored to London to attend performance about Princess Winnie, *An Evening with the Princesse de Polignac*. A taxi from Heathrow passed us and John Julius [Norwich] lent out and waved to us, holding out a copy of one of my paperbacks which he had evidently been reading. Performance so long that I had to leave in the interval to motor home. What I saw and heard I much enjoyed. Barbara Leigh-Hunt was splendid, though not looking the least like Winnie. Spoke well and audibly. London Sinfonietta performed pieces by Ravel and Stravinsky, all dedicated to the Princess. Photographs of those numerous distinguished

---

* *Superior Person: A Portrait of Lord Curzon and his Circle in Late Victorian England* (1969).
† They had married on 23 July.
‡ Theatre and opera director.
§ Actress (b. 1935).
¶ Bass singer who had known Princess Winnie, and been a close friend for many years of her protégée Nadia Boulanger (French musician and teacher of composition [d. 1979]).

composers, writers, painters she patronised flashed on screen. It was a good arrangement, she and Doda talking like old friends, both reading from script; but too long.

Wednesday, 27th August

To London yesterday in pouring rain and bitter cold. But a good day none the less. London Library in morning, actually finding two books I wanted. Then had M. to lunch at Cavalry Club which is offering hospitality during summer closure of Brooks's, full of ghastly memories for me of the luncheon with my father in 1927 when he motored me to London to find me a job, and ran into Major Percy Battye in the dining room.* M. intrigued by the portraits of field marshals and generals. What a silly little instrument is a baton, and what did they do with it? I imagine it is a truncated version of some deadly medieval weapon. Paintings with titles like *A Military Skirmish*, dozens of high-ranking officers identified but not the artist. One of Lord Valentia in the 1920s; hard to imagine him as the 'Caryl' whom Regy fell for and tried to make his son Maurice have an affair with.† A fearsome one of Penelope [Betjeman]'s father Lord Chetwode.‡

At three went to interview Felix Kelly§ at his smart flat in Prince's Gate. Charming man, un-arty to look at, short hair smarmed down and tidy suit. I must say his paintings are irresistible. Very professional, and better than Rex Whistler. The avant-garde, like Richard [Shone], would despise. I did not dare tell him that my article would also deal with three other artists, but did say it was limited to 1,500 words.¶ He

---

* This story is recounted in Chapter IV of *Another Self*.

† Caryl Annesley, 12th Viscount Valentia (1883–1949), soldier and farmer. Regy Esher wrote to his son Maurice at Eton in 1899: 'Altogether I don't know when it is that I last saw any human being of either sex so better worth while loving.' He described Caryl's charms as 'not feminine yet not wholly male'. (Quoted by J.L.-M in *The Enigmatic Edwardian*, p. 111.)

‡ Field Marshal Lord Chetwode (1869–1950; cr. Baron, 1945); Commander-in-Chief of the Army in India, 1930–5.

§ New Zealand-born artist (d. 1996), specialising in atmospheric paintings of country houses in their landscapes; his best work includes a series of spectacular murals at Castle Howard, Yorkshire.

¶ J.L.-M. had been commissioned by the *American Architectural Digest* to write an article on four contemporary painters of country houses – Felix Kelly, Julian Barrow, Alexandre Sebriakoff and Jean-Marc Winckler. The article, 'Contemporary Masters of a Venerable Genre', appeared in March 1989.

told me that he last saw Johnnie Churchill at a crowded cocktail party. Johnnie, so drunk that he had to be supported, said to Kelly (who is I imagine abstemious), 'Whereas you get tighter and tighter, I get looser and looser'.

Sunday, 31st August

I motored to Stourhead to meet Audrey – her 81st birthday – and was not as nice to her as I should have been. Bloody of me, for she had put off motoring to the Mill to stay with Richard and Linda [Robinson] owing to high blood pressure. We had a good luncheon at The Spreadeagle, then visited the house, which I have not entered for ages. Full of memories of the work Eardley and I did there; hardly any of the pictures or furniture we placed have been altered.* Well kept, crawling with public. Somehow I was detected, for the curator came to me in the Library and introduced himself. Poor Audrey talked nonsense to his wife until I became embarrassed. When this was over I went home, instead of returning to tea with her and the Suttons as she wished.

All this week A. has had her great-granddaughter to stay. It has nearly driven me mad. I have been reading a life of Bill Bentinck, present and final Duke of Portland.† A good man, treated abominably by the Foreign Office, which he served with distinction (rising to be head of wartime secret service committee), on account of his divorcing his wife. Bevin did not even allow him a pension.

In the Italian Room at Stourhead, which happened to be empty of humans, I was touched by a photograph of the room taken in 1900. Against one of the chairs, Alda Hoare had written, 'In this chair Harry sat on the last day of his leave'. Harry was killed in the Great War, to his parents' indelible grief. Lady Hoare never changed the style of her dress from that day until the day of her own death in 1947.

---

* Stourhead, Wiltshire, was donated to the N.T. by the will of the kindly but eccentric Sir Henry Hoare, who died in March 1947. During the following two years (as described in *Caves of Ice*, *Midway on the Waves* and *People and Places*), J.L.-M. and Eardley Knollys worked tirelessly and almost single-handedly to sort out its chaotic mass of contents (much of which was removed and lent to other N.T. houses) and prepare it for opening to the public.
† Victor Frederick William Cavendish-Bentinck, 9th and last Duke of Portland (1897–1990); career diplomatist; Chairman Joint Intelligence Committee, 1939–45; Ambassador to Poland, 1945–7.

Thursday, 11th September

We were sitting cosily in front of the fire last night at 7.45 when the doorbell rang noisily, to accompaniment of barking from Folly. A pathetic boy at the door presented an identity card and explained that he and his friends, who were from Nottingham, were travelling round the country selling household goods rather than go on the dole. At once suspicion seized me and I kept him talking while calling for A. Boy produced a large roll-bag from which emerged dish cloths, car sponges, dusters. We wanted none of these things, and I was irritated by the infringement of privacy and element of blackmail implied in this unsolicited touting. Nevertheless we gave him £10 for an assortment of things he calculated cost £9.50, and wished him good luck. He thanked us politely, adding that it was a good day whereas the day before he had only sold £4-worth of stuff. He smelled dreadfully, the poor youth. For the rest of the evening I was tormented by a mixture of shame at my original suspicion and irritation, distress that this boy has to descend to this sort of livelihood, and admiration that he chooses to work this way rather than live off the state. Youth unemployment has become a national cancer.

Friday, 12th September

A lady with a notebook accosted me as I was coming out of Waterstone's bookshop in Milsom Street, asking if I had two minutes to spare. 'Well, I suppose I might spare half a minute,' I replied grudgingly. She belonged to some research unit, and wanted to know how many books I read a year. When I said about two hundred, she was aghast. 'You don't mean it?' I explained that many of them were library books which I did not buy, nor did I read every book from beginning to end.

Then, out of devilry, I went and bought a small bust of Lord Melbourne for £275, by a sculptor called W. Jones. It is signed 1846, and Lord M. died in 1848. Was it done from a sitting, or a portrait? The same might be asked of my bust of Henry Brougham. Do I deceive myself in thinking that these late neo–classical English portrait busts may one day have a value? My parents' generation hated and despised all busts.

Monday, 15th September

On Saturday we lunched with Billy [Henderson]* and Frank [Tait].†
Michael and Anne Tree‡ present, he full of anecdotes, she very clever
and direct with the most upper-class accent in the world. Michael says
David Beaufort is fed up with hunting, and sometimes prays for a
socialist government which will stop it. An enjoyable luncheon for
there was conversation, rare these days in the circles in which we move.
Billy told me that the little picture of a carnation which he gave me
for my seventieth birthday was done on the bark of a tree from
Yucatan.

On Sunday we lunched with Elspeth [Huxley]§ and the Murrays
from Moorwood. She is Nick's godmother and they have a house in
the West Indies, where he advises governments on sugar. A. is now
determined that we go there in February for sun and bathing.

I watched 'Last Night of the Proms', Raymond Leppard¶ conduct-
ing. He made an excellent little speech saying the Promenaders were
the best audience in the world, and BBC Radio Three was the best
wireless channel. Also saw Dirk Bogarde** being interviewed by
Russell Harty.†† Rather queenly in his gestures. He struck me as vain
and shallow, saying nothing of any depth or consequence, and contra-
dicting himself at times. Yet clearly a sad and sensitive man. Norah
[Smallwood] adored him.

Wednesday, 17th September

To London for the night. At Sidgwick's I signed copies of Regy. A.
keeps telling me not to give away so many copies, at least to the rich.
But it is often the only way I can repay their kindnesses. Already I have
given fifteen copies, including those to The Queen and Oliver
Everett. To the Queen, I put 'Her Majesty The Queen with humble
duty from her grateful and loyal subject J. L.-M.' Am not sure whether

---

* Painter (1903–93); former aide to Lord Linlithgow and Lord Wavell as Viceroys of
India.
† Australian child psychiatrist (b. 1923).
‡ Michael Lambert Tree, painter (1921–99); m. 1949 Lady Anne Cavendish.
§ Elspeth Grant (1907–94); m. 1931 Gervas Huxley (d. 1971); writer.
¶ Conductor (b. 1927).
** Professional name of Dirk van den Bogaerde (1921–2000), film actor, novelist and auto-
biographer. J.L.-M. had briefly met him four years earlier: see *Holy Dread*, 13 July 1982.
†† Television chat show host (1934–88), who later died of Aids

this sort of address is too flowery and deferential for these days, but I wanted to get in the 'humble duty' because that is how Regy began all his letters to King Edward.

In the evening A's publishers, Viking, gave a party in Hardy Amies'[*] rooms in Savile Row to launch her new book, *The English-man's Room*, which promises to be a great success. Many old friends. The Enoch Powells[†] there, she sweet and simple, he difficult and rather deaf. When he asked me on what subject A. was now engaged, I mumbled, 'gardens'. He turned to A. and said, 'Your husband tells me you have chosen an interesting new subject – gowns'. She replied that 'gowns' was not a word I would use. Derry told him I was not a business man. 'That's good,' he replied. 'A useless profession.' I said I thought business men were what the country needed, as we pro-duced too little. 'Rubbish,' he said, 'we don't need to produce any-thing. There are other troubles.' M., whom A. had invited, reported a similar snatch of unsatisfactory conversation. He drew Powell's attention to the unpublished diaries of Sir Ronald Storrs[‡] in a Cambridge library, including interesting descriptions of visits to country houses in Powell's Downshire constituency. He replied, 'Diaries are useless, because they are written with an eye to publica-tion.' End of talk. Powell is a small, compact, greyish man. I have long wished to meet him, but on such occasions I cannot click with dis-tinguished strangers.

Rosemary Chaplin[§] present, sweet and tiny and rather aged. Seeing her with A. and myself, Junie [Hutchinson] called us 'the incestuous trio'. 'Yes,' I said, 'but we all had such fun, and loved each other.' This shocked some people at the time.[¶]

---

[*] Dressmaker By Appointment to HM The Queen (1909–2003).
[†] J. Enoch Powell (1912–98); writer and politician, known for his brilliant oratory, his opposition to Commonwealth immigration and British membership of the European Union, and his support for Ulster Unionism; Conservative MP for Wolverhampton SW, 1950–74; Ulster Unionist MP for South Down, 1974–92; m. 1952 Margaret Wilson.
[‡] Colonial administrator (1881–1955).
[§] Hon. Rosemary Lyttelton (b. 1922), dau. of 1st Viscount Chandos; m. 1951 3rd Viscount Chaplin (formerly husband of A.L.-M.).
[¶] In *Midway on the Waves*, published the year before, J.L.-M. had described how he, his future wife Alvilde, her then husband Anthony Chaplin and Chaplin's future wife Rosemary all stayed together at Alvilde's house in France in June 1949.

Thursday, 18th September

Went through entries on Venice in London Library subject index
before going to see Julian Barrow* in Tite Street. I am taking more
taxis in London than ever before, no longer able to face slogging on
public transport with parcels and luggage. Julian B. delightful, as is his
wife. He has a studio at No. 33, whose past owners include Sargent,
Glyn Philpott and Augustus John. Huge window at rear. On one wall
a vast reredos dated 1610 which Sargent saved from a Venetian church.
Julian's pictures are less tight that Felix Kelly's, but sun-dappled and
slightly impressionistic. Some very covetable. At four I went to M's to
listen to a discussion about *Ancestral Voices* on Radio 4. I was nervous
lest I should yet again be accused of being a snob. On the contrary,
the main speaker seemed to see me (as I see myself) as a social historian. I shall listen to the repeat on Sunday.

Friday, 26th September

On Monday I went to stay with Diana [Mosley] at Orsay for two nights.
Enjoyed myself enormously. We talked and talked, scarcely stopping to
go to bed. She told me all kinds of things without reservation.

Before O[swald] M[osley]'s death she was advised to obtain a copy
of their marriage certificate (the original having perished in a fire at
their Irish house), since in the event of his predeceasing her she would
have to pay massive French death duties unless she could prove she was
his widow. This was difficult, as they had married in the garden of
Goebbels' house, in Hitler's presence. She applied to the West German
government who told her she must write to the East German government, as the site was now on the eastern side of the Berlin wall.
Amazingly, such is German efficiency, she obtained it, though house
and garden long gone.

I told her about the *Berlin Diaries* of Missy Vassiltchikov† which I
so much enjoyed. She denied that Hitler watched a film of the slow
strangulation by piano wire of those involved in the attempt on his life
in 1944. It was not the sort of thing he would do. She said Hitler

---

* Painter of portraits, landscapes and country houses (b. 1939); m. Serena Harington.
† Princess Marie 'Missy' Vassiltchikov (1917–78), Russian aristocrat who was stranded in
Nazi Germany on outbreak of war in 1939, and employed as a translator in German
Foreign Ministry. Her *Berlin Diaries* (1985) are a fascinating source for both wartime social
life in the German capital, and the 'resistance' to the Nazis in official circles.

would never have declared war on England, which he loved even more than the Kaiser did. He wept when Singapore fell to the Japanese. Had we not declared war on him, he would have defeated Russia. She despises Stauffenberg for being a coward, bolting from the scene before his bomb went off. Cowardice is what she most despises in humans, even more than disloyalty.

Hitler, she said, had the most delicate hands, and beautiful blue eyes. Everyone he met fell under his charm. I tackled her about the Jews and concentration camps. She admitted that what had happened was dreadful and inexcusable, but wondered whether he was aware of it, for he was not naturally cruel or callous. But she said that we in England overlooked the fact that the German Jews bled the economy in their own selfish interests, much as the blacks do in Britain today.

At Chatsworth, O.M. met the Prince of Wales, who talked to him with fascination for three-quarters of an hour and asked to see him again. But O.M. begged to be excused a further meeting, as it would not be in the Prince's interest. They talked of the future of the monarchy.

Diana once asked K[enneth] Clark what the attitude of King George VI and the Queen Mother towards the Duke and Duchess of Windsor really was. 'Vicious,' he replied.

A. awfully cross when I told her these stories on my return. Thinks me weak for being taken in by Diana's charm. Possibly.

Saturday, 27th September

A. and I flew to Holland, arriving early afternoon. We landed at Amsterdam and took train to The Hague, staying two nights in comfortable but very expensive Hôtel des Indes in centre of Old Town. Spent evening strolling. Very pretty streets, and houses with autumnal gardens on the canals charming. Friendly people who stop and talk. Nevertheless town spoilt by tower blocks in the wrong places. Our new friends the van Lyndens* have a flat next to the hotel. We met them in England dining with our neighbours the Fachs, both couples being Dutchmen married to Englishwomen; we took to each other and they suggested the trip. The Baron has just retired from an ambassadorship; she is perfection, clever, bright, friendly and pretty. They organised our entire visit.

---

* Baron Diederic Wolter van Lynden (b. 1917); m. 1945 Anne Heathcote.

Sunday, 28th September

Van Lyndens motored us to Wallenburg, an old house restored some twenty-five years ago by an architect called Canneman whose wife is a gardener. Before we arrived, the van Ls explained that, since they made the arrangements, Mr C. had been taken to a nursing home following a succession of strokes and Mrs was about to join him there, but she first wanted to show A. her garden. It was charming, a deserted, sleeping-beauty, overgrown garden surrounded by trees. I thought how much Vita [Sackville-West] would have loved it. A divine, autumnal morning. Mrs C., frail, fair, elderly, with large teeth and gentle manners, reminded me of Ethel Sands.* Her husband's collapse was a shock, but she is now resigned. I was haunted by this living ghost sitting in the midst of her own creation which she was about to abandon forever.

We were then taken to lunch nearby at Hardenbroek, with Countess of that name. Very different set-up. Rich lady, twice widowed. Very amusing, reminding me of Catherine d'Erlanger with her greying red hair and assured manner. Large house with straight avenues in park-like setting. Both these houses moated, as many Dutch houses seem to be. Country very ugly, flat as a pancake, spoilt by ribbons of motorways, Vermeer's open skies now streaked with pylon wires.

After luncheon we drove to Doorn, which the Kaiser acquired in 1920, after staying at Amaronger with the Bentincks after his flight from Germany in 1918. He was allowed to send forty-eight wagons to fetch his favourite possessions from Germany. So house full of excellent French and German furniture, along with family pictures and usual mass of knick-knacks. Taste not half bad. I expected it to be hideous. In his study, the Emperor had a stool consisting of his old saddle mounted on a swinging-post, so that when writing letters he had the illusion of reviewing troops. Something fascinating about this man, half-cad, half-visionary, kindly yet imperious.

Back in The Hague, the van Lyndens gave a dinner party for ten. Rather a struggle, the rooms low and hot. Guests included the next Dutch Ambassador to London and wife, dull, middle-class couple.

---

* See *Ancestral Voices*, 2 May 1943 and note: 'An intellectual, Europeanised American artist', then in her early seventies.

Monday, 29th September

Packed, left our comfortable double room, settled hefty bill of £250. Continental breakfast £8 each extra. Van Lyndens motored us to Het Loo, main object of our visit. Lunched at Appeldoorn in smart pub with Vliegenhart, the curator, and wife, charming couple, and an old, stout, jolly Princess Salm who motored across border from Germany. The curator personally showed us around the palace, it being a 'closed' day. Great privilege. Miraculous restoration to its former state. Unsightly annexes demolished, original furniture collected from Dutch museums, even from America. Rooms now exactly as William of Orange and Queen Mary created them. Original marbling found and re-done, old fabrics copied at vast expense. Daniel Marot left coloured drawings of each room. The whole exercise is said to have cost £40 million, borne by the state. A few rooms wisely left as they were when lived in by Queen Wilhelmina and her parents. Garden also restored to formal parterres and walks and arbours, with fountains, cascades, and pleached hornbeam tunnels. A truly amazing re-creation by a small country, owing much to enthusiasm of Vliegenhart.

Returned to Heathrow after dark. Difficult drive home owing to fog.

Wednesday, 1st October

Strange occurrence at Lansdown Tower* meeting this evening. After the usual boring agenda – maintenance costs, dry rot, drop in number of visitors during season, etc. – we were shown a portrait of Beckford as a child which the Duke of Hamilton† offers to us for £20,000, along with three oils by Maddox of Beckford treasures, painted for the coloured lithographs in the book of 1844 of which I have a copy. We

---

* Having moved from Fonthill to Bath in 1822, William Beckford commissioned the architect H. E. Goodridge to build an ornate Tower (1826) on the hill above Lansdown Crescent, where he spent much time in his later years, reading and admiring the view. On his death in 1844, he was buried next to it. It later became the property of the local parish church, and deteriorated through neglect. A couple named Hillyard, Bath doctors, bought it in the 1970s, restored it, established a museum there, and set up a trust for its conservation (later incorporated in Bath Preservation Trust).
† Angus Douglas-Hamilton, 15th Duke of Hamilton (b. 1938); descendant of William Beckford, whose daughter had married 10th Duke.

decided that we could not afford the portrait, but would offer £6,000 for the Maddoxes. Then Graham Cave* produced a loose flannel bundle from which fell a cascade of gold spoons which had belonged to Beckford, also the Duke's who wants to get rid of them. With eyes glistening like werewolves, we greedily examined this loot, clawing at teaspoons, sugar tongs and tea-caddy spoons, all with Beckford's crest, pelican with fish in beak or Latimer Cross. We decided that the Trust should buy the pick, some to exhibit, others to keep in the bank as an investment, and that we ourselves might buy any of the remainder which we wanted. I took six tea spoons and a pair of silver gilt dessert spoons, for which I paid £150, less than they would have fetched at auction. As we left, Sidney Blackmore† said to me, 'How Beckford would have hated that scene.' He would indeed, and may well haunt me at No. 19 for being a participant.

Monday, 6th October

Have finished Venice book, including preface. Must now re-type the whole thing. The young no longer type. All done by computer. Lucky they are. I can't possibly grasp the intricacies.

Alexander Mosley told me that some twenty years ago he was in an air crash, the thing I most dread. It was a smallish machine. Pilot managed to 'pancake' on sea near the shore. Water came pouring in. Ali, a brave and hefty man, took charge of an old lady. As he helped her out, she said, 'Oh dear, I have left all the Christmas presents for my grand-children behind.' He said, 'Come along, just think what a welcome Christmas present *you* will be for them.' They waded safely ashore.

I have discovered a delicious bitter chocolate in slabs, obtainable at chemists. It is low in sugar, so won't make me fat. As good as any chocolate I have ever eaten.

Reading Goncourt *Journals.* The death of the younger brother Jules, from syphilis aged thirty-nine, is one of the most harrowing death scene descriptions I have ever read. They were of one mind and almost body, though eight years between them. No wonder the Pope-Hennessy brothers, equally clever, sharp, intolerant and arrogant, were sometimes compared to them.

---

* Poultry farmer; trustee of Beckford Tower Trust.
† Civil servant and art lecturer; trustee of Beckford Tower Trust, later Secretary of Beckford Society.

I met Charles Tomlinson, lunching on Saturday with Bob Parsons[*] at Newark. There is still a stuffiness and lack of humour about him, but he is no longer chippy, having become assured through success. Had been lecturing in Italian in Liguria, and visited the catacombs in Palermo, of which I had never heard. There are some thousands of bodies in a perfect state of preservation, mostly middle-class people from the early nineteenth century, wearing coats, hats, etc., all awaiting Judgement Day.

Went to poor old Osbert Lancaster's memorial service last week. Although he was a very old friend from Oxford days, I was not deeply moved. The church in Covent Garden is so gloomy (awful little card lampshades dangling from the ceiling like paper caps), and the fact that O. died weeks ago did not call for mourning. And I did not love Osbert as I did John Betjeman. He was too much the actor, too much the echoer of that horrid Maurice Bowra. That he was the best cartoonist since Beerbohm one cannot doubt. Lesson read by his son William, the living (or should I say dying) image of Osbert, squat, hunched, round-faced, bad-complexioned, mustachioed, resembling an old carpenter in a back-street of Florence. Anne still extremely pretty, slim, tall and distinguished. Before I could escape she caught me at the church door and kissed me. She was upset but controlled, poor dear.

Tuesday, 7th October

Glyn Boyd Harte[†] came from London to do a drawing of me in the library. It must have been ten years ago that he made the same expedition to paint me. I was so horrified by the result that I could barely look at it and never referred to it again. Yet his friend Colin McMordie told me he was pleased with it and hung it in his house. This time he is doing a sort of fantasy, including me in my writing chair reflected in the mirror. Took innumerable snaps of me with minute camera the size of his hand. He works rapidly. The rough sketch seemed pleasing. A nice, chatty young man, grey-haired at thirty-eight. Could just be my grandson. Is a great friend of Edmund Fairfax-Lucy. When I praised Edmund's work and said I presumed he

---

[*] American architect (1920–2000); tenant and repairer of Newark Park, Gloucestershire, N.T. property.
[†] Artist and illustrator (b. 1948).

had large sales, he replied, 'Not as large as mine, or so expensive.' Says that Edmund and Lucy already live in separate houses, and meet but seldom.

Saturday, 11th October

We dined tonight at the House. In Caroline's absence, I found myself sitting next to David's mistress Miranda Morley,* whom I have hitherto avoided for diplomatic reasons. Very sweet and pretty, and unobtrusive. She did not take the head of the table, or welcome guests or seat them. Yet I was assailed with a slight feeling of disloyalty to Caroline, and wondered what the servants thought about her being in the House. On my other side was Liliane Rothschild,† Poppy Pryce-Jones's sister. A dumpling with snow-white hair, white face and currant eyes. A great friend and patroness of Winckler,‡ the French artist I have to meet in Paris next week. I gathered that neither she nor her husband, Baron Elie, had a high opinion of Alan Pryce-Jones.§

Tuesday, 14th October

Day in London. To Tate Gallery to visit *Golden Age of Scottish Painting* exhibition. Lovely and unexciting. Only with the arrival of Raeburn does Scottish painting excel. Not enough of John Watson Gordon, and none of Macnee. My funny little McCullough looks homely and proud to be among such illustrious company. Called on M., still in pyjamas. Felt irritated that this young man leads such an unhealthy life. As Stuart [Preston] says, he is going the way of Jamesey [Pope-Hennessy], without the latter's Lady Crewe¶ background. Met

---

* She married 11th Duke of Beaufort in 2000, five years after the death of his 1st wife Caroline.

† Liliane Fould-Springer; m. 1941 Baron Elie de Rothschild.

‡ Jean-Marc Winckler (b. 1952); French artist whose country house paintings, as J.L.-M. was to write in his *American Architectural Digest* article, 'might be taken for late Georgian engravings': see entry for 15 October 1987 below.

§ Writer and journalist (1908–2000); Eton contemporary of J.L.-M.; editor *Times Literary Supplement*, 1948–59; his first wife Poppy, *née* Fould-Springer, Liliane's sister, had died in 1953.

¶ After 1945, J.P.-H. had befriended the Marchioness of Crewe, widow of a Liberal statesman (and daughter of Lord Rosebery), and written biographies of her husband and father-in-law.

Kenneth Rose at Geales, a superior fish and chip shop. Was bored by his cynicism. But he has reviewed my book kindly in *Sunday Telegraph*. Then to Madame Lobanov's nearby to be shown water-colours of the Sebriakoffs.* Charming they are too, in the professional manner of one's great-aunt. Then took my armorial soup plates to Howard in Grafton Street, who pronounced them to be Chamberlayne Worcester, early nineteenth-century, the arms and crest of Parker, although the tinctures were wrong. His knowledge of such things phenomenal. On his walls were hanging two small portraits of Prince Charles and the Cardinal King.† I said, 'I suppose very expensive?' 'Very,' he replied, assuring me that I would not be able to afford them. I skipped Paddy [Leigh Fermor]'s party at John Murray's. Could not face the din, the heat, and the adulation of P., which I recognise to be deserved, but which irritates me because he basks in it. Were he to ignore or deprecate it, I should not mind. Then to Eardley's where we ate delicious smoked salmon before going to a tiny, grotty theatre in Chalk Farm, entered through a newsagent's. Not more than twenty in the audience. Macallan, or some such name,‡ impersonated Harold Nicolson, wrestling with his conscience in a shabby hotel in Croydon during the 1947 by-election in which he stood for Labour and was beaten by the Tories. Very well done. Resemblance to H. not bad, though he was too smartly dressed and unable to catch H's slurry voice. In bed at Brooks's by ten o'clock.

Wednesday, 15th October

Left Brooks's at 7.30 for Heathrow. Arrived Paris 10.30, took taxi to Grand Palais. Filthy day, pouring with rain, whereas London had been divine. Spent rest of morning at François Boucher exhibition. I do not like Boucher – ladies with blue ribbons round their necks, tending

---

* Alexandre Sebriakoff, émigré Russian painter of country house interiors, and another subject of J.L.-M's article for the *American Architectural Digest*. He came from a famous family of Russian artists, and was nephew of the stage designer Alexander Benois. His sister Catherine did the figures in his paintings.
† In the Jacobite canon, Prince Charles Edward Stuart, 'the Young Pretender' (1720–88), reigned *de jure* as Charles III and his brother Prince Henry, Cardinal Duke of York (1725–1807), as Henry IX.
‡ Possibly Ian McKellen (b. 1939; kt 1991), actor and gay rights campaigner.

sheep or goats; even a cook courted by a baker's boy is a Dresden shep-
herdess being seduced by a swain. In landscapes, the sunlight on
broken tree-trunks is a favourite trick. He is a Rococo painter, and
Rococo is only tolerable as architectural decoration. Though it was
only a few yards away, I had some difficulty finding the Travellers'
Club, as no one could tell me where it was. Lunched there with
Stuart, who showed me around this hideous but interesting Second
Empire residence of some renowned odalisque.* Horrid luncheon.

S. accompanied me to the Elie de Rothschilds' extremely posh residence in the rue de Courcelles. Really, these Paris town houses.
Concièrge at gate; forecourt; butler at front door; entrance hall with
curved staircase and elegant railings. Several grand people in large
first-floor drawing room drinking coffee after luncheon. Was introduced to Jean-Marc Winckler, young, merry, plain youth of thirty-
four who insisted on kissing my hand. I looked at coloured
photographs of his interiors and conversation pieces. Liliane de R.,
the youth's patroness and impresario, has other works of his hanging
upstairs in her bathroom. Pastiche, yet competent and attractive. The
four artists whose work I must write about are near-indistinguishable
in style, with their revived eighteenth-century miniaturist technique.
Liliane is intelligent and social, with excellent taste and lovely possessions. One room full of portraits of and objects which belonged to
Marie Antoinette.

Despite Stuart's help, I had much trouble finding a taxi in the rain
to take me to the airport. Was glad to get away. Don't feel happy in
Paris. Never have. Hope never to go there again.

Sunday, 19th October

Am extremely depressed as Regy has been almost totally ignored by
the press. Only two reviews by friends, Kenneth Rose and M. Whole
thing a flop after the pains of more than four years. Yesterday received
aggrieved letter from Angela Thornton,† horrified by revelations of

---

* 25 Champs-Elysées, built in the 1860s by the courtesan Thérèse, Marquise de la Païva
(born Esther Lachmann), and prized today as a surviving example of the sumptuous decoration of the period, became the Travellers' clubhouse in 1904.
† Angela Brett (b. 1911), eldest child of 2nd Viscount Esher's yr son Maurice (whose
incestuous relationship with his father was described in J.L.-M's book); m. 1934 Kenneth
Thornton. She wrote to J.L.-M.: 'You are so right, it *was* a shock, & a most unpleasant
one. I wish with all my heart I had not read it . . .'

the intimacy between her grandfather Regy and father Maurice. Asked me not to write to her again. The only cheering thing has been a telephone call from that distinguished man Noël Annan,* whom I barely know, to say how good he thought it was. I shall never write another book after the silly little Venetian volume I am now finishing. I am a third-rate failure and must recognise it.

Thursday, 30th October

To London. Had tea with poor Ros, looking better but blinder than ever. After all her operations she still cannot see to read more than a page of any book. She told me a curious story about Jamesey [Pope-Hennessy], who towards the end of his life, when he was writing about Robert Louis Stevenson, visited her in Eaton Square by taxi. On arrival, the driver said to him, 'A few minutes ago, I saw another figure sitting beside you. He had a downward-curling white moustache like a Chinaman, and was wearing a green eyeshade and large white hat. He seemed to be carrying a funny old typewriter.' Jamesey at once recognised this description to be of Stevenson, who was one of the first writers to use a typewriter, and mentioned this to the driver. 'Never heard of him, I'm sure,' said the driver, 'but I quite often see people like that. I have the gift.'

I stayed the night with Eardley, and we dined with Jack Rathbone at Jack's house. He seemed slightly better than formerly, but his mind all over the place. Much 'Dear Eardley', 'Dear Jim', 'Darling'. He seemed to enjoy my telling him stories about the good old days at the National Trust, yet never once laughed. His face used to crease with laughter.

Friday, 31st October

Driven by Dudley Dodd to Clandon [Park, Surrey], where I yet again took the chair of the Arts Panel in John Julius [Norwich]'s absence. Not so unwieldly a party as met last year at Canons Ashby. I found it hard to hear in the large empty saloon where we sat. There was a division of feeling between those who had known John Fowler, who

---

* Provost of King's College, Cambridge, 1956–66, and of University College, London, 1966–78; Vice-Chancellor of London University, 1978–81; cr. life peer as Baron Annan, 1965 (1916–2000).

thought we ought not to alter anything he had done at Clandon (the one N.T. house where he had a free hand), and those who had not, like Michael Jaffé* and Chrissy Gibbs,† who were all for making changes. I secretly sympathised with the latter, for it is absurd to turn a great country house of the past into a memorial to a modern decorator, even one as outstanding as J.F. However, we agreed to let another decade pass before making any further changes. The truth is that Mrs Gubbay's‡ furniture is too small in scale for these huge rooms. John was aware of this and did the best he could. I really ought to retire from the Panel at my age, but it is such fun and the N.T. boys and girls are so nice.

Tony Mitchell motored me to Chippenham, where I had left my car yesterday. On the way we stopped at Yattendon, where a very unusual and talented member of the Panel, Alec Cobbe,§ lives with wife and children. It turned out to be the house where Alvilde's cousin Robert Bridges¶ lived. The rooms are now covered with rich red damask hangings rejected by the Wallace Collection. Large *seicento* paintings lit by curved metal shell-shaped shades. Rooms full of musical instruments, including a forte piano made by Erhard for Marie Antoinette, which Cobbe played for us. He cleans pictures for the N.T. No legs to speak of.

Saturday, 1st November

We lunched with the Trees at Donhead St Mary. A couple called Bridge** staying, who live in the village at Firle, she a cousin of Nancy

---

* Professor of History of Western Art, Cambridge, 1973–90 (1923–97).
† Christopher Henry Gibbs (b. 1938) of Clifton Hampden Manor, Oxfordshire; collector, connoisseur and antique dealer.
‡ The N.T. exhibited at Clandon a collection of eighteenth-century furniture, porcelain, textiles and carpets assembled in the 1920s by the connoisseur Mrs David Gubbay.
§ Richard Alexander Charles Cobbe (b. 1945); artist and designer, arranger of pictures and interiors for N.T.; m. 1970 Hon. Isabel Dillon. In 1987 he became tenant of Hatchlands, N.T. house near Guildford, which he redesigned in theatrical style, filling it with his family pictures from Newbridge House, Co. Dublin and his collection of early keyboard intruments.
¶ Poet (1844–1930); Poet Laureate from 1913.
** Christopher Bridge (b. 1918); director of Hambros and sometime High Sheriff of East Sussex; m. 1953 (as her 2nd husband) Hon. Dinah Fox (b. 1920), yr dau. of 1st and last Baron Brand.

Lancaster. As we went into the dining room, Anne whispered to us, 'Be careful what you say. The butler's wife is black.' The butler, very efficient and professional, was one Prince Ercole Rospigliosi. What a topsy-turvy world.

Anne talked of the Bachelor Duke.* He was stone deaf by middle age, which is why the Paxtons acted as host and hostess to his friends at Chatsworth. He was madly in love with George IV's daughter Princess Charlotte, but considered not good enough to marry her. He never got over his disappointment and never looked at another woman. Anne said that Lord Lansdowne,† the statesman who tried to stop the First World War, was her great-grandfather. In his case too there are masses of papers but no biography, and one should be written.

A. and I have been agonising over whether to go with Andrew Devonshire and Selina in search of the sun in February. We both decided that Andrew was too high-powered for us. So A. has written that her health does not at the moment allow her to have injections against all the ills that tropical countries are heir to – which is true.

Sunday, 2nd November

While A. and I were kneeling together in Little Badminton Church this morning and reciting the Confessional, it suddenly occurred to me that millions habitually made this act of contrition, yet their names were forgotten on earth, and probably unrecorded in the scrolls of Heaven. I was reciting something which, within five years at most, I shall have ceased to recite, 'I' having vanished forever, and with it all my resolutions. Yet I felt I was not wasting my time, but rather contributing to the contrition of the whole of mankind, of which I was so fragmentary a part as to be of no importance to God. This came

---

* William George Spencer Cavendish, 6th Duke of Devonshire (1790–1858); Whig states-man, collector, and patron of Sir Joseph Paxton. Debo Devonshire was trying to persuade J.L.-M. to write his biography (see diary for January–March and October–November 1987 below).

† Henry Petty-Fitzmaurice, 5th Marquess of Lansdowne (1845–1927); Unionist states-man; Secretary of State for War, 1895–1900, and Foreign Affairs, 1900–5; member of War Coalition, 1915–16. In a private letter to Asquith in November 1916, and again in a con-troversial public letter to the *Daily Telegraph* a year later, he suggested how the First World War might be ended by negotiation.

almost as a visionary understanding, and not one that was wholly agreeable to me.

Friday, 7th November

Shopping at Sainsbury's is a terrifying experience. Hundreds of women, their trolleys piled high with tins, milling at the paying desks, of which there is a row of some thirty, each staffed by a lady punching buttons like some furious automaton. How I would rather be at my little shop at the end of Lansdown Crescent, even though everything there is much more expensive.

Robert Smith of Sidgwick's telephoned to ask if I had seen today's *Daily Telegraph*. Very favourable review of Regy by Anthony Powell, just when I was resigned to the book being totally ignored. Smith also told me that Philip Ziegler had asked for copies to distribute to judges of the W. H. Smith Prize, but I told him not to bother.

Saturday, 8th November

As I was walking across the park with the dogs on leash, sun very low on horizon, long shadows, the herd of red deer dashed across my path. One hind was several paces ahead of the rest, who were so densely packed one could not separate them with a finger. They were like a train, in closest formation, three abreast, galloping in order. Some six or seven stags in the rear. A beautiful sight.

Wednesday, 12th November

A. having gone with Caroline to Italy for four nights, staying with the Brandolinis, I went to London. M. lunched with me and we went to Felix Kelly's exhibition at Partridge's. Very dream-like his paintings, deadly silent scenes as if some calamity about to happen. Then to Agnew's to see Fyvie Castle picture collection, including a dozen Raeburns, and Martyn Gregory Gallery for eighteenth-century watercolours of country houses. After tea I went to the Cartoon Gallery in Lamb's Conduit Street where I bought one of Osbert's drawings. There were about a hundred of them, like postage stamps in rows, not collectively a pretty sight, but I have always admired his work, and wanted to have one.

Saturday, 15th November

We lunched at the House, about twenty at the long table. Sat between Cosima Fry,* to whom I had little to say, and Claire Ward,† as sweet as once was her mother,‡ who is now out of her mind. Talked afterwards to Tony Lambton, writing yet another biography of Mountbatten, whom he hates and regards as the vainest, stupidest and most scheming of men. Before Prince Philip married, Mountbatten summoned him and said, 'You know where your duty lies. For twenty years you must be absolutely faithful.' Mountbatten was obsessed with the interests of the Hesse family, but may not have been one of them himself, as his father was probably illegitimate. Lambton dark, balding, saturnine.

We dined with Rupert Loewenstein to meet Littman§ and wife. He said to be the cleverest lawyer alive, she American and pretty. Littman said that, at a dinner party in the 1930s, the name of Oliver Cromwell was mentioned. A very old lady present said, 'Ah, Oliver Cromwell! My first husband's first wife's first husband knew him well.' I suppose just possible, assuming vast age-gaps between spouses.

Sunday, 16th November

Filthiest day imaginable, and a motor rally attended by 22,000 taking place in the Park. We lunched with Woman at Caudle Green to meet Diana, who had been driven there by the Osborne Hills.¶ This millionaire couple keep permanent suites in the most expensive hotels in Rome, Paris, New York and London, and invite friends to stay there as their guests, everything paid for. Burnet adores them; but would he and others do so if they were rat-poor?

---

* Lady Cosima Vane-Tempest-Stewart (b. 1961), ostensibly yr dau. of 9th Marquess of Londonderry (though in 106th edition of *Burke's Peerage* she claims paternity of Robin Douglas-Home); m. 1st 1982–6 Cosmo, s. of Jeremy Fry, 2nd 1990–6 Lord John Somerset, yst s. of 11th Duke of Beaufort.

† Claire Baring (b. 1936); m. 1956–74 Hon. Peter Ward, yr s. of 3rd Earl of Dudley; close friend of Lord Lambton. Her daughter Tracey Ward (b. 1958) married the Beauforts' heir, Harry, Marquess of Worcester, the following year (see entry for 13 June 1987).

‡ Mona Husband, *née* Hubbard.

§ Mark Littman, QC (b. 1920); m. 1965 Marguerite Lamkin of Louisiana (b. 1932).

¶ Wealthy anglophile American couple based in Seattle: see entry for 6 July 1987.

Sunday, 23rd November

I invited my new friends the Alec Cobbes to luncheon. A. made cross by their asking to bring their schoolboy son, an amiable boy. The others Coote [Heber-Percy], and Polly and Andy Garnett.

Monday, 24th November

A bungled day. Went to London in the afternoon, mistakenly thinking it was the day Feeble* had asked me to dinner. Had also meant to go to Glyn Boyd Harte's exhibition at Kyle Gallery, but could not face the heat and crowds. So ended up dining at Brooks's alone, or rather with Merlin Sudeley,† who is still going on about his genealogy. When he laughs he makes a cretinous sound. Saw Alan Clark. Just back from the Balkans, and says that in Hungary you can say whatever you like. Everyone grumbles about the regime, from cabinet ministers downwards. He is a great ally of Mrs Thatcher, against whom there is much disloyalty. I went to bed early, reading Paddy [Leigh Fermor]'s book about Transylvania,‡ admiring his beautiful prose and poetic descriptions but rather bored by his dissertations on language derivations.

Tuesday, 25th November

Lunched in expensive fish restaurant in Dover Street with Dan Franklin and Simon King of Collins. They are pleased with *Venetian Evenings* and also want to reissue *Roman Mornings*, though unable to accept all my additions and corrections to the latter. At Heywood Hill, John Saumarez Smith told me that he had been unable to secure the Duff Cooper Prize, of which he is a judge, for my *Regy*, because of 'those damned dons'. Had I been John, I would not have mentioned this. Meanwhile I have had a praising letter about it from Michael Howard,§ and a kind one from Lady Shuckburgh;¶ and a review by

---

* Lady Elizabeth ('Feeble') Cavendish (b. 1926); dau. of 10th Duke of Devonshire; Lady-in-Waiting to Princess Margaret; long-standing friend of Sir John Betjeman.
† Merlin Hanbury-Tracy, 7th Baron Sudeley (b. 1939).
‡ *Between the Woods and the Water.*
§ Sir Michael Eliot Howard (b. 1922); Regius Professor of Modern History, Oxford, 1980–9.
¶ Hon. Nancy Brett (b. 1918), dau. of 3rd Viscount Esher; m. 1937 Sir Evelyn Shuckburgh, diplomatist (1909–94).

John Grigg* in the *TLS*, approving my estimate of Regy's character, but saying my political history is faulty. No wonder the dons rejected it.

Geoffrey Agnew† has died. He was exactly my age. He resembled a huge ram and had a deep, resonant voice. Earned a position for himself as the confidant of ministers. The art world set less store by his expertise, but then they are bitches. He wanted me to join his little committee for redecorating Brooks's and hanging the Dilettanti pictures, but I declined, for he had no taste, and brushed aside all criticism. I shall miss him at the club.

Went this morning to Kyle Gallery to see Glyn [Boyd Harte]'s picture of my library, with me reflected in the mirror. A nice picture. I am just recognisable by the shape of my head, though given a halo which I don't deserve. Already a red spot, indicating it is sold. For how much, I asked? £2,600. I wonder who bought it. There are several of his pictures I would like to have. He has found his style – detailed and fantastical, with glowing, polished colours.

Sunday, 30th November

St Andrew's Day and the date of my poor father's death [in 1949]. To the Rodin exhibition, a disappointment. His drawings of nude women, lying on their sides and exposing their nude pudenda, I find offensive. Oh how I loathe sex these days. Is this my middle class upbringing? Or resentment? Or my neutrality? Or is it a right and proper attitude, simply revolting from something disgusting? A beautiful head of *La Pensée*, 1886, redeems him by its beauty and purity.

Saturday, 6th December

A. and I off on errands of mercy. First to the Droghedas for luncheon. Garrett had also asked a Mrs Haig, boring woman who paints plants in watercolour. He arrived with her from the station at precisely the moment we did, which proved bewildering for Joan. Joan now not

---

* Writer (1924–2001), official biographer of Lloyd George; succeeded father as 2nd Baron Altrincham 1955, but disclaimed peerage 1963; m. 1958 Patricia Campbell.
† Sir Geoffrey Agnew (1908–86); Managing Director (from 1937) and Chairman (from 1965) of Thomas Agnew & Sons, Fine Art Dealers; m. 1934 Hon. Doreen Jessel.

just senile but a mad woman, with a look in her eyes. Had no idea who we were. Got up at least ten times during luncheon and had to be restrained by the nurse from leaving the room. Poor Garrett almost at the end of his tether, though refuses absolutely to send her to a home. He is pale and wan, all looks departed, his nose hooked like K. Clark's became.

We left at 3.15 for Loelia [Lindsay]'s. She had a stroke three weeks ago, and cannot communicate easily; knows what she wants to say, but cannot get the words out. Says things like, 'that place down the road', meaning the church, or 'that rich man with the houses I used to be married to', meaning Bendor. Yet in her courageous way laughs while she struggles for a word and we make frantic guesses. Is not physically impaired, and can walk.

I am reading Tommy Lascelles'* early diaries. He is not likeable, and in the youth one can see the father of the man – arrogant, supercilious, cagily queer. But I can't help admiring his style. He is also shrewd about George Lloyd,† whom he describes as unable to relax and unlikely to make old bones. How true.

Friday, 12th December

I am restless, with little inclination to start new books. To London for the day. Visited M. in his flat to see his new bed. It looks like one of those baldaquins assembled in the houses of Black Families in Italy in which to receive a visiting Pope. All of dark oak, the tester fitted with mirror panels in which one sees one's reflection. M. sweetly suggested we christen it with a cuddle, which we did. How satisfactory to embrace someone one truly loves without a trace of sexual appetite, as with Missy at home. Again I gave him a talking-to about his lamentable indolence and bad habits, and not getting down to his new book. He protests he will heed my scolding.

Jamie Fergusson lunched with me at Brooks's. He has greatly

---

* Sir Alan Lascelles (1887–1981); courtier; Private Secretary to HM King George VI and HM Queen Elizabeth II, 1943–53. The first volume of his letters and diaries, edited by Duff Hart-Davis under the title *End of an Era* (Hamish Hamilton, 1986), describes his life up to 1920, when he began a ten-year stint as Assistant Private Secretary to the Prince of Wales.
† J.L.-M's sometime employer (see notes to 19 September 1985) had married Lascelles' sister Blanche.

matured; has a quiet, quizzical manner, and is very clever. Asks for another obituary from me – of Sachie [Sitwell]. Am not sure I know Sachie well enough.

Saturday, 13th December

We lunch at Sudeley Castle with the Ashcombes.* Extraordinary how rich the upper classes are. This vast house has been done up in the Fowler style by Stanley Falconer,† who was present. Others present Metcalfe, son of Baba, tall, ugly man;‡ John Bowes Lyon,§ intelligent gossip; Margaret-Anne [Stuart] and John Wilton; Loelia [Lindsay]. I sat between Elizabeth Ashcombe, a friendly and unpretentious little thing, and Loelia, who seemed dreadfully ill, though full of laughter. Says she misses Martin Lindsay. 'Of course, he had his faults; little humour, and our friends strangers to him. He was much in love with me, whereas I never was with him.'

Sudeley is a difficult house to write about. Nothing about it is genuine. It was a ruin when the glove-manufacturing Dent brothers bought it in the 1830s. Their restoration of it was scrapped by Walter Godfrey in the 1920s, and they are now scrapping that. The house full of good Morrison pictures. The Elizabethan exhibits mostly fakes. The situation surrounded by hills is fine and the gardens are spectacular. But quite impossible to take proper notes on a social occasion.

Sunday, 14th December

Elspeth Huxley said that to be made a literary dame or knight you must accept every invitation to lecture or make speeches. They are the only ones which qualify. You can be a Milton or a Dickens, but if you

---

* Henry Cubitt, 4th Baron Ashcombe (b. 1924); m. (3rd) 1979 Elizabeth, widow of Mark Dent-Brocklehurst of Sudeley Castle, Gloucestershire. (Lord Ashcombe's mother, Sonia *née* Keppel, was the sister of J.L.-M's friend Violet Trefusis [1894–1972].)
† Interior decorator (b. 1927), director of Colefax & Fowler (former close friend of John Fowler).
‡ David Metcalfe (b. 1927); o.s. of Major E. D. 'Fruity' Metcalfe, companion of Edward, Prince of Wales, and Lady Alexandra, dau. of Marquess Curzon of Kedleston; m. 1st 1957–64 Alexandra Boycan, 2nd 1968–73 Comtesse de Chauvigny de Blot, 3rd Sally Cullen.
§ John Francis Bowes Lyon (b. 1942); sometime director of Sotheby's.

do not speak in public, you will not be recognised. She laughed at my question whether she would like to be made a dame herself.

I am reading Alan Pryce-Jones's autobiography* – which is not yet out, but [John] Saumarez [Smith] is always ready to oblige. The book is typical of Alan, reads just like him speaking, is very brilliant and sparkling and one enjoys every word. Yet somehow one does not admire him for it. It is like a highbrow's Jennifer's Diary, names dropping like autumn leaves – my aunt Mary Minto, my uncle Hillingdon, my cousin Harewood, all presumably through his Dawnay mother, for the Pryce-Joneses were quite dim, like my family. All the while there are protestations against snobbery, and veils are tightly drawn over his propensities. One is expected to believe that his relationship with Bobbie Pratt Barlow† was totally avuncular and disinterested, that he is a tolerant hetero, amused by the venial peccadilloes of his queer friends. Interesting that, like myself, he feels the Church let him down after he became a Papist. Had he known what John XXIII was going to do he would never have signed up.

Sunday, 21st December

Have been looking through my diaries for the early 1970s, when we were still at Alderley. Diaries of a Provincial Lady, less readable than Parson Woodforde. Will they ever be published?‡

I believe everyone has a secret spark of *Schadenfreude*. So when told that Bruce Chatwin,§ who is suspected to be suffering from Aids, felt better, I experienced a momentary pang of disappointment. This was instinctive rather than rational, for were God to ask me point-blank, I should express an unhesitating wish that Bruce should recover. It is a case of the civilised self banging down the brutish self. They say old people enjoy reading of the deaths of their old friends in *The Times*. I am not sure what my own true feelings are in this respect.

At Foyle's luncheon on the 17th I sat between Fay Weldon¶ and my

---

* *The Bonus of Laughter* (Hamish Hamilton, 1987).
† In his book (pp. 69ff.), A.P.-J. describes how, from 1931 to 1934, he was supported by this rich and languid bachelor, with whom he travelled all over the world in sumptuous style. 'No doubt this looked strange to some. I was twenty-two – Bobbie was in his forties . . . At no time did his private life impinge on mine.'
‡ They were – as *A Mingled Measure* (1994) and *Ancient as the Hills* (1997).
§ Travel writer and novelist (1940–89).
¶ Novelist (b. 1931).

friend Christina Foyle.* Chief speaker David Frost,† an extremely second-rate man. An endless string of anecdotes, half a dozen of which might have amused, whereas I nearly cried with boredom. Then Lord Forte‡ spoke. Both have written books we would not dream of buying. Fay W. told me she thought less and less of Tolstoy. 'Oh, but he is wonderful,' I protested. 'He has recorded all the thoughts that have flitted through my mind and never been able to express.' 'That's the trouble,' she replied. 'I need a novelist to tell me things I have *not* thought about.' 'Like Proust?' I suggested. 'Perhaps,' she said. Christina amazed me by telling me that Daisy Ashford,§ author of *The Young Visiters*, is still alive in her nineties. I loved her book when it appeared in the 1920s. The film of it on TV last week was abominable, whereas that of Vita's *All Passion Spent* was admirable and moving.

Wednesday, 24th December

We have Clarissa and Igor staying. Church at Great Badminton in the morning, then the four of us lunch at the House. All given presents. David tells A. that he hates Christmas and longs for it to be over. Sebastian Walker¶ there, unshaven but apparently sane, talking about the continuing success of his children's publishing house. David Ford** is its prop and stay. Walk dogs in afternoon, and after dinner we watch Horowitz for an hour. A. and Igor lie on the floor taking flash photographs of his hands and funny faces. H. says there is nothing he cannot play. His wife watching him apprehensively.

Friday, 26th December

While we are having breakfast, Sebastian telephones A. from the House to say he must see her. She tells him to come in the evening.

---

* Christina Foyle (1911–99); Managing Director of W. & G. Foyle Ltd, booksellers (founded by her father); started Foyle's Literary Luncheons, 1930; m. 1938 Ronald Batty.
† Television presenter and producer (b. 1939; kt 1993).
‡ Sir Charles Forte (b. 1908); Italian-born restauranteur and hotelier; cr. life peer, 1982.
§ The famous child author had in fact died in 1972, aged ninety-one. She dictated her masterpiece *The Young Visiters* in 1890 at the age of nine, though it was not published until 1919.
¶ Children's publisher (1942–91).
** Assistant to Sebastian Walker, formerly a fashion model (b. 1946); picture researcher for J.L.-M's book *Images of Bath* (1982).

Then, while we are waiting for Audrey and the Robinsons to come for luncheon, Caroline telephones to say Sebastian has gone off his head. He came into her bedroom at two in the morning demanding to 'consult' her. She gave him short shrift. He then apparently came round to our house (this must have been when Folly barked in the night) and, getting no response, went round to Daphers [Moore]. She was terrified, thinking it must be the man who tried to disinter Master two years ago, who when released from prison was heard to vow vengeance on all inhabitants of Badminton. She rang the police, waking up PC Earle, who said he couldn't come himself but would send someone (he didn't). Finally S. woke Daphne Fielding who took him in and let him sleep on her sofa. This morning he returned to the House, where he made another frightful scene, following which Caroline bundled him into a taxi and sent him back to London. This breakdown, not apparently the first, is thought to have been induced by heavy drinking and probably drugs over Christmas.

Igor wanted to go to the meet* so I accompanied him on foot to Worcester Lodge and back, dogs on leads. Nearly died of the cold. So many people, cars and horses that we could hardly see the hounds. I saw Julian Barrow and had a word with him about my article for the [American Architectural] Digest. On our return through the courtyard we met Daphers, who recounted the story of the drunk hammering on her door.

Igor asks the dottiest questions. Were the Somersets aristocratic? Was the fox let out of a box at the meet? Did the hunters drink the fox's blood? I can't make him out. He is very sweet and gentle, but ignorant of everything most twenty-one-year-olds would take for granted. I gave him the silver hunter which belonged to my Great-uncle Neale† for his birthday. Mallory's in Bath had overhauled it and engraved his name on the lid, for £71.

Sunday, 28th December

After motoring Clarissa and Igor to Chippenham to catch the long-distance bus to London, I overheard two elderly ladies chatting in the

---

* The traditional Boxing Day meeting of the Beaufort Hunt.
† Neale Thomson of Camphill House, Renfrewshire; brother of J.L.-M's maternal grandmother.

queue. One said, 'The papers say Princess Michael is buggering' (I think I heard aright) 'off to America.' 'Good riddance, I say,' the other replied. 'So do I,' said the first. 'Prince Michael is a good chap,' said the second. 'A very good chap,' said the first. 'He's so gentle,' said the second. 'Yes, so gentle,' echoed the first.

Monday, 29th December

I called on Joanie Altrincham* on return from Bath this evening, the first time I'd seen her since Diana Westmorland's[†] death. I like her in spite of her incessant grumbles. She has a strong, masculine face and firm voice, and moves with agility. We drank whisky. I remarked on her son John [Grigg]'s many interesting articles lately, one in today's *Times* about the Honours List. 'I haven't seen any of them,' she said. 'He never tells me what he writes.' Then I said, 'You must be pleased about his new job.' 'What new job?' she asked. 'Obituaries editor of *The Times*,' I said. She had no idea. Yet she is going to John and Patsy tomorrow. Says it is horrid staying with them in Blackheath. They are out all day, he working, she sitting on the local bench. Blackheath has no shops or galleries and is too far from the centre of town.

Joanie says that as she gets older and lives increasingly alone, seeing hardly anyone, so she ruminates on the Great War when she, a débutante, found herself plunged, untrained, into nursing – in France for six months in 1915, then in London for remainder of war. It was appalling watching the young men die in hundreds of gangrene, before antibiotics. She would never condone war of any description after that. As a girl she attended Diana's first marriage to Wyndham in 1914, but was not allowed to go to the reception given by Lord Ribblesdale in the Cavendish Hotel,[‡] where he had rooms, for the Cavendish was not considered respectable. Said Diana had a terrible time with her second husband Capel, and was perpetually in tears. Joanie was there when he walked out on her. There was madness in

---

* Hon. Joan Dickson-Poynder (1897–1987), o.c. of 1st Baron Islington; m. 1923 Sir Edward Grigg, MP (1879–1955), cr. Baron Altrincham 1945; mother of John Grigg; she lived at Tormarton near Badminton.
† Hon. Diana Lister (1893–1983), yst dau. of 4th and last Baron Ribblesdale; m. (3rd) 14th Earl of Westmorland; late neighbour and close friend of J.L.-M.
‡ Hotel in St James's owned by the former courtesan Rosa Lewis; it was satirised by Evelyn Waugh in *Vile Bodies*, and inspired the television series *The Duchess of Duke Street*.

the Ribblesdale family, both Barbara Wilson and Laura Lovat* were tinged with it.

Tuesday, 30th December

Michael Howard lunched with me in Bath. I was slightly shy about having him, but he was delightful, if not exactly cosy. Wore a stiff academic suit with buff waistcoat and chain. We chatted about Regy, on whom he expressed positive views. Talked about John Sparrow's appalling sloth and hatred of change. But he owes his career to John who invited him to co-author the wartime history of the Coldstreams, John contributing not a word. As a former Vice-Chairman of the Institute of Strategic Studies, Howard is passionately in favour of retaining our nuclear deterrent. To my objection that the stockpiling of armaments leads to war, he replied that nuclear weapons soon become out-of-date, and few are needed; they merely need to be better and more up-to-date than the potential enemy's. Alistair Buchan† was his friend and colleague, a workaholic as well as an alcoholic who died of epilepsy. Normally slept with wife who knew how to deal with his fits, but one day he came in late and exhausted, retired to his dressing room, and smothered himself during the night.

Wednesday, 31st December

We lunched at Combe [near Newbury] with the Moores and the Hendersons. Roy and Dame Jennifer Jenkins‡ there too. Though we had met before at Ann Fleming's,§ he said to me as we shook hands

---

* Hon. Barbara Lister (1880–1943), est dau. of 4th Baron Ribblesdale; m. 1905 Capt. Mathew Wilson, e.g's son of Sir Mathew Wilson, 2nd Bt; Hon. Laura Lister (1892–1965), 2nd dau. of 4th Baron Ribblesdale; m. 1910 Simon Fraser, 14th Baron Lovat (1871–1933).
† Hon. Alistair Francis Buchan (1918–76); yr s. of 1st Baron Tweedsmuir (and bro. of J.L.-M's friend Alice Fairfax-Lucy of Charlecote); war correspondent; Professor of International Relations, Oxford, 1972–6; m. 1942 Hope Gilmour.
‡ Roy Harris Jenkins (1920–2003); Labour politician and cabinet minister; President of European Commission, 1977–81; Leader of Social Democrat Party, 1981–3; cr. life peer, 1987; m. 1945 Jennifer Morris (b. 1921; DBE 1985; Chairman of N.T., 1986–90).
§ Ann Charteris (1913–81); m. 1st 1932–44 3rd Baron O'Neill (brother of J.L.-M's friend Midi Gascoigne), 2nd 1945–52 2nd Viscount Rothermere, 3rd 1952 Ian Fleming (1907–64), novelist. J.L.-M's meeting with the Jenkinses at her house is described in *Deep Romantic Chasm*, 28 January 1979.

that he had looked me up in *Who's Who* before setting out. He said Asquith had the best brain of any Prime Minister of our history, but was not creative; Dizzy was an exhibitionist; Gladstone was not clever, but immmensely honourable and religious, tormented by doubts. Praised Regy to me, but told A., next whom he sat, that I had made mistakes in the politics. She said he should tell me so. When he told her he was now writing on Baldwin, she said I had known B., and Jenkins should ask me about him. He did neither, must be a shy man. Nico Henderson in raptures about Regy, which embarrasses me, coming from someone so much more intelligent than myself. After luncheon I sat in the long window overlooking the wide, totally unspoilt downland landscape, and talked to Dame J. about the National Trust. She is worried about many things, such as the Kedleston Appeal, which has not even been launched. I praised the way historic houses were shown these days, far better than when I was in charge. But you were starved of money, she said. True, I replied, we did everything on a shoe-string. Nevertheless, men like Martin Drury and Gervase [Jackson-Stops] are extremely competent and clever. I cracked them up.

1987

I wonder if M. is bored with me. His attentiveness and kindness never cease to amaze me. But have they become perfunctory? We never seem to write letters these days, or exchange tokens of affection as we used to. I am still devoted to him, though anxious. He is idle and slothful. Although loyal in his friendships, would he put off doing a friend a service if he was bored by the idea? He keeps bad company, and may end up like Jamesey,* as I keep warning him. I am beginning to wonder whether I have done the right thing in making him my literary executor. What worries me most is whether he will ever be recognised as a writer. He is a procrastinator, and puts off his work to fritter away his time on the tiles.

I lunched with the Loewensteins today, A. having gone to London to take the 'greats' to a pantomime. I tell her she will kill herself on behalf of those ungrateful Lukes; and this makes her cross with me who, she says, hates them all. I think I may do so. The Loewensteins had a dinner on New Year's Eve (which we refused to attend) for the Michaels of Kent. They pity her because Princess Margaret causes such mischief between her and the Queen, instead of giving her kindly hints on how not to irritate HM.

I motored to Broughton Poggs this evening to Eliza Wansbrough's† ninetieth birthday party. Had no idea when invited she was that old. A great crowd present, poor Eliza, a tiny, shrunken figure, bent like a hoop, surrounded by congratulators. I arrived late with a copy of Regy which I knew she wanted for a present, and forced a way to her. She took me by the hand and almost dragged me into the passage to talk, subsiding into a chair while I knelt on the stone floor. Even so, bawling, I could not make her hear nine words out of ten. I suppose the attention and tribute (someone made a speech which she answered) gave her pleasure, but tomorrow she will be worn out. Standing is torture to her

---

* As described in *Ancient as the Hills*, James Pope-Hennessy was done to death in January 1974 by ruffians whom he had invited into his flat in Ladbroke Grove.
† Elizabeth Lewis (1897–1995); dau. of Sir George Lewis, 2nd Bt (and granddau. of Sir George Lewis, 1st Bt, famous late Victorian solicitor); m. 1928–38 George Wansbrough.

back, with her curvature of the spine. J.K.-B. there, and we talked in a corner. Also Mark Girouard who has become friendly and attentive, advancing towards me instead of retreating taciturnly, and assuring me his father* would welcome a visit. And Monsignor Gilbey,† who presented himself to me with fulsome congratulations over my book.

Wednesday, 7th January

Poor little Missy has returned from the vet, wobbly, dopey, dazed and surprised at herself. I feel a brute when A. says that she may never recover her puppyishness and her whole character may have changed for the worse.

Thursday, 8th January

Selina [Hastings] lunches at Franco's in Jermyn Street. Much gossip about her commitments, she recently made literary editor of *Harper's* and about to take a deep dive into Evelyn Waugh. I told her about my quandary over the Bachelor Duke.‡ She does not think Debo will be difficult, notwithstanding her partiality to the B.D. Had my usual tea with M. in his cosy but chaotic flat. He admits he will have nowhere to keep my papers and suggests I sell them to an American university through Rota;§ but I shall not do so with my remaining diaries. He must have these.

Saturday, 10th January

Susanna and Nicky Johnston¶ lunched. Susanna talked only of Rosie, now languishing in gaol. She gave me Rosie's address and has told her

---

* Richard Désiré ('Dick') Girouard (1905–89); stockbroker, member of Georgian Group; m. 1st 1927 Lady Blanche de la Poer Beresford, est dau. of 6th Marquess of Waterford (mother of Mark Girouard, died in road accident, 1940), 2nd 1944–5 Beatrice Grosvenor, 3rd Monica Trafford (d. 1965). See entry for 4 February 1987.
† The Rt Rev Monsignor Alfred Gilbey (1901–98); Roman Catholic Chaplain to Cambridge University, 1932–65; resident at Travellers' Club, Pall Mall.
‡ See notes to 1 November 1986.
§ See entry for 20 January 1987.
¶ Nicholas Johnston (b. 1929), architect; m. 1926 Susanna Chancellor. Their daughter Rose (b. 1964) had been sentenced at Oxford Crown Court in December 1986 to nine months' imprisonment for supplying heroin the previous June to her closest friend Olivia Channon (dau. of Rt Hon. Paul Channon [b. 1935], Secretary of State for Trade and Industry, 1986–7), who had died of an overdose.

to expect to hear from me, but I can't think for Adam what to say to this child, whom I hardly know. Susanna noisy and overbearing; Nicky a quiet, saintly man, with a sense of humour.

Wednesday, 14th January

We are truly in the grips. This morning deep snow and I remain in Badminton. The cold intense, and I was not warm in bed last night despite Missy cuddling beside me and the electric blanket on all night.

My face is corrugated like Aunt Jean's* used to be, Auden's[†] was, and Fanny Patridge's[‡] is. As though the skin had been scratched with a strigil. I never imagined this would happen to me. I really am extremely ugly, quite bald, a permanent shining red nose, pendulous chin and sagging mouth. A horror to behold.

Thursday, 15th January

The appalling cold persists. Television and newspapers revelling in the deaths of the old from hypothermia, inviting us to blame the Government for not being prepared. But England never is prepared for extreme temperatures, though they arrive annually. I might have got to Bath today, but as we are enjoined not to stir unless our journey is really necessary, I obeyed. But more snow due tonight. M. telephoned on his return from Paris, where conditions are even worse than here. He found himself walking in the streets entirely alone, the severe weather coinciding with a transport strike. Felt like Hitler when the streets were cleared for him. This afternoon, while I was walking with dogs down the verge and back through the woods, the sky suddenly became the colour of gunmetal. It was very still. No shadows, only pools and walls of darkest green. Nothing stirring except an occasional pheasant's cry and a crackle of snowy ice. On reaching home I noticed that the sky had turned from gunmetal to black ink. The leaves of the privet hedge were a vivid orange rust colour.

---

* Jean Muir, e. dau. of Sir John Muir, 1st Bt (1861–1941); m. 1887 Lieut-Col. (later Lieut-General Sir) Ian Hamilton (1853–1947).
[†] W. H. Auden, poet (1907–73).
[‡] Frances Marshall (b. 1900), diarist and critic; m. 1933 Ralph Partridge (d. 1960).

Sunday, 18th January

Yesterday we lunched with the Loewensteins, who had staying a Dutch-born woman married to an Austrian count (did not catch name), an attractive sophisticated lady with long fair hair and red stockings. We think Oenone* models herself on her, for the Countess is a great friend and admirer of Michael Luke. A. and I made no bones about what we think of his upbringing of the children. She told us that her husband is an uncle of Princess Michael of Kent, brother of the mother, who is a splendid woman, with no airs and graces. Reduced to penury after the war, she (the mother) went to Australia where she made a living out of a beauty parlour – not exactly a hairdresser, as alleged by the press. The Countess wonders if Princess Michael's behaviour is an embarrassment to the nice, gentle Prince. Then we dined at the House. Dotty Lady Lambton there, enthroned on a chair with diamanté wings in her hair, cracking jokes in a silent, inarticulate voice, rather oblique and in riddles, like Daphne F[ielding]. These people have no idea how uncultivated they are.

Such a contrast to the luncheon party we gave today – Elspeth Huxley, Simon Verity and the Duff Hart-Davises.† A successful little gathering of genuine, intellectual, broad-minded, interested people. The H.-Ds a delightful couple. Duff, like Desmond Shawe-Taylor,‡ takes one up with 'What exactly do you mean by that remark?' – which alarms A., but I rather like. I love Elspeth. As for Verity, he is a beautiful creature. Fine, delicate yet strong face. Slight of build and full of zest. Wearing the same redingote made of rusty-green velvet, short tails and gold-embossed buttons. He said it had belonged to Ernest Gimson,§ and was one of the Bathurst livery jackets given each year up to 1914 to the estate keepers. Also velvet knickerbockers and curry-coloured stockings. A splendid appearance. Told me he was brought up by his great-uncle Oliver Hill¶ at Daneway. Simon's father

---

* J.L.-M's step-granddaughter (b. 1960), 2nd dau. of Hon. Clarissa and Michael Luke; m. 1992 Richard Gladstone.
† Writer and journalist (b. 1936), son of Sir Rupert Hart-Davis; m. 1961 Phyllida Barstow.
‡ Music critic (1907–95); co-tenant with Pat Trevor-Roper of Long Crichel, Dorset.
§ Cotswolds arts and crafts designer (1864–1919); he and the Barnsleys built themselves cottages at Sapperton in Glouscestershire, and used Daneway House at Sapperton as workshops and showrooms.
¶ Architect (1887–1968); lived at Daneway 1948–68.

disapproved of his wish to be a sculptor, while Oliver did all to encourage him. Says he owes everything to Oliver, though agreed he was a ruthless man who would sacrifice anything and anybody to the immediate necessity. Today's company was really sympathetic to me.

Monday, 19th January

Weather still bitter, but thaw on way. A. and I went to London for the night to attend Nigel Nicolson's seventieth birthday dinner at Escargot Restaurant, in private room upstairs. Arranged by Rebecca,* Nigel unaware of it. Was expecting to dine with children alone. Some thirty guests assembled, drinking champagne. At eight lights dimmed, company silenced. Nigel walks in. Shades his eyes to take in crowd before him. His face breaks into smiles, and he utters cries of delight. Great success. George Weidenfeld† made a speech in which he paid high tribute to Nigel, his first helper when he started as a penniless refugee, the most loyal friend and collaborator, his beloved best friend, etc. Nigel gave a splendid impromptu reply, as only a sometime MP could do. Because of the tremendous din I could hear but little, though I think it was a splendid occasion. I had many compliments for Regy, which I take with a grain. Terence de Vere White told me – I wonder how truthfully, for he is Irish to the core – that at a recent meeting at Chatto's, it was said that Paddy L. F., I and someone else were the three best prose writers today. Baba Metcalfe, suddenly shrunk to a small old lady, made a touching speech. Stayed at Brooks's.

Tuesday, 20th January

Went to Rota's in Long Acre to discuss the disposal of my papers. Mr Rota‡ was at a board meeting, which to my embarrassment he dismissed in order to talk to me. I explained that Misha was to be my literary executor but I didn't want to burden him with sorting and storing my papers. Mr Rota will pay us a visit to look through A's and my papers to assess their worth, and decide which American libraries to approach.

---

* Yr dau. (b. 1963) of Nigel Nicolson; m. 1988–96 Hon. Guy Philipps.
† Austrian-born publisher (b. 1919); co-founder with Nigel Nicolson of Weidenfeld & Nicolson, 1948; cr. life peer as Baron Weidenfeld of Chelsea, 1976.
‡ Anthony Rota (b. 1932); managing director of Bertram Rota Ltd of Long Acre, dealers in books and literary manuscripts; m. Jean Kendall.

John Julius [Norwich] asked me last night if I researched each chapter
individually before writing it. No, I said, I did all the research for
the whole book, taking copious notes, and then began writing. But,
he asked, do you not find you have forgotten the research for a particular chapter before you have reached it? I admitted this was often the
case, and that I had to rely on the completeness and good order of
my notes.

Friday, 23rd January

Rosemary Verey and the Mitchells dined. After dinner, Rosemary and
A. went through Hardy Amies' preface to their next gardening book,
furious with their editrix for having altered Hardy's little jokes, while
I went through my draft list of Cotswold Houses with Tony. The
trouble is that, apart from a few great houses like Badminton,
Cirencester and Stanway, nearly all the lesser houses, which I wish to
concentrate on, have changed ownership within the past few years,
and are now owned by rich commuters and stockbrokers. It will be a
problem finding out what they look like within, even if the outsides
seem unspoilt. My nice David Burnett is still keen for me to do the
book, and is lunching with me the week after next to discuss.

Saturday, 24th January

We lunch with Ian McCallum at Claverton. Ian much aged and
suffering, he says, from emphysema. Is bent at shoulders, and has new
teeth, always a give-away. When A. suggested he was left-wing, he
indignantly denied this, saying he had never voted Labour in his life.
But he has always been hostile to the 'Establishment' and in particular the police, possibly the result of his having been in prison during
the war, about which he reminded me when we talked of Rosie
Johnston. Incidentally, Susanna rang this morning to say Rosie was
pleased with my letter.

Dined at Didmarton with the Westmorlands, just the four of us. An
extremely 'posh' house, with an air of opulence and fashion. Rather
dreadful large sketch of David as Master of the Horse, with head-gear
and feathers, his face the image of the late lamented Master. The Queen
thought it made him look like Captain Bligh of the *Bounty* about to
lash his crew. He explained that it was done at the lowest period of his
life, when he was ill and having trouble at Sotheby's. David is irritated

by [his half-sister] June [Hutchinson]'s constantly tackling him about the corruption and immorality in the City. He is not censorious of the Guinness transactions,* and says it is now impossible to know where sharp business dealing ends and corruption begins. But the BBC is discussing nothing else, and the voters are shocked.

The Westmorlands said they once lived in Ormesby Lodge, Ham Common, which was badly haunted. Jane often saw a woman and a ghost dog. When they thought of selling, Princess Alexandra was interested in buying and paid a visit. She walked into the hall, sniffed the air, and turned on her heel, saying she could not possibly live in a house with such an unhappy aura.

Sunday, 25th January

Really, we are being too social by half. Lunched today with Isabel and Michael [Briggs] at Midford. The Knight of Glin and Olda† staying; he greeted me with the remark that he was glad I was writing the biography of the Bachelor Duke. I suppose Debo told him. I wonder if I ever shall? I said to A. when we left that I like the tone of this house. It is like ours rather than Didmarton or Badminton, not opulent or fashionable, but simple and slightly shabby.

Monday, 26th January

I go to Sudeley Castle. As I was early, I motored up to the Wadstray,‡ which I last visited when it was inhabited by Addie Rodocanachi,§

---

* In November 1986 the DTI had appointed inspectors to investigate allegations of an illegal share support operation in connection with Guinness's recent acquisition of the Distillers Company. As a result of the inspectors' report, criminal charges were brought during 1987 against Guinness's managing director Ernest Saunders and three other businessmen. After a trial of immense length and complexity, all four were convicted in 1990 – though it was widely felt in informed circles that they were scapegoats at a time when City practices were coming under intense public scrutiny, and the European Court at Strasbourg later ruled that their human rights had been infringed by the inspectors and prosecuting authorities.
† Desmond Fitz-Gerald, 29th Knight of Glin (b. 1937); architectural and art historian, President Irish Georgian Society, Christie's representative in Ireland; m. (2nd) 1970 Olda Willes.
‡ Presumably Wadfield House near Sudeley, described in Pevsner as 'an elegant house in a very beautiful setting . . . with a hipped sprocketed roof'.
§ Miss Ariadne Rodocanachi (1886–1966); scion of Anglo-Greek mercantile dynasty.

fifty or sixty years ago. From what I saw (I did not get out of the car), the house still very pretty, hipped roofs, grey stone. But the approach awful – drive caked in mud and horrid farm buildings of corrugated iron in a great mass. The view from the front, which I did not see, must still be lovely. At Sudeley, Elizabeth Ashcombe very friendly, and Stanley Falconer to meet me. Spent the morning going round the house at leisure, omitting wing shown to public. They do not want it described. Only their part, and the wonderful transformations, of which they are proud. A brand-new house within old walls, the 'improvements' of each generation having obliterated those of its pre-decessor. Difficult to write about – all history and no antiquity.

Wednesday, 28th January

Put out to receive letter from Mark Girouard this morning asking if he may quote several extracts from my published diaries in the country houses anthology which he is compiling. Of course I do not mind his quoting, but I do mind that he is doing the very same book that I am pledged to do. Tried all day to telephone Collins. Failed to get through owing to British Telecom strike, all lines from Bath to London blocked. It would be wonderful if Mark and I could amalga-mate, but I fear unlikely. He has presumably got his own publisher, and being a giant will not want to associate with a pygmy like me. Perhaps it will be a blessed way out of a book my heart is not in. Yet I deplore a whole month's wasted labour.

Sunday, 1st February

We lunched with the Lloyd Georges at Freshford. Pretty stiff party too. On arrival I was greeted by two middle-aged ladies who claimed to have known me when they were in their nurseries. One was Serena, daughter of the Michael Petos, those dears of yore; the other, Mary-Anne Murray that was, Barbara Moray's* eldest daughter, whom I knew less well than her two sisters. Serena looked younger than when I last saw her as a very large, brown bride, but her husband, General Sir Torquil Matheson,† bored A. with his endless complaints

---

* Barbara Murray of New York; m. (2nd) 1924 Francis Stuart (b. 1892) who s. 1930 as 18th Earl of Moray and d. 1943.
† Sir Torquil Matheson of Matheson (b. 1925), 5th Bt and Chief of Clan Matheson; m. 1954 Serena, o. d. of Lieut.-Col. Sir Michael Peto, 2nd Bt.

that plans for the bridge from the Scottish mainland to Skye had been abandoned. Owen Lloyd George told me that old Sylvester* is still alive, living all by himself in that lodge on the road to Corsham. He is ninety-eight and becoming forgetful. He spends his time trying to decipher his shorthand notes of private conversations of Lloyd George during the Peace Conference of 1919. No one will be able to interpret these notes once poor old Sylvester dies, which he is bound to do soon.

Wednesday, 4th February

To London and Pat Trevor-Roper for eye test. He gave me a prescription for reading glasses to help me see the scripts I am typing without bending too low and developing a dowager's hump. Full of gossip as usual. He told me that Sheridan Dufferin,† Bruce Chatwin and Ian McCallum all have Aids; that they might seem to recover from some mild ailment, only to get another, but when a serious attack of pneumonia or the like assailed them, they would go under. Very terrible. Derek Hill, who is rather proprietary of Bruce, naively denies it in his case, insisting to Pat that Bruce caught a mysterious disease from bathing in the South Seas too close to a whale, or some such nonsense.

M. lunched at Brooks's. He spoke of Ribbentrop, by whose biography he is now gripped. All the English disliked him when he was Ambassador here, and even Hitler could hardly bear his company, though considering him a useful tool. In the London Library, Douglas Matthews told me he was indexing Victoria [Glendinning]'s short life of Rebecca West.‡ He said that Stanley Olson,§ who under Rebecca's will was to write the definitive life, is still knocked out by his stroke and cannot speak, though he is sane and keeps fretting about the book, which he will never write. He is not yet forty.

Went to tea with Dick Girouard¶ in Colville Road, miles the

---

* Albert James Sylvester, CBE (1889–1989); Private Secretary to Lloyd George during and after his premiership, and author of works about him.
† Sheridan Blackwood, 5th and last Marquess of Dufferin and Ava (1938–88); o.s. of J.L.-M's friend and contemporary Basil, 4th Marquess; m. 1964 Serena Belinda ('Lindy') Guinness.
‡ Pseudonym of Cicily Fairfield (1892–1983), writer; DBE 1959.
§ Scholar and aesthete (1947–89); biographer of Elinor Wylie and John Singer Sargent.
¶ See notes to 3 January 1987.

wrong side of Paddington. He is very immobile, struggles around his nice flat with a frame. Is pot-bellied and much older, now eighty-one, otherwise little changed. We gossiped, yet I found it difficult to pick up threads after some thirty years. He said that, were she only alive, he and his first wife Blanche would be celebrating their diamond wedding today. She was a cousin of Master. He remembers Duchess Louise,* and liked her. Blanche's aunts referred to her as the Bristol Brat. How snobbish. After all, the Harfords, who were Bristol bankers in the eighteenth century, are very much Gloucestershire landed gentry now. We talked of Gerry Wellington. Dick told how, when he was staying at Stratfield Saye, the butler came to Gerry with some grave news. Dick tactfully withdrew. Then Gerry came to him with an ashen face and said, 'A dreadful thing has happened. You've no idea how difficult it is to get an odd man these days.' 'I can imagine it must be,' replied Dick, 'though I've never needed one myself.' 'The butler tells me that ours has wetted his bed for the third time,' continued Gerry, 'and the dining room ceiling is in serious danger.'

Thursday, 5th February

Received a long and heart-warming letter from Dadie [Rylands] about Regy. The sort of letter any biographer would be overjoyed to receive. Yet I notice that all the raves come from friends and acquaintances. None from strangers, and no prize.

Friday, 6th February

Bruce Hunter writes that Penguin have turned down my novel. We must regard it as dead now. He can do no more. Sends me their letter in which the usual things are trotted out – excellently written, but characters not sharply enough drawn, etc. Now, it may not be brilliant, but I know parts of it are good, and thousands of worse novels are published every year. I have thanked Bruce and also told him that I am joyfully chucking the anthology, which leaves me with the Cotswold Country Houses only. After that, which should keep me busy for most of this year, it is the end. I don't want further suggestions such as the

---

* See notes to 26 January 1986.

ones I have lately received – travel books on Northern Italy, picture books with young photographers. I am finished. Debo writes to A. that Joan Haslip* wants to write about the Devonshire House set (she is welcome), and Jim had better hurry up with the Bachelor Duke. But I am not sure. Who has heard of him? And do I wish to spend years researching a biography which will sell two thousand copies and get no reviews? No, I don't.

Sunday, 8th February

Freda Berkeley, who is staying with us for a well-earned respite from poor demented Lennox, tells me that someone is already writing his biography. But it is of course too late, for communication with Lennox is out of the question now. Freda said that, before she and Lennox met, he was madly in love with Benjamin Britten (this being before Peter Pears came on the scene). She possesses all Britten's letters to L., and L's to B. are preserved among the Britten archives in Aldeburgh. A very interesting connection. Freda says it did not do Lennox much good and gave him an inferiority complex, Britten's genius being overbearing as well as overpowering.

Pat Trevor-Roper also stayed for two nights. He is a most generous and intelligent man, but there is a piggy side to him which neither of us two fusspots likes. A. told Freda that she should see that he had his suits cleaned more often because they stink. I too was rude to him when I realised he was having a pee on the grass by our front door. 'Must you do this?' I said angrily, as he came in, doing up his flies. When I later told Freda that I regretted having lost my temper, she said there was no need, for Pat never takes offence at a rebuke. It just slides off him.

Monday, 9th February

That charmer David Burnett lunched in Bath, and we drew up plans for the Cotswold Country Houses book. The odd thing is that, when he arrived, I did not at first recognise him, though finding him no less attractive than when we met last May. I have now written six letters to owners of those houses we most want to include.

---

* English writer living in Florence (1912–94).

Tuesday, 10th February

Saw my first snowdrops this morning in Somerset Place. Still in unfolded stage, like pendulous, opalescent pearls, glistening with dew. Also the birth of a primrose. Couldn't believe it. Bent down, and there was the unmistakable leaf. Just a peep of pale yellow on the ground.

I now realise I made a terrible mistake in having poor Missy spayed. She has ceased to be a puppy and become a dull, ordinary little dog. Also unresponsive. Never looks up when I return home in the evening. Meanwhile a terrible accident has befallen Folly. A. walking with both dogs in Westonbirt woods put up a hare. Folly gave chase and ran headlong into a barbed-wire fence enclosing a cricket pitch. She was torn to shreds. A. somehow carried her to the car (she is heavy), and drove at top speed to the vet in Chipping Sodbury, holding F. together with her left hand.

Sunday, 15th February

Have been reading through letters to Uncle Robert [Bailey] from Mama and Aunt Doreen during the last year of his life, 1917, when he was serving in Palestine. Interesting to read what my mother wrote about Dick and myself. That we adored returning to school (which we hated). That I was fearfully proud of my school (which I wasn't). That she was vexed by my colour-blindness because I wanted to be a sailor (which I didn't, loathing it when, some years later, I was made to stay with Victor Campbell* on his destroyer). In one letter to Robert, Doreen wrote that both our parents jumped on us, and my father snubbed us so often, that we were cowed. She was worried about it.

In Mama's letter of 11 February 1917, I came upon a postscript which enables me to correct one false memory, namely that my father held me on his shoulders to watch King George V's coronation in 1911, when I was not even three. She writes: 'I forgot to tell you

---

* 'My mother and her sister, Doreen Cunninghame, were great friends of a strikingly handsome Victor Campbell, captain in the Royal Navy during the First World War. My mother admired him very much and my beautiful aunt may have done more than that, I fancy. My mother, who had always longed for me to become a sailor (an idea obnoxious to me from the very start), sent me one holiday from my preparatory school to stay with Victor on his destroyer . . . To this day I have detested all sailing and being on the ocean wave.' (J.L.-M., *Fourteen Friends*, p. 1.)

that I took Jim to the Mall to watch the [royal] procession from Buckingham Palace to open Parliament. The whole route was lined with special constables, such cheery good sorts who let Jim stand with them so he had an uninterrupted view. When the King passed, Jim stepped out and yelled Hurray and waved his bowler so violently that the King saw and saluted him. It was *too* nice and Jim the proudest kipper* in the world. It was such an excitement for a country bumpkin seeing all the colonial troops & Jellicoe† & Fisher‡ & French,§ Connaught¶ & all the celebs & I am glad he came for it, as he'll never forget it. We then waddled up to Buck Palace and stood & gazed wondering which was the King's bedroom window! We then went to Fortnum's & armed ourselves with a huge cake and chocs for school and sent you your parcel. It was a memorable day in Jim's life.' Memorable it should have been, and I got it all wrong.

Tuesday, 17th February

To London for the night. In afternoon I went to see Ros. Her eyesight no better. Reading an agony. She is eighty-six, and says she wants to die. Would like to stay away, but what friends can have an immobile guest for a week or ten days? The trouble with Rosamond is that she has been a star, and is now a decayed old lady whom a few friends visit out of kindness. Conversation is not easy. I did a terribly unkind thing. She produced a rather ugly mauve bottle with stopper and children engraved in white on the bowl. She said, 'I am giving things away and was going to give this to you, but now I can't because I find there is a hole in it.' I looked at it and admired it rather coldly because I didn't like it. Put it down and went off without it, not having referred to it again. I think I should have gushed and put it immediately in my coat pocket and taken it with me. Oh dear.

    Before dinner, A. and I went to Christie's to watch film of

---

* J. L.-M's note in text: 'What an odd word for her to use.'

† 1st Earl Jellicoe (1859–1935); Admiral of the Fleet; commanded Grand Fleet at Battle of Jutland (1916); Governor-General of New Zealand, 1920–4.

‡ Admiral of the Fleet Sir John Fisher, 1st Baron Fisher of Kilverstone (1841–1920); First Sea Lord, 1904–10 and 1914–15, resigning in disapproval of Dardanelles Expedition.

§ Field Marshal Sir John French, 1st Earl of Ypres (1852–1925); commander of British Expeditionary Force in France, 1914–18.

¶ HRH Prince Arthur, Duke of Connaught (1850–1942); 3rd son of Queen Victoria; Governor-General of Canada, 1911–16.

Kenneth Clark speaking at I Tatti about Berenson.* Accompanied by many stills of B.B. and Nicky Mariano[†] and Alda Anrep, and the beautiful villa and country around. Brilliantly done as K. did everything. Yet somehow I was a little put off by his exaggerated emphases. He addresses his audience too graciously. K. said that B.B. was far better value walking round the garden with a friend than he was on paper. The Florentine countryside which he loved inspired him to make Goethe-like statements about nature and art which were stupendous. It was a tragedy that they went unrecorded.

Then dined at Boodle's with Derek Hill, Anne Norwich[‡] and the Snowdons.[§] Tony's present wife is not pretty but charming. So easy and relaxed after Princess Margaret. Had a long talk with him after dinner. He had just come from Liverpool, and was appalled by the disintegration, the deserted streets, the empty and decaying terraces, the smashed churches, the hooligans. Thinks it hauntingly awful. 'Does the Government know? And does it care?' I said I had the same impression when last there, but did not know what could be done about it. He said what he could do was to take photographs and get the popular press to publish them.

Stayed the night at Brooks's. When I got to my room, telephoned M. who is down with 'flu. Said he had been interviewed by the police, as a man he met at a party, to whom he gave his telephone number, was subsequently suspected of a murder which took place on the night in question, and gave M's name as an alibi. After the interview, the police presented him with an illiterate statement for him to sign. He refused, saying he was a writer by profession and couldn't oblige.

Wednesday, 18th February

Nick breakfasted with me at Brooks's. His very presence does me good. He arrived like a breath of fresh Scotch air in a neatly-fitted

---

* Bernard Berenson, American art historian (1865–1959); lived at Villa I Tatti, Florence (now the Harvard University Center for Italian Renaissance Studies).
† Signorina Nicola Mariano; devoted secretary, housekeeper and companion to Bernard Berenson.
‡ Anne Clifford; m. 1958 (diss. 1985) John Julius Cooper, 2nd Viscount Norwich.
§ Antony Armstrong-Jones (b. 1930); son of J.L.-M's friend Anne, Countess of Rosse by her 1st marriage; photographer; m. 1st 1960 HRH Princess Margaret, 2nd 1978 Lucy Davies; cr. Earl of Snowdon, 1961.

tweed suit. I explained to him the dispositions in my new will, which names him as residuary legatee. He understood, as he understands everything. I asked him when he was going to settle and cease being a gypsy. He said he might marry, but wasn't certain. 'Be very certain,' I said, like any old grandfather.

Lady Howard* telephoned me after dinner to say that Hubert Howard[†] died in Rome this morning, without having appointed a President to his Ninfa Foundation. How I lament him. One could not be intimate with him, but he was very companionable. One could talk with him for ever, and he was a mine of information on subjects historical, genealogical and ecclesiastical. He laughed as he spoke in a slightly self-deprecatory manner. Had no illusions about the Italians, whom he loved; indeed, his mother was an Italian princess. His wife, Lelia, very quiet, diffident, correct, a little stiff as was Hubert. Very devout papist, very patrician. I am glad I saw Ninfa in its glory. It can never be what it was, however well kept up, for it will not be a private place. It is my idea of the Garden of Eden.

Saturday, 21st February

Gervase Jackson-Stops stayed two nights with us. He is preparing two articles on the House for *Country Life*. This morning I accompanied him to the House. For the first time I entered the Muniment Room, which is the South-East pavilion on the East front, approached from outside. Very pretty inside with shelves and gallery, copied by Stephen Wright from the Kent[‡] pavilions which were adaptations of Gibbs's[§] designs. Looked at several drawings in a portfolio. They prove beyond dispute that Kent took over from Gibbs, presumably on the death of the 3rd Duke [in 1746] who was a man of culture as well as a sportsman, probably the last Duke of Beaufort to combine these qualities. One fascinating discovery was an outline drawing – I'm sure a projected design for it is very simple, without

---

* Anne Hotham; m. 1944 Francis, 2nd Baron Howard of Penrith.
† Hon. H. J. E. Howard (1907–87), yr s. of 1st Baron Howard of Penrith; m. 1951 Donna Lelia Caetani (d. 1977), o. dau. of 17th Duke of Sermoneta. They lived at Palazzo Caetani, Rome and maintained the famous garden which had been created by the Caetanis at Ninfa south-east of Rome, interspersed with the ruins of a town abandoned in the fourteenth century.
‡ William Kent (1684–1748); artist and architect.
§ James Gibbs (1682–1754); architect.

adornments – of the Almshouses and our Essex House. It is signed
one T. Hayward, and I feel sure is seventeenth-century. Moreover,
in pencil, Hayward calls Essex House 'the Parsonage'. He also indi-
cates that the East elevation, now obliterated by the Victorian lodge,
was the same as the North elevation. Then G. and I went round the
House with Caroline. I learnt much from Gervase, who is extremely
quick. In the dining room he remarked that the dentils of cornice
were all of different flower heads. They must be by the Rococo
carver Poynton, who is known to have made the doorcases with
involuted pediments. A really remarkable craftsman. He also did the
panel in the library which David has now scrapped in favour of the
fine Lely of 1st Duke [d. 1699] and Duchess. This panel, which
David thought Victorian, is dated 1732 from a drawing.

We went up to the roof, where I had not been before. The top floor
remarkably dilapidated, ceilings fallen in, rooms stuffed with furniture
gathering worm. Roof rickety. Both cupolas are not of stone but
wood; and more remarkably still, the rather ponderous pediment
added by Kent, with heavy trusses, is also of wood, and not in good
condition. Gervase found a letter from Smith of Warwick* warning
the Duke that the proposed pediment by Kent would be too heavy
for the frail walls of the top storey. Presumably Kent got his way by
making this addition of wood. I have never noticed this before, but
on descending today it was apparent when I examined it searchingly.

Sunday, 22nd February

To church at Acton Turville at 9.30. Usual smattering of some half a
dozen parishioners, and a young woman sitting in front of me whom
I did not recognise, wearing a scarf which partly concealed her head.
When we left the church she smiled at me, to which I responded. The
Vicar told me she was Mrs X.; that she had never been to church
before, but this was her third Sunday running, making him wonder if
there was something wrong with her. When I told A., she said that
X. had recently started a wild affair with another woman, on learning
of which Mrs X., in a towering rage, had kicked him in the balls.

I asked Vicar why it mattered so much if the Synod voted for

---

* Francis Smith of Warwick (1672–1738), builder and architect, altered the exterior and
remodelled the interior of Badminton House for the 3rd Duke from 1728 onwards.

women priests.* He is dead against it because (1) it has been traditional
for two thousand years that only men are priests, and (2) it would
mean never a getting-together with the Orthodox and Catholic
Churches which are fundamentally opposed to the idea. Nevertheless,
I support the proposal because women are generally more devout than
men, and there is a dearth of theological students. Our own vicar has
four parishes instead of one.

We lunched with the Johnstons. Much talk of poor Rosie. She has
no sanitation in her cell, just a pot, which she has to empty out of the
window to avoid beastly encounters at latrines. Owing to the wide
publicity of her case, all the inmates know about her. Being girls of
the criminal class, they hate her and bully her. During the exercise
hour in the prison yard, they cover her with jeers and taunts. 'Does
the Queen fart, Rosie? You know, Rosie. Tell us, Rosie!' On one visit,
Susanna noticed Rosie had a black eye, caused by inmates hitting her.
When they do not brutalise her, they make lesbian advances. On
hearing of Susanna's concern, Lord Longford, aged eighty-two, by
virtue of his privileged access to any prisoner at any time, made an
expedition to Essex during the worst weather spell. Stayed with Rosie
for an hour and a half, bringing her newspapers and books. He will
give a luncheon for her at the House of Lords on her release. Never
again will I scoff at him, says Susanna.

John Fleming and Hugh Honour† staying. Very affectionate. Francis
Watson‡ lunched, too pontifical, yet genial. Told me he had bought a
pair of candlesticks which he is sure belonged to Beckford at Fonthill.

Wednesday, 25th February

To Chatsworth by train, changing twice. Was ushered into Debo's
little room with the green pleated hangings, and the little spy window
overlooking the entrance gate. We were alone the first night. Debo
full of excitement at the prospect of my doing the Bachelor Duke. I
soon discovered what I had feared, that his handwriting is appalling

---

* The General Synod voted to ordain women priests in 1992. Almost 500 clergy left the
Anglican ministry as a result. The first women were ordained at Bristol Cathedral in 1994.
† Hugh Honour (b. 1927) and John Fleming (1919–2001); writers, separately and
together, on art and architecture.
‡ Sir Francis Watson (1907–92); Director, Wallace Collection, 1963–74; Surveyor of
Queen's Works of Art, 1963–72.

and gets worse as his life progresses – or as it ebbs, as mine is doing. There are masses of box-files of diaries and letters, and a variety of other matter. At the end of the day Michael Pearman, one of the librarians, gave me a straight talk. He said he dared not say what he was going to tell me in front of Her Grace, to whom the B.D. was hero and god, but he wondered whether he was a sufficiently important subject for a biography. Would it not involve years of hard labour, resulting in a book which might be remaindered after six months? This was wise counsel, and I took it well of him. Debo, when I put these points to her, dismissed them, assuring me that any publisher would jump at the biog. There was sex (which seems to amount to his having kept a mistress at the Rookery for several years, like any other aristocrat, and hardly exciting); there was royalty (true, relations with George IV and William IV may prove interesting); he was one of the greatest collectors of books, pictures, furniture, and, above all, sculpture; and he was a great builder and gardener, with Paxton. Friendship is another quality which Debo emphasises. So I find myself in the predicament of trying to respond to D's immense enthusiasm while having grave doubts – about my ability to read the writing, about my having to spend months here, or near here (for I don't suppose they will let me take the papers away), and about my state of health, for I doubt if I can summon the strength to embark on another long book of this sort. Luckily the Cotswold Houses will give me some months to think it over.

Thursday, 26th February

Andrew [Devonshire] returned. He is such a clever man. With him, never frivolous talk, always about a subject. I committed an indiscretion. After dinner we were discussing Nancy [Mitford]. Debo said that none of her brothers-in-law liked her. I volunteered that I did not really like her either. 'Oh really?' said Debo. I quickly added that I was not fond of her when she was absent, but when I saw her, I succumbed. My principal reason for dislike was her being too pleased with her own writings. Oh, said Debo, I never thought she was that.

Friday, 27th February

Left in the morning, not having stepped outside the house once during my visit. Left notebook behind. Telephoned. Andrew found it somewhere. Fatal to put anything down in that palace. Luckily it just contained notes about the Bachelor, not my diary or anything compromising.

We lunched with the Waterparks at Bletchingdon [Park, Oxfordshire] to meet the French Ambassador and wife. A very long journey down twisting roads, Missy crying from beginning to end. Poor food and sticky party. Caryll amusing in that casual way he shares with his sister Pat. After luncheon, A. asked him for the names of the ambassadorial couple and their French friends who had come down with them. He replied that he hadn't a clue. When they had all gone, we got the details from Daniele. Ambassador, much older than plain little wife and looking like a shopkeeper, has grand-sounding name, Vicomte Luc de la Barre de Nanteuil. Tall cadaverous woman who came with them is the Duchesse de Magenta, Napoleonic title. Very difficult lady, horribly grand in French way. Other Frog couple better, he French chairman of Channel Tunnel. I said I was a friend of Nico Henderson. Oh, he said, horrible man, I have had a row with him. A. told him she disapproved of the Tunnel. He said it would only take three hours from London to Paris. She replied that it took less than one hour by air. Neither of us a great success.

When we got home, Folly bit A. in the cheek. I insisted on her seeing Dr King, although the poor man was dining at home. I motored her to the surgery, but in the commotion was wearing my reading glasses. Driving round a corner I went up a bank and we rolled back onto the road, A. on top of me. Luckily the car did not turn over, but we were both shaken. She then took the wheel. She was given an anti-tetanus injection, and mercifully seems all right. The truth is that my eyes have deteriorated during the past nine months, and I cannot see properly except in daylight.

Thursday, 5th March

I have written a long letter to Debo and told her frankly that unless I may be allowed to have the Bachelor Duke's diaries (if no other papers) on loan in Bath, I cannot tackle his biography. Mentioned that Churchill College had allowed me to have all the Esher papers, and Nigel Nicolson the Harold papers, on these terms. That at my age I should not be away from A. for months on end, kind though she was to offer to put me up in the house. I don't know whether I hope the business is off or on.

A. says she gets very cross when women say 'Poor Mr L.-M.' after I have done something asinine. Like today, when I was about to make off with my wire basket at Sainsbury's, until a row of kind ladies reminded me that I must leave it in the pile by the cash desk. A. is maddened when Peggy says 'Poor Mr L.-M.' when I have allowed Missy to be sick on my bed, whereas it would never be 'Poor Mrs L.-M.' if Folly were sick on her bed.

Tuesday and Wednesday, 10th–11th March

Two blissful days being motored by David Burnett round Cotswolds, reconnoitering houses for our book. From the outside, we must have seen twenty. It is a long time since I have driven round the counties and looked at houses with a critical eye. I am shocked by the dreadful examples of in-filling in villages, and the appalling invasion of the remote Cotswolds by London weekenders. At Eastington Manor, for example, we saw a humble little house slightly tarted up with a neat, trim garden. David found a farm worker in a barn, of whom he asked the owner's name. 'A Mr Docker from London, who comes down about four times a year,' was the reply. 'How dreadful,' said David. 'It be,' was the answer. The village people don't like these fly-by-night, new-rich, suburban-minded, totally non-country folk, who bring their middle-class friends and cocktail bars for a few days and are of no use to the community. Then, so many of the large country houses are being converted into flats. This is a good idea in principle, but seldom are the conversions sympathetic. As for Northwick Park, the spectacle was horrifying. There stands the great house in the middle of the erstwhile park, a mile from Blockley village in an area of outstanding natural beauty. It was unapproachable, for one drive was blocked up, the other so churned by tractors and tree-felling vehicles that we could not get up to it. A long row of hideous garages with blue doors newly erected; pegged strips in the park where new residences will be built. Northwick, where George Churchill* lived surrounded by precious pictures and works of art, can henceforth be erased from the memory. Dowdeswell Manor has been divided into three. The charming Georgian gazebo made into a residence, with ghastly window inserted.

---

* Captain E. G. Spencer-Churchill (1876–1964), grandson of 6th Duke of Marlborough; inherited Northwick Park from his mother, stepdaughter of last Lord Northwick; High Sheriff of Worcestershire, 1924; a Trustee of National Gallery, 1943–50.

Carriage lamps abound. Broadwell Manor under scaffolding, having recently been bought – by whom? Adlestrop Park by Sanderson Miller* now a second-rate preparatory school with flimsy shack annexes like so many public lavatories surrounding it. And so on.

David a perfect companion. Treats me as though I were Dresden porcelain. Always solicitous as to whether I am not too cold, too tired, etc. He leaps from the wheel to ask directions and questions while I sit like Buddha wrapped up in front seat poring over the map. We eat deliciously in pubs, make jokes and laugh. He has the sort of humour that I appreciate.

Only once did we encounter an owner – at Whittington Manor, a prominent Elizabethan house we saw from the road and drove to. Met owner in drive. Nice modest professional from Surrey and sympathetic wife. They showed us round this empty, dilapidated white elephant. The wife left it by friends. Feel it their duty to restore and inhabit, bringing daughter and her children to share. What an enterprise. I suspect they already regret that cosy villa in Chobham.

Saturday, 14th March

There on breakfast table is reply from Debo. Make A. read it. Answer is yes, Andrew will allow me to take away papers. So now I am committed, and nothing but a stroke or death can prevent me embarking upon this vast enterprise.

Lady Butler† rings me up. Apologises because she doesn't know me. Wants permission to quote something I wrote somewhere about intellectuals not suited to being prime ministers. She is writing a book about her husband Rab. I express surprise, because one is being reviewed in the papers at the moment. Yes, she says, but hers is to be a personal memoir. She is a clever woman, I believe. Charming on telephone. 'May I take this opportunity of saying how much I hope there will be more diaries? You bring back a world that has passed', etc.

Received first letter from M. for months. To say how happy he is, now immersed in Ribbentrop, working like fury, reading books in German, meeting people who knew R. Is glad to be rid of the Duke

---

* Gentleman architect in the Gothic style (1717–80); friend of Horace Walpole.
† Mollie Montgomerie; m. 1st Sydney Courtauld, 2nd 1959 (as his 2nd wife) Rt Hon. R. A. Butler, Conservative statesman, cr. life peer as Baron Butler of Saffron Walden 1965 (he d. 1982).

of Windsor and says that life has opened up exciting new vistas. Am so pleased.

Today we lunched with Tanis [Guinness],* I the only man among five women. Loelia driven over from Send. Her articulation is bad, and she struggles for words. I look dazed, smile and say yes. 'You don't know what I am driving at,' she justly retorts. Tanis in sweetest way asked if I received reproaches for things written in diaries. 'You wrote that my sister Mérode† was a moron, or quoted someone else as saying it. In fact she is extremely well-educated.' This veiled in sweetness and friendliness, and made me feel a brute. After luncheon, we sat in the conservatory in full sunshine and radiators on, sweltering. Zita and Teresa [the Jungman sisters]‡ came over. Teresa said she was tearing up all letters and papers relating to the Twenties. Why? Because she is sick of her past. Zita says she has reached 1984 in reading back numbers of the *Daily Telegraph*. Daughter Penny§ gave them a subscription to the *Spectator* for a present the Christmas before last. They dare not confess to her that they have not opened the first number yet. They buy books they have seen reviewed, but never read them.

We dine again at the House. I tell A. this is a mistake; we are becoming bores, and have little to say to them. I know David loves A. and Caroline is fond of her; but they tolerate me just. I feel awkward.

Wednesday, 18th March

David Burnett called at ten, having taken his children to school somewhere near Bournemouth, and off we set on our third recce. A fine,

---

* Yr dau. (b. 1906) of Benjamin Guinness of New York (and sister of Loel Guinness, MP for Bath 1931–45); m. 1st 1931–5 Hon. William Montagu, 2nd 1937–51 Howard Dietz, 3rd 1951 Charles Phillips.

† Elder sister of Tanis (b. 1904); m. 1929 Alvaro Guevara, Chilean artist. On 23 October 1943 (*Ancestral Voices*), J.L.-M. wrote of her: 'She talked a lot about Russia and communism. She shouts one down like everyone else these days. She said she was trying to like England and Englishmen again without succeeding. Stuart [Preston] says she is stupid and dull. James [Pope-Hennessy] says, "Let's face it, she's a moron." Emerald [Cunard] says she is billiant. I don't know what to think.'

‡ Teresa ('Baby') Cuthbertson and Zita James, daughters of the rich socialite Mrs Richard Guinness by her first husband, Dutch-born artist Nico Jungman. As girls in the 1920s, the sisters attracted attention through their ribald antics, and started a craze for masquerades and treasure hunts in country houses.

§ Penelope Cuthbertson; m. 1985 Hon. Desmond Guinness (b. 1931) as his 2nd wife.

bright day but piercingly cold. At first I thought that the first fine care-
less rapture must have passed, but after an hour's motoring I started
enjoying the outing as much as before, recapturing the sympathy, the
empathy (a word coined by Gerard Manley Hopkins, I believe, and
much used incorrectly today). We saw ten or twelve houses, most of
which we instantly dismissed. But the first visited was Alderley Grange,
which D. was much taken with and wants included. I must say the
Acloques* have filled it with wondrous things, and it looks a charming little country house. Extraordinary experience at Holcombe and
Hilles, two houses beyond Painswick once owned by Detmar Blow.†
At the first we saw a coal-black negro in the garden. David leapt out
of the car to ask him who the owner was. 'I am,' he replied. Thinking
he had misheard, David asked again very politely. With exquisite courtesy the blackamoor replied, 'I am the owner and have been these forty
years.' Gave his name as Pollock and said we were welcome to see over.
However we didn't, and went on to Hilles which Blow built. Liked
both houses and decided to put the two together under one heading.
On getting home, I rang Simon Blow‡ to ask to whom at Hilles I
should direct myself. He said to Mrs Gopal, the Indian widow of his
cousin Jonathan Blow, now remarried to another Indian. Strange
squires to find cheek-by-jowl in the deepest Cotswolds.

We liked what we could see of Ablington [Manor, Bibury,
Gloucestershire], beside the rushing River Coln; and that's about all.

David Burnett makes me realise how old I am by his rapidity. He
jumps out of the car in a flash, backs the car down wrong lanes as fast
as if he were going forward, and gobbles his food before I have begun,
withal being so patient and charming. I said to Zita on Saturday that
we old people were a menace on the roads, that I drove with little of
my former *élan*. She disagreed, saying, 'No, I am a safer driver now.
When we get to a roundabout we go round at least three times before
deciding which road to take, to make sure.' Then she asked, 'Do you

---

* Guy Acloque; m. 1971 Hon. Camilla, dau. of 9th Baron Howard de Walden. They had
purchased Alderley Grange from A.L.-M. in 1974 and maintained the garden she had
created there.
† Architect and sometime adviser to 2nd Duke of Westminster (1867–1939).
‡ Writer, former racing jockey (b. 1945); yr. s. of Purcell Blow (e.s. of Detmar Blow) and
Diana Bethell (dau. of Hon. Clare Tennant by her 1st marriage); his publications include
works of family history and autobiography including *Broken Blood* (1987) and *No Time to
Grow* (1999).

think we ought to keep to the left or the right when circumambulating?' There is nothing that enrages younger motorists so much as old creatures weaving their way on roundabouts.

Thursday, 19th March

During the night, deep snow fell on dry ground. Woke up to see cedar trees weighted down. Had to brush snow from doorsteps; mail and paper late and warning of bad roads. So postponed driving to Bath. Took two dogs to The Slates. A thick light carpet of snow, unwalked-on, virginal. The dogs adored it. Was surprised on looking at the snow that it does not lie smooth, in spite of there being no wind today. It lies with faint marks as of a net having covered it. Walked to the flagstaff. A gorgeous morning. Far warmer than yesterday. The sky ice blue; figures of riders down the lanes like silhouettes in the distance. The west front of the wall to Park Piece swathed in snow. None the far side. All snow disappeared by afternoon.

Sunday, 22nd March

A. and I went to see Nan Bernays. She was in bed facing a huge picture window, though now blind. Greatly changed since we last saw her. Her round face is in its present gauntness quite beautiful. She is extremely weak and frail, talks softly and wanders, yet still craves the company of her friends. She talked of her approaching demise, hoping she would survive into April, which is rather touching. Says she is giving presents right and left to her friends, and money to those who need it. What a good, affectionate woman. Strange, this death confronting one who is still normal in mind.

Amury Blow, cousin of Simon, telephoned me, I having written to ask his mother, Mrs Gopal, if we might include Hilles House in the Cotswold book. His voice is exactly the same as Simon's, for whom I first mistook him. Since they are at daggers drawn and have hardly spoken all their lives, how comes it that two cousins have the same voice, unless voices are hereditary?

Tuesday, 24th March

A ghastly morning in Bath. How can I be expected to write books? The plumber who promised to arrive at 10.30 came at 11.30, and then had to go off to get the parts he needed. Then a man came about the gas boiler in the basement, where the tenant is currently without heat or hot water. Man said flue is blocked, and he would report to head-quarters and advise me of what needed to be done. I rang the HQ all afternoon to ask when they would repair, without getting through to anyone who knew about the trouble. Terrible interruptions. Then, while talking on the telephone to Prince Michael's secretary, I see Folly retching. Desperately with my leg I manoeuvre her off the Persian carpet onto the linoleum floor, where she is sick. In the evening I tell A. that I want to live in a 'home' where there are no responsiblities. She says, 'You are living in one now, with minimal responsibilities.' The darling.

Thursday, 26th March

Went to London yesterday, arriving at Westminster Cathedral just in time for Hubert Howard's Requiem Mass. This building is extremely beautiful and rendered mystical by there being no decoration on the vaulting whose bare brown brick recedes into the eternal night. Glimpses of sparkling mosaics in a side chapel to right of presbytery. Could not see from where I sat those lovely ones by Anrep,* among the best works of art in London this century. (Freda Berkeley tells me that Anrep left her his model for mosaicing the presbytery, never carried out for lack of money. I think just as well the money ran out over the marbling.) The papists can still run these shows beautifully. Officiating priest called Father Jock (odd) Dalrymple, a youth who looked eighteen and may be twenty-eight, very handsome, fair and devout. He never faltered. Referred to Hubert's soul, to the devout and fervent Catholicism of Hubert and Lelia. Francis Howard's son Esme† gave address about Hubert's personality. Very correct, satisfactory service without being moving. Met Francesca Wall‡ coming out. Said she was the only Lindsay present. And met Burnet Pavitt limping after knee operation.

---

* Boris Anrep, Russian mosaicist (1883–1969).
† Hon. Esme Howard (b. 1945); e. s. of 2nd Baron Howard of Penrith.
‡ Francesca Fummi (b. 1935); m. 1961 Christopher Wall (b. 1929), N.T. Historic Buildings Rep. for Thames & Chiltern Region, 1956–94. Her mother Lady Cynthia – sister of David Lindsay, 28th Earl of Crawford, Chairman of N.T. 1945–65 – was connected with the Caetani family through her paternal grandmother.

Lunched with Isabel Napier,* recently bereaved. Her flat very Sunningdale taste, as are her clothes and manner. Is eighty-one and told me Joanie† – mother of my still-born son? – was born in 1899. She was very sweet, but is not warm, or intellectual.

Then to Collins, she kindly motoring me there. Spent two hours with Ariane Goodman‡ going through *Venetian Evenings*. Very few queries and hardly a correction, whereas my last lady from Sidgwick would have produced dozens. Ariane said that Joy Law§ went through the typescript, and she is the best arts critic she knows. Ariane's husband has cancer and is in hospital. Yet they have bought and are doing up a cottage in Derbyshire.

I gave a dinner party at Brooks's of Midi [Gascoigne], Freda [Berkeley], Geoffrey Houghton-Brown and, thank goodness, M., wearing a new suit of dark corduroy. Geoffrey has a snow-white spade beard and is very deaf and old. Deeply furrowed face like a ploughed field. Poor Geoffrey, so gentle and lonely and resigned. Midi unchanged and full of fettle and fun. When they left M. stayed behind and gossiped. Is off to Geneva to see Sotheby's sell the Duchess of Windsor's jewels. His affection unvarying.

Saturday, 4th April

I object, in so far as I still mind anything, to a reviewer referring to me as 'dear old Lees-Milne' and adding, 'It is nice to know there is someone whom fate treats more unfairly than myself.' I am much out of sympathy with the modern critic who is gratuitously rude. Something distasteful about the brutal cynicism, the carping disparagement, the mockery, in the advanced intellectual journals like the *Literary Review*. And how badly they behave. *Books & Bookmen* has just

---

* J.L.-M's second cousin Isabel Surtees (b. 1906); m. 1931 Sir Joseph Napier, 4th Bt (d. 1986).

† Isabel's sister Dorothy Joan 'Joanie' Surtees (1899–1939); m. 1st Colonel Sir James Holt Hutchison, 1st Bt, 2nd Eric Smith. She is probably the voluptuous 'Janie' portrayed by J.L.-M. in Chapter III of *Another Self*, with whom he had an amorous encounter in his late teens (he gives 'Janie' the surname Puleston – another family to which he was related, which had however died out). J.L.-M. once told the editor that he believed himself to have been responsible, early in life, for a stillborn child conceived out of wedlock.

‡ Publisher's editor (b. 1955), working for Collins 1980–88; m. 1984 Andrew Bankes.

§ Art historian and publisher; as editorial director of George Rainbird Ltd, she invented the coffee table book.

packed up without warning, pocketing one's quarter-used annual sub-scription. Dear old Lees-Milne with his perpetual grumbles.

We motored in pouring rain to lunch at the Chantry. Tony Powell appeared in his striped butcher's apron from the kitchen, where he was cooking his special curry dish. Both he and Violet looked older, he smaller, shorter, but mind as alert as ever. I love these two. Violet always in shining, ringing cheer. Had long talks with Tony on sofa after luncheon, about genealogy. He says his interest in the subject is entirely unsnobbish. He gave us a signed copy of his *Fisher King*, I having tactlessly mentioned that I had been unable to get it at Waterstone's. There is to be an album by Thames & Hudson of his novels in the autumn.[*]

Wednesday, 8th April

On Sunday last David Burnett motored me to Bourton House, Sezincote and Batsford. The first has changed hands eight times since Miss Bligh lived there when I visited in 1944 or thereabouts. It has suffered much in consequence. Land below the great barn was sold by one owner to a speculator who has built two cheap little houses cheek-by-jowl. Some very bad things done to the building. The old thick sash bars removed from the south front and thin ones substituted, and four panes for the original three across. Some ghastly decoration, a sort of velvet paper splashed on the undersides of the staircase. One big room made out of two on the garden side and Rococo fireplace substituted for the original William and Mary. Nice bedint couple have now bought it, and love it. Intend to improve it gradually, though what we saw of their taste was pretty poor.

A very different state of affairs at Sezincote, where we lunched. The owner, Mrs Peake, daughter of Cyril Kleinwort,[†] very distinguished-looking. Charming husband, City man, intelligent too. The house in excellent taste and well kept up. From there we hopped across the road to Batsford. Tony Dulverton[‡] has the same teasing manner as he had when a boy. I pulled the bell and when I did not hear it ring was about

---

[*] It was compiled by Lady Violet Purcell (J.L.-M. having earlier rejected the suggestion that he should do the job himself: see entry for 25 September 1985).
[†] Susanna Kleinwort (b. 1942); m. 1962 David Peake.
[‡] Anthony Hamilton Wills, 2nd Baron Dulverton (1915–92); m. (2nd) 1962 Ruth, dau. of Sir Walter Farquhar, 5th Bt.

to walk off to find another entrance, when he opened the door and said abruptly, 'Aren't you going to say how do you do to your host?' Nice friendly wife, sister of the late Peter Farquhar.* We were quite impressed by the hall and the ballroom, but a beast of a house really.

The following day, Monday, we went to Nether Lypiatt [Manor, Gloucestershire] in the morning, losing our way as we tried to cross the deep valley above Stroud. Taken round the outside by gardener-cum-clerk-of-all-works with enormous nose like spout of a teapot. This house likewise spoilt since Mrs Woodhouse† had it. The fire escape an eyesore. The garden ruined. Hideous rose maze of flori-bundas within wooden curbs. Lamps down the lime avenue for benefit of guests gazing after dark from drawing-room window. The house also too tarted-up. More and more I admire the taste of Mrs Woodhouse's generation in doing up old houses – Reggie Cooper,‡ Ted Lister, Gerry Wellington and the like. The next house we visited, Ablington Manor, was a disappointment. Again too tarted-up. It has changed hands several times since the war and is now owned by a rich scrap-metal merchant whose children won't live there when he is dead. So it goes on. No one stays long. Each owner undoes what the previous one did. No owner leaves well alone. Still, the outside is attractive – alterations of every date, all in the traditional style, of gables and harling, a motley of yellow and orange.

The Beauforts dined last night, having cancelled the Three-Day Event because of incessant rain, the parking fields a bog.§ I asked David if he would lose money thereby. He said he would not lose, as he was insured, but he would not make the £176,000 he depended on making, and would thus be unable to carry out improvements to the estate he had planned for next year.

---

* Sir Peter Farquhar, 6th Bt (1904–86).

† Violet Gwynne (1870–1948); m. 1895 Gordon Woodhouse; harpsichordist and bohe-mian, who lived in a *ménage à cinq* with four men, as well as having lesbian associations (see biography by Jessica Douglas-Home, *Violet: The Life and Loves of Violet Gordon Woodhouse* [1996]). The *ménage* moved in 1923 to Nether Lypiatt, where J.L.-M., who greatly admired the house, visited her on several occasions towards the end of her life (as described in his early diaries).

‡ Lieut.-Col. R. A. Cooper (1885–1965); school friend and sometime diplomatic col-league of Harold Nicolson; garden designer and restorer of country houses, some of whose work may be seen at Cothay Manor nr. Wellington, Somerset where he lived 1930s.

§ The Badminton Three-Day Event customarily took place in late March or early April, but was later moved to May after a succession of disastrously wet springs.

John Lehmann* has died. I telephoned poor Ros who is sad but
philosophical. 'It feels odd being the only one of us four left,' she said.
She was not pleased with the *Times* obit., saying it did not give him
credit for his poetry, and he was a good poet if not a great one. Said
he became nicer towards her as he got progressively iller, but always
remained hostile to her religious beliefs. 'Poor old boy,' she said, 'he
will be having a strange surprise now.' How can she be so sure? And I
have never understood the precise nature of Ros's Christianity, for she
never goes to church or takes Holy Communion.

Monday, 27th April

Very successful ten days with Eardley, staying at Banyalbufar in
Majorca. Our hotel run by a charming and efficient brother and sister,
the brother's wife the cook and their sons the two waiters. In the
mornings I read two of Ros's novels, *The Echoing Grove* [1953] and
The Ballad and the Source [1944], and wrote a long obituary of her for
the *Independent*. Was greatly impressed by the novels, and in writing
to Ros pretended I had read them when they came out, but in truth
I don't think I had. Each afternoon we walked up the mountains, or
along coastal paths reached from the main road. Beautiful walks but
arduous for us. We retired to our bedrooms to read between five and
eight, on our beds or balconies. Much sleep, much eating, much
reading, and a good deal of walking. On best of terms with E. who
seems to have regained his dear old serenity. When together we
chatted endlessly as of yore.

I asked E. who he would most like to walk into the dining room
and join us for dinner. He said Duncan Grant.† We talked of De-la-
Noy‡ and the book on Eddy [Sackville-West] which he has now
begun. He is a great fan of Eddy's and has discovered papers and writings of his quite unknown to Eardley, his executor.

E. surprises me over the people of the distant past whom he has
known intimately. Jean Cocteau§ was one. They met in Villefranche
in 1926. Cocteau was furiously smoking opium and tried to induce

---

* Writer, poet, publisher and critic (1907–87); brother of Rosamond.
† Bloomsbury artist (1885–1978).
‡ Michael De-la-Noy (*né* Michael Delaney Walker), writer (1934–2002). His *Eddy: The
Life of Edward Sackville-West* was published by The Bodley Head in 1988.
§ French poet, artist, librettist, dramatist, novelist, actor and film director (1889–1963).

E. to join him, but E. withstood his persuasions, although he says no
smell is more delicious than opium smoke. Cocteau would seduce
French boys to be his lovers by inducting them into smoking, and
when bored with them would sack them. Pretty bloody behaviour.

Saturday, 2nd May

Have been reading Simon Brett's[*] anthology of diaries, unable to put
it down. His arrangement, running through the calendar and choosing
extracts for each day, is a good one. One quickly gets to learn the character of each diarist as his extracts appear, though I don't know that my
character emerges very clearly. It becomes obvious that the majority of
diarists write for their own glorification and pathetic immortality.

I am appalled by my bad temper. This week I was enraged by our
tenant in the basement at Bath, demanding £100 compensation for
having been a fortnight without hot water. I asked why, in my
absence, she had not chivvied the gas company to come and fix the
boiler. She assured me she had done so. They promptly came and fixed
it when I telephoned myself. I told her I want her to leave, whereupon she said it would be difficult for her to find other premises, and
I would be hearing from her solicitor. I shall now write to her giving
notice and pointing out that the £160 a month which she pays is
ridiculously little. Then I lost my temper with poor little Missy who
seems to have collapsed, takes no interest in anything, hates going for
walks, and might almost be a stuffed dog for all the notice she takes of
A. and myself. When obliged to return to the foot of a steep hill on
the golf course I had climbed for her benefit to find her still standing
there, I put on her lead and literally dragged her up the hill in a rage.
Am overwhelmed by depression as bad as before I went to Majorca,
if not worse. Poor Alvilde. Oh the guilt and *Angst*, as bad as ever, even
in extreme old age.

This morning, Miriam Rothschild[†] turned up. We had not seen her
before and it was a great surprise. Splendid presence, not a Rothschild
for nothing, like a sibyl with long, fine face, craggy nose, wearing
flouncy, chintzy dress to ankles, head swathed in blue kerchief, large
owlish spectacles. Talked to A. about wild flowers, saying she is
spreading the gospel, and the results are beginning to show. The popu-

---

[*] Novelist and playwright (b. 1945).
[†] Hon. Miriam Rothschild (b. 1908); zoologist; m. 1943–57 George Lane; DBE 2000.

lace are mad about cultivating them now. She has just returned from a wild flower mission to Texas, USA. Stayed with Lady Bird Johnson[*] who is a very intelligent and enterprising woman, behind all the good things her husband the President did, and who has sown 75,000 acres of road verge with wild flowers. Miriam R. said the beauty of some of the forests in Texas where wisteria has been planted to rampage around the dark pine trees is staggering. She left to lunch at the House, while we had Anne Lancaster and Rosemary Verey to luncheon. Alvilde intended to show these two gardening ladies her video of Ninfa, but couldn't make it work. So she telephoned Caroline at 2.30, who came round. After much fiddling it transpired that A. had wiped out the Ninfa film by recording an episode of *Dallas*[†] on top of it. Great disappointment. Caroline seemed in no hurry to return, but announced that the Waleses were lunching at Badminton. We said, 'But you must go back at once!' No, she said, I think I have worked my passage all right, or words to that effect. Anyway, shortly after she motored back, saying she was intrigued to know what David thought of Princess Diana who sat next to him at luncheon. She is what used to be known as 'a card'.

Tuesday, 5th May

A. is in France again. Whenever she flies to Paris I wonder whether I shall hear on the news that her 'plane has crashed. I don't have the same fears when she goes by train; but I do when she motors to London. Sally Westminster telephoned today and spoke of the death in a motor accident of Duchess Viola.[‡] 'Maybe it was a good thing,' she said. 'She was getting deaf which was a great worry for her, being musical. And she was in another world, you know, in touch with the other side.'

Friday, 8th May

I am too conscious of my failing powers. They accelerate week by week. I notice how my knees grow feebler, how I walk shorter

---

[*] Claudia 'Lady Bird' Taylor; m. 1934 Lyndon B. Johnson (1908–73), President of USA 1963–9.

[†] Popular 1980s television soap opera about family of newly-rich Texan tycoons.

[‡] Hon. Viola Lyttelton (1912–87), dau. of 9th Viscount Cobham; m. 1946 Robert Grosvenor (1910–79) who s. 1967 as 5th Duke of Westminster.

distances, get puffed and tired. Always tired. Little things upset me inordinately. My eyes give constant trouble; I find it difficult to focus, to see any print in a dim light. Now I have developed a red patch on the left cheek. I dabbed it with TCP, only to find next morning that it had doubled in size. I fear it may be skin cancer, brought about by the sun-drenching I got in Majorca. I know sunshine does not agree with me, although it was delicious there owing to the air being cool. Nevertheless it was very strong and I was obliged to buy a straw hat which I did not always wear.

I chucked the dinner party to be given tonight at Fenton House [Hampstead] for Betty Hussey's* eightieth birthday. What with my face, and having broken my bottom dental plate, I could not confront a host of people I knew but slightly. The idea of going without A. has worried me for the past week, making me miserable and inducing needless *Angst*. I have grown like those floppy plants that must always have a stake to cling to.

M. went to the funeral in Cambridge of his Russian friend Vera Traill,[†] who although totally agnostic directed that she was to have an Orthodox service. Her last words to a group of friends round her bedside were, 'Entertain me, I'm bored.' At the service the mourners held candles and were invited to walk past her open coffin and kiss her embalmed face. I asked if it was not rather gruesome. No, he said, it was very beautiful. I said that I hoped that his Ribbentrop book would criticise the Nuremberg Trial, which I always thought abominable and a terrible foreboding of what might happen after future wars. He knew an impressive amount about the Trial and thought it had done a favour to the Germans, helping them purge their soul.

Tuesday, 12th May

Rupert and Josephine Loewenstein have just returned from taking Princess Margaret on a tour of her German relations. Rupert very shocked that she did not know who any of them were. Stranger would come up, kiss her, and say Hello Margaret. Rupert would explain that this was the daughter of Missy or the grandson of Ducky, as she must know. She would reply, 'I don't know and I don't care. Mummy hates

---

* Elizabeth Kerr-Smiley (b. 1907); m. 1936 Christopher Hussey, architectural historian (1899–1970); of Scotney Castle, Lamberhurst, Kent, whose gardens she donated to N.T.
† Film critic (1906–87); daughter of the Tsarist politician A. I. Guchkov.

the Germans, who killed her brothers and killed Papa.' The last a slight exaggeration surely, George VI having died seven years after the War. He also told me that Peg Hesse,* that charming woman I once met at Ian [McCallum]'s, had refused point-blank to let Tony Lambton see the Hesse papers for his book on Mountbatten; she would not have him poking around, scavenging for scandal. Then she told Rupert an astonishing thing – that her father-in-law, the Grand Duke of Hesse who was the son of Queen Victoria's daughter Alice,† was homosexual, and had been seduced by his uncle, Edward VII. I asked Rupert what earthly proof she had for this astonishing statement. He said he would ask her the next time he saw her.

We had James Fairfax‡ to stay. A perfectly agreeable, dull Australian journalist. He owns all the [Australian] newspapers which Rupert Murdoch doesn't own, as well as our *Spectator*.

A. and I stayed Saturday night at Englefield Green with the Droghedas. Joan much worse, far frailer, bent, tiny and shuffling. Conversation out of the question. One smiles at her and she kisses one without knowing who one is. Nurses round the clock, costing Garrett £40,000 a year. At meals, she sits at table between Garrett and the nurse. Too much attention I think. The result is that the moment G. leaves the room she goes to look for him. Clings to her tattered handbag which contains only a handkerchief, which she takes out and twirls round her fingers. It is all piteous.

Wednesday, 13th May

Lunched in London with M. at his new club, the Savile in Brook Street. He is very proud of it, but the food was poor and the company not very distinguished. M. took me upstairs to see the bathroom in which poor Loulou Harcourt§ took his overdose. Bathroom remosaiced since his time but I thought the tub might be the same,

---

* Hon. Margaret Geddes (1913–99), dau. of 1st Baron Geddes; m. 1937 Prince Louis of Hesse (1908–68), who succeeded as head of the Grand Ducal House of Hesse when the plane carrying his elder brother and children to his marriage in London crashed with no survivors. For J.L.-M's meeting with the Princess, see *Holy Dread*, 9 July 1983.
† Grand Duke Ernst Ludwig (1868–1937); reigned in Darmstadt from 1892 to 1918.
‡ Australian media tycoon (b. 1933).
§ Lewis, 1st Viscount Harcourt (1863–1922); Liberal politician; committed suicide at 69 Brook Street after 'pouncing' on J.L.-M's Eton contemporary, Edward James.

though lacking the mahogany which would have gone with it. Two fixed cupboards against the bedroom walls are clearly Edwardian French, what in this building is termed 'Loulou Quinze'. M. said he had received a letter from one of Ribbentrop's sons excusing himself from helping with his biography, saying he was only ten when his father was hanged. I told M. I felt sorry for this man.

Then J.K.–B. had tea with me at Brooks's. He was in fine fettle, most affectionate, and forgiving about my having forgotten our lunch at Brooks's last week, the day I was to have attended the dinner for Betty Hussey. He is slightly better-off, having paid off the mortgage on his house, and seems happier generally.

Friday, 15th May

I went last night to the opening of an exhibition in the Victoria Gallery of some excellent paintings of Venice. By Canaletto, Guardi, Bellotto, Vanvitalli, the lot. I hoped to have a word with Joe Links[*] who opened the proceedings, but I could not get near him, nor hear a word of his talk. We rushed off at 7.30 because David Beaufort had asked us to dine with him alone, Caroline away in Albania. Very nice it was too. David said how much he regretted the evening when he had lost his temper with poor Derry [Moore].[†] His father once told him that to lose one's temper was an indulgence, and that no colonel ever lost his temper with a general. But sometimes a duke with a viscount, I suggested?

Saturday, 23rd May

I find the general election not only boring but horrifying.[‡] Every news on wireless and television is concentrated on politicians abusing one another, telling outrageous lies, making promises they will never fulfil. They are a contemptible race. If we had a Green candidate I might vote for it, because at least their programme concerns itself with the fundamental issue of the future of this earth and whether human

---

[*] Canaletto expert, author of *Venice for Pleasure*, and furrier by appointment to HM The Queen (d. 1997); m. 1945 Mary Lutyens.
[†] See entry for 28 June 1986.
[‡] The election took place on 11 June and returned Mrs Thatcher's Conservative Government for a third term with a majority of 102.

life will continue or no – though I sometimes think no the preferable outcome.

M. told me on the telephone that the retiring British Ambassador to Paris* invited himself to tea with Maître Blum. The old lady, now eighty-eight, supposed he and the ambassadress wished to say goodbye and thank her for all her efforts on behalf of the Duke and Duchess of Windsor. Not at all. The Ambassador came without wife, but with a private secretary clutching an important-looking envelope addressed to the Maître, bearing royal ciphers on the flap. The Ambassador announced that the Queen had commissioned Mr Philip Ziegler to write the official life of King Edward VIII, and hoped the Maître would co-operate to the extent of lending such papers and photographs as she had in her charge, and giving permission as executor to quote copyright material. She resolutely refused, saying she had her own official biographer lined up, namely Misha. Having been given a dusty reception, the Ambassador left, not without giving a nod to the secretary which apparently conveyed that he was not to deliver the clutched envelope, presumed to be some honour from the Queen, only to be conferred if the old lady complied. M. is upset by this news, which means he must now put aside Ribbentrop to finish his book on the reign of Edward VIII, which he was hoping to do later on. He fears Ziegler's book, despite being an official royal biography, is bound to be ungenerous and unsympathetic, for Z. is given to unsympathetic biogs (*vide* his Mountbatten), and generosity is unimaginable with the Queen Mother alive who loathed the Duke. I sympathise with poor M.

The last few days I have been incensed by my bitch of a tenant declining to answer my letter of three weeks ago giving her six months' notice (though I am only obliged to give her three under our signed agreement). I am further enraged by my Bath solicitors, who are cautious and pessimistic, warning me that under current legislation it is not easy for landlords to rid themselves of undesirable tenants. A sense that one is in the right, but apparently unable to do much about it, engenders a sense of frustration and arouses one's most aggressive instincts.

David Burnett and I had an enjoyable day at Stanway [House, Gloucestershire] on Wednesday the 20th, spending so long there that

---

* Sir John Fretwell (b. 1930); HM Ambassador to France, 1982–7.

there was no time to visit Sudeley as we had intended. We arrived for luncheon and were surprised to find the drive littered with cars, wondering if we had come on the wrong day. But it was just a gathering of businessmen for the afternoon's clay pigeon shoot. Jamie Neidpath met us and took us round the garden, up to the Belvedere, and ambled so slowly, talking all the while, that we did not get back to the house and luncheon, famished, until three o'clock. Luncheon in the kitchen, very *intime*, with wife Catherine and small boy. I like him immensely. He is extremely bright. Loves Stanway, knows its history, very well informed and clever on every count. Could not have been kinder. Took us over the house, explaining every picture and piece of furniture. Catherine also easy and friendly. She has none of the beauty of her grandmother Diana [Mosley], being plain with a large chin. The so-called Elcho boudoir, with its portraits of Lady Mary Elcho and The Souls, includes William Acton's* drawing of Diana, now a Stanway ancestress.

Sunday, 24th May

Dear Freda staying. Lennox now completely gaga. Yet they still sleep in the same bed, and she takes him to pee several times during the night. She is utterly worn out and miserable and longs for him to die. Today we drove to luncheon with the Hobsons† at Whitsbury [Hampshire], a long drive. Were greeted by Anthony saying that Tanya not present, having slipped on Friday on the polished floor, breaking her right leg and left ankle. She was being operated on as we ate. John Julius [Norwich] and Molly staying. Conversation very jolly during luncheon. Anthony has good taste and excellent pictures and furniture. I suppose he is rich, being a director of Sotheby's, of which his father was Chairman.

Tuesday, 26th May

These past few days I have been in a rage with the tenant in Bath. It is nearly a month since I wrote telling her she must leave, out of the goodness of my heart giving her six months' notice instead of the agreed three. I have since written her two further letters but heard

---

* Artist, brother of Sir Harold Acton.
† Anthony Hobson, bibliographical historian (b. 1921); m. 1959 Tanya Vinogradoff.

nothing and last Friday I called to see her to ask why she had not replied, nor thanked me for the cheque I had sent at her request to compensate her for a fortnight without hot water. She said she was writing to me that very day – I told her I required merely a word of acknowledgement – but this morning there is still no reply from this bloody bitch of a girl. So I have asked my Bath solicitors to write to her, but they warn me that I have little chance of getting rid of her if she is determined to stay. It is monstrous that the law prevents a landlord sacking an undesirable tenant. I am determined that, come what may, I shall rid myself of this pestilential female.

This afternoon Michael De-la-Noy came from London to talk about Eddy [Sackville-West]. He produced the inevitable dictaphone, which was so silent that I forgot it was there and doubtless said many indiscreet things. I found myself liking him more as the interview progressed. He is very quick and clever, and has discovered many interesting papers of Eddy's.

Wednesday, 27th May

A. being in France, I dined with Alex [Moulton] at Bradford. Not having seen him for several months I was shocked by his appearance. He said he had been suffering from pneumonia for six weeks. 'At least I cannot have got Aids,' he added. Nevertheless he was brisk in his movements as he took me round the garden. He is very pleased with what he has done there, which would not meet with A's approval, I don't think. Talked much about death. Feels happy that he has put The Hall into first-rate condition, which will count to his advantage on Judgement Day. I asked if he believed in a future world. He said he didn't quite, but he did believe there was a kind of a twilight world inhabited by those caught up in the endless process of death. He had a glimpse of it when he was very ill the other day, and saw his mother and his best friend, both dead, lying on beds, breathing peacefully. Their presence gave him confidence and happiness. Yet he was tormented by remorse for his sins, countered to some extent by satisfaction at the good work he has done on The Hall. We talked of the election. He thinks it of the utmost importance that Mrs Thatcher gets in again. If she does, and survives her third term, Socialism will be dead, as it is in America. There, people may be democrats, black people may be deprived, but there is no envy of the rich, as there is here. I said they valued money too much there.

Sunday, 31st May

We lunched today with Audrey and the Suttons.* James a gloomy man
with something to be gloomy about, as Westons, the firm he joined
four years ago, announces that it will sack many of its employees, and
he fears he will be made redundant. Says we have no idea how beastly
it is awaiting the news. Indeed I sympathise. The Suttons' house is a
menagerie – two Alsatians; a scratchy little Yorkshire terrier; flocks of
wild pigeons; macaws by the dozen; two horses; and a python. When
I asked about the python, Dale suddenly remembered she had not fed
it for six weeks. They give it a whole dead sheep or goat – must be
dead – and slowly it eats, the sheep etc. visibly descending down its
body. Python then becomes torpid. I saw it, beautiful colouring, lying
in a sort of centrally-heated glass coffin. It is now fourteen feet long.
They do not know its age, having had it for thirteen years, pythons
said to live about forty. They carry it onto the lawn and let it lie in the
sun. It weighs a ton.

Audrey very sweet and touching. We had tea in her garden. She said
to me in her kitchen, 'None of my children or grandchildren will
know that that dish was given to me by Matthew, that plate by a dear
black servant in Barbados, and so on. When I tell them, they are not
interested, and my beloved treasures will be scattered, their associations forgotten.' Is this not the case with all of us? As we leave, she
picks a large bunch of lilies-of-the-valley which she presents to me.

Wednesday, 3rd June

To London for the day. A first class ticket is now £26 return for our
age group, no matter what train one takes; second class is £13 provided one does not go too early. I take the second class. Go straight
to London Library, but all the books I want are out. At 12.30 meet M.
at Oxford and Cambridge Club for half an hour. He and Andrew
Best† are meeting Tiny Rowland‡ this afternoon, to see if the *Observer*
will publish the important papers of the Duke of Windsor which

---

* See notes to 30 March 1985.
† Michael Bloch's literary agent (b. 1933), director of Curtis Brown Ltd.
‡ Rowland T. Rowland (1917–98), born Rowland T. Fuhrop in India; tycoon who made
his fortune in Africa, and was said by Edward Heath to represent 'the unacceptable face
of capitalism'; owner of *Observer* from 1983; rival of Mohammed Fayed, who obtained the
lease of the Windsors' former Paris house and acquired many of their possessions in 1987.

Maître Blum wants M. to edit before Ziegler's book comes out. Then I lunch along the street with Hugh Massingberd. Sweet man, I am truly fond of him. He asks me to write obituaries for the *Daily Telegraph*. Suggests dowagers such as Anne Rosse, Sybil Cholmondeley, Debo Devonshire (not yet a dowager); also Eardley. I say I cannot do John Summerson,* which would call for much research and re-reading of his books.

Then to Tate to see Turners in new Clore Gallery. He is surely the greatest English painter, and stirs me into a turmoil of emotions and admiration. The impressionist paintings, which I take it are the latest, are fantastic. It is years since I looked carefully at the *Téméraire*, and *Rain, Speed and Steam*. They have all the freshness for me they had forty and more years ago. The sparkle, the imagination, the depths of vision merely hinted at. What a man! How did he come to these wispy, pearly, sketchy yet finished pictures? How did he invent the technique which the French developed years later? I feel a great urge to re-read Ruskin's *Modern Painters*. Strange that he should have liked Turner, considering his Gothic prejudices.

Wednesday, 10th June

We have returned Missy to the Lowes, who are keeping her and returned A's cheque. I sent the cheque back and begged them never to let anyone else have her without our first being given the chance to take her again. My sense of guilt reduced me to tears, for I fear I may have caused the dislocation of her little spine by dragging her down the road when she wouldn't come for a walk the last day. Cruelty to a dog is far worse than cruelty to a child, which can make the reasons for its suffering known. I still love her and miss her at nights terribly, and my guilt is fearful. A. says I am being absurd; but I know how I have behaved, and she doesn't.

Thursday, 11th June

This morning I put on my dark blue pullover and found it covered with Missy's little hairs. If this isn't 'coffee cups' with a vengeance, I don't know what is.

---

* Sir John Summerson (1901–92); architect and architectural historian.

Saturday, 13th June

Margaret-Anne Stuart staying, she and A. just returned from the Worcester[*] wedding which I did not attend. Instead I lunched with Mrs Pollock who owns Holcombe House [near Painswick, Gloucestershire], one of my chosen Cotswold Houses. I hardly know her, and accepted her invitation just to see the house. A very rich American lady from Newport, Rhode Island, rather pretentious. I was one of ten guests, the others all unknown to me. We did not sit down until two, or rise from the table until four, then moving to the library where liqueurs were dispensed. Mrs P. friendly and agreeable – but oh, these women! The sort of visit which wears me out nowadays.

Margaret-Anne and I walked Folly in Park Piece. An aeroplane was releasing parachutists over The Slates. As they jumped, the 'plane's engine cut out, and for a moment it seemed that it might crash – but it landed gracefully on the airstrip. M.-A. said, 'It's a terrible thing to say, but in a way I was disappointed that it did not crash. Not that I want anyone to be killed, or even hurt.' I said, 'Yes, it is very wicked, but when I hear that someone who is rumoured to have Aids seems to be better, I too have a pang of disappointment.' M.-A. said, 'It's not a thing many would own up to, but I don't believe there is anyone who does not sometimes feel like this.' She said that Peter Quennell[†] once admitted to her that he secretly rejoiced in the misfortunes of his friends. I honestly don't believe I do, though I am sometimes jealous of their success.

Monday, 15th June

I motored to Hinton Ampner[‡] to join a party of N.T. men – Brinsley Ford, Bobby Gore and Christopher Rowell.[§] A podgy millionaire ex-son-in-law of Tanis [Guinness] aged forty[¶] is now the tenant,

---

[*] Henry Somerset, Marquess of Worcester (b. 1952), heir to 11th Duke of Beaufort, had married Tracy Louise (b. 1958), yr dau. of Hon. Peter Ward and Claire *née* Baring.

[†] Sir Peter Quennell (1905–94); writer, editor and journalist.

[‡] Estate in Hampshire, owned for 400 years by ancestors of Ralph Dutton (see notes to 26 April 1985), who bequeathed it to N.T. on his death in 1985. He created a famous garden there in the 1930s, and rebuilt the house in the Georgian style after it had been gutted by fire in 1960. The N.T. had decided to let the house, and open the gardens to the public.

[§] N.T. Historic Buildings Representative for Southern Region, 1986–2002 (b. 1952).

[¶] Christopher Shaw.

inhabiting the whole house (he owns several others) with all Ralph Dutton's furniture and contents. Nothing altered; everything well kept. I didn't much care for being back in Ralph's old house, although he would be pleased with the present arrangement.

Tuesday and Wednesday, 16th and 17th June

These two days spent with my dear new friend David Burnett, visiting, in filthy weather, Snowshill [Manor] (good, keen and knowledgeable custodian), Hilles [near Harescombe], Rodmarton [Manor] and Eastington Manor. The last a dud house of no interest. A mistake to choose it, as there is absolutely nothing to write about. Ghastly inside. Hilles has an oriental flavour and the half-Indian Blow who showed us round was as dark as my hat, with the manner of an English squire.

Sunday, 21st June

Elizabeth Cavendish to stay for the weekend. A perfect guest whom we are delighted to see again. She is the easiest person to have in the house; does not ask endless questions like our last guest, dear Midi [Gascoigne]. Much talk about John Betjeman. She says the first volume of Bevis Hillier's[*] biography is about to come out, though he has seen few of John's old friends, and she has refused to have anything to do with him. Feeble confirmed that John died without fear of death, though without any certainty of another world. He was perplexed towards the end that his poetry was so popular, thinking himself a fraud and a failure. Yet she believes that his was a happy life – which I can vouch for since Oxford days when I first knew him. He may have been misunderstood in childhood, but no more so than many children with intellectual and enquiring minds who have unimaginative or philistine parents. Feeble accompanied me to church this morning, just as Midi did a fortnight ago.

Garrett [Drogheda] arrived at midday, driven by motor. Looked ghastly, white, drawn and thin. I walked with him to the House and realised before we got there that he was exhausted by the effort. He says it is awful returning home and having Joan there in the flesh yet

---

[*] Writer, journalist and critic (b. 1940); Antiques Correspondent of *The Times*, 1970–84. His *Young Betjeman* was published by John Murray in 1988.

not being able to tell her where he has been, whom he has seen and what he has thought.

Friday, 26th June

Only on Sunday I was showing Feeble Master's tombstone by Verity. She thought it rather pretentious, with the coronet on the cushion. I said I admired it very much, but couldn't for the life of me see how Mary [Beaufort] would fit in when her time came, as the coffins have to be concreted down to guard against vandalism. Then, on Wednesday, poor old Mary died. James Fergusson asked me to write an obituary for the *Independent*, which I composed within an hour this morning and dictated down the telephone. Hugh Massingberd, who is writing about her for the *Telegraph*, also asked me for anecdotes; I gave him some, and felt a bit of a cad.

On Wednesday I went to London to collect proofs of *Venetian Evenings*. Had Jamie Fergusson, M. and J.K.-B. to luncheon at Brooks's. Thought it a good way of getting the last two to meet without previously warning either. They seemed to like one another, and M. much taken by Jamie who has developed a distinction with his tall, upright figure, thick dark hair and whimsical mouth.

I went to Turnbull & Asser* to buy some yellow socks, and ran into Horowitz and his wife choosing ties. As I passed him I stopped, turned to him and, without saying a word, made a deep bow to him with a faint smile. He seemed surprised but not displeased. At least I did not bore him by shaking his hand and saying what a wonderful musician he was. The youth who served me seemed totally uninterested when I told him that his other customer was the greatest pianist in the world.

Saturday, 27th June

Yeterday David Burnett motored me to Cirencester Park. At the Estate Office it transpired that Lord Bathurst† was in his jeep on the estate and had forgotten our appointment. They telephoned him and he returned, not best pleased. While waiting, we asked the girl if we could look around the back premises. 'Don't,' she cautioned, 'his lordship does not like his privacy invaded.' I had forgotten what a tiny man he is. After a

---

* Shirtmaker in Jermyn Street.
† Henry Bathurst, 8th Earl (b. 1927); m. (2nd) 1978 Gloria Rutherston.

while he warmed up, but he is nervy, fidgety and fussy. It is a hideous house, though portraits interesting. Bad taste, too. New wife has painted the Adam mirrors red, the gilt having worn off; previous wife had painted them cream. It was too hot to walk to see the follies and temples and we failed to find an entrance, having motored all round the park.

Stopped at Cherington church on return. Not interesting save for a sentence in the history leaflet which reads, 'The school was not a success. Certain irregularities were recorded.' David and I laughed over this. Approaching Tetbury, we saw a notice that Tetbury is twinned with Zwinnenberg. The idiocy of this sort of thing.

Last week I went to a new oculist, a pupil of Pat's called Tom Casey. I begged him to be discreet, as I felt rather disloyal to Pat. 'Mum's the word,' he said, having become used to such defections. Anyway, he told me my left eye was very bad indeed. It has glaucoma, which can be treated to prevent worsening, and cataract, which must be operated on as soon as convenient. Well, that is a bore.

Tuesday, 30th June

Attended Mary Beaufort's funeral after much deliberation and changing of mind. Church very full of grand relations and royalty in the front pew. The Queen Mother in deep black looking minute, scuttling up the aisle like a beetle; the Prince of Wales, small and balding; Princess Alice, small but handsome; Prince Michael. On leaving the church, still lachrymose from singing 'All Things Bright and Beautiful', so appropriate to Mary's gentle childlike nature, I was accosted by a BBC reporter at the door, thrusting a trumpet at me and asking fatuous questions as to what the service had been like, how well I had known the Dowager Duchess, etc. I made a few asinine remarks which mercifully were not broadcast. How do public figures always manage to say something which makes sense on these occasions?

Thursday, 2nd July

I went to the National Portrait Gallery and bought their complete catalogue, with stamp-sized illustrations, for £25, an essential addition to my reference library. As I approached the building, Harold Wilson was emerging in a long blue raincoat, looking undistinguished. I imagined how different Disraeli or Gladstone would have looked, top-hatted, cravatted, imperious, gracious, noble.

I was obliged to attend *Spectator* party at 6.30, having refused to accompany A. to dine with unknown American Attingham* visitors this evening, making this party my excuse. A crowd such as one would not believe. I had hoped to meet Mark Amory,† but there was no visible host. At first I saw no one I knew, but mercifully Richard Shone appeared, and then, of all people, the Sarge‡ from Paris. I stayed half an hour and then bolted to Paddington where I waited for next train home.

Monday, 6th July

Burnet [Pavitt] called for me at Brooks's at 2.30 in a huge hired Rolls-Royce. Coote Lygon and himself teed up in evening splendour in the back. I, scruffy by comparison, in a dark blue suit, white shirt and bow tie, sat with driver in front. We took two hours to reach Glyndebourne. As we drove through Brixton I remarked to the driver on the scruffiness of the streets. He replied that no one would clean them for fear of getting beaten up. For the same reason, he was eschewing various short cuts through side streets lest the inhabitants throw bricks at his expensive motor. I felt embarrassed at the expense Burnet must be incurring until he explained that the entire evening was being paid for by the Osborne Hills, including our seats and dinner in the restaurant. (The latter included champagne, which I hardly touched, costing £57 a bottle.) Coote was going to stay with them at St Moritz tomorrow, they having sent her a cheque for £1,000 for her travelling expenses. Mrs O.H. said quite seriously to Burnet the other day, 'I honestly don't know how people can manage on less than £700,000 a year.' Coote told us that the happiest periods of her life had been the poorest; and she has been rat-poor at times, in fact most of her life I guess.

Burnet told us an extraordinary thing – that Lady Poole and Garrett

---

* The annual summer school at Attingham Park (see notes to 9 July 1985) had been started in 1952 by Sir George Trevelyan, 4th Bt, to promote the study of the English country house. It still flourished under the direction of Helena Hayward, though no longer based at Attingham, which had recently become a regional headquarters of N.T. It always attracted many American students.

† Writer and editor (b. 1941); for many years literary editor of *Spectator*.

‡ Stuart Preston (see notes to 19 June 1986) was known as 'The Sarge' from his days in London with the US Army during the Second World War, when he was a sergeant 'attached to Headquarters'.

[Drogheda] had Joan christened the other day by a clergyman who came to the house. Joan, who has never been a believer, never gone near a church except for the Garter Service in St George's Chapel, and who is now out of her mind. What can have been the idea?

Tuesday, 7th July

I saw Stuart [Preston] at Brooks's. He had just read a letter written by Mrs Keppel* to Lady Astor† on her marriage, which contained the following advice: 'Don't do anything for nothing, and do very little for sixpence.' Sums up Edwardian society neatly. Then to New & Lingwood where they had polished an old pair of brown shoes for me. Got into conversation with a nice old shoemaker who spoke lovingly of his craft. He let me see, touch and feel a large sheet of Russian leather which was recently retrieved from the wreck of a ship bound from St Petersburg to Plymouth in 1786, preserved in sand. It was soft and pliant. He told me that no leather of such quality has come their way for a hundred years. One pair of shoes is to be made out of it for the Prince of Wales, who as Duke of Cornwall has foregone his right to the trove. Then to Winifred Nicholson‡ exhibition at Tate. Her still lives and seascapes are typical of the Twenties under the influence of Picasso – colourful but not moving.

Saturday, 11th July

Very hot day. We drove to Oxford to lunch with Leslie Rowse.§ I told A. that were I younger I would certainly sniff cocaine or take heroin to get me through occasions such as this luncheon, which I presumed would be of intellectuals unknown to me. Like Diana Cooper who had to drink before she could face a party. A. replied that it was a form of conceit, this feeling that I must shine. But I feel it is just a case

---

* Alice Edmonstone (d. 1947); m. 1891 Colonel The Hon. George Keppel, yr son of 7th Earl of Albemarle; mistress of King Edward VII.
† Nancy Langhorne (1879–1964); m. (2nd) 1906 Hon. William Astor, late 2nd Viscount (1879–1952); the first woman to take her seat as a British MP (1919), and a noted political hostess at Cliveden, Buckinghamshire.
‡ Winifred Roberts (1893–1981), 1st wife (1920–31) of painter Ben Nicholson (1894–1982).
§ A. L. Rowse (1903–97); historian and Fellow of All Souls.

of sheer nerves, from which I have suffered all my life, and which seem if anything to get worse in old age. Impossible to find a parking space when we got to Oxford, which must be the worst city for parking in the British Isles. We drove round and round until the porter at All Souls took pity on us and let us park in the Warden's drive. I enjoyed the luncheon immensely, sitting between Christina Foyle and Lady Monson.* Christina, with her clipped, bedint little voice and inattention, is very sweet. Lady M., a daughter of Anthony Devas whose painting I have always admired, very bright and sympathetic. Henry Thorold[†] also present, and Leslie's literary agent and wife. Leslie a dear old pussy cat. He has become rather deaf, but is as voluble as ever and an excellent host. Called us all 'dear', irrespective of age or sex. Afterwards he took us round the College. The Codrington Library has perfect proportions, though the ceiling is not as Hawksmoor intended and could do with some gilding. Unsuitable marble-topped table just given by Simon Codrington[‡] which might have belonged to Beckford. Chapel screen fine, early Georgian but Leslie says not by Hawksmoor. He showed us a pair of fine fifteenth-century statues taken down from the towers and put in the crypt for preservation, of Sainted Henry VI and Archbishop Chichele, founder of All Souls. Is it possible that they were done from life? That of the King is very tragic, lean and worn and devout; one senses the hair shirt under the emaciated figure; the crown is broken, whether by accident or design. The Buttery by Hawksmoor splendidly Baroque, small oval tables and kidney-shaped benches to fit. Before we left, Leslie said to A., 'Jim writes for me, and I write for him.'

Friday, 17th July

When I rang up Sam Vestey[§] to ask if I might have a look at the old front of Stowell Park [near Cirencester, Gloucestershire] on Sunday, he said he would be delighted but feared he *might* be going to New

---

* Emma Devas (b. 1936); m. 1955 John, 11th Baron Monson (b. 1932).
† Revd Henry Thorold of Marson Hall, Lincolnshire (1921–2000); clergyman, schoolmaster and architectural historian; author of Shell county guides, and books on cathedrals.
‡ Sir Simon Codrington, 3rd Bt (b. 1923), formerly of Dodington Park near Bath (see *Holy Dread*, 1 November 1982).
§ Samuel Vestey, 3rd Baron (b. 1941); m. (2nd) 1981 Celia Knight.

Zealand 'this evening'. A. and I agreed that it would take us three months at least to make up our minds and another three to prepare to go to New Zealand.

Sunday, 19th July

We walked around Stowell Park. Not a soul in sight, though I rang the doorbell to announce our presence. It is a richly, well kept-up establishment, on a splendid site, but ugly. The central garden front and a return wing might be of the same date as Compton Castle, but have been much altered. An ugly hotch-potch on the whole.

We lunched with Richard and Linda Robinson at Audrey's old Windrush Mill. They have repaired it well and made it into a proper little residence. She is a bright little thing; Richard improved in looks, filled out and more mature, though with the skin of a teenager despite his thirty years. They adore the Mill which is very picturesque.

After dining last night with the Beauforts at the House, we were taken upstairs to see Mary's bedroom. Rather 'how', with bedside photographs of her plain soldier brother killed in the Great War, and other mementoes untouched. David and Caroline quite without sentiment in deciding what things to remove and what to throw away. Charming watercolours in matching rope frames of Lord Arthur (Podge) and Lord Henry [Somerset], both rather plain-featured, which Caroline decided to hang in her bedroom. I wonder how much Mary knew about the two delinquent males.*

Sunday, 26th July

Selina [Hastings] left today. I enjoy having her to stay immensely. She is as clever as a monkey. Very amusing about her visit to Mrs Thatcher's elder sister, married to a rich farmer in East Anglia and

---

* Lord Henry Somerset (1849–1932; Comptroller of Royal Household, 1874–9; m. 1872 Lady Isabelle Somers) and Lord Arthur Somerset (1851–1926; sometime Equerry and Superintendent of Stables to Prince of Wales) – younger sons of 8th Duke of Beaufort – were both obliged to live abroad for most of their lives owing to homosexual scandals. Lord Arthur fled in 1889 after the police raided a male brothel of which he was a client in Cleveland Street, Marylebone; he was helped to avoid arrest through the influence of his friend Regy Brett, future 2nd Viscount Esher. Lord Henry, who settled in Florence where he achieved some distinction as a poet, was great-grandfather of the L.-Ms' friend and landlord David, 11th Duke.

bored stiff by Margaret and all the fuss about her. When the Thatchers last stayed the sister was wildly irritated by all the security men, and said she would never go through *that* again. Selina has not begun her Evelyn Waugh biography yet, although paid a huge advance over a year ago. A. N. Wilson* told her that the golden rules in writing a biography were to choose a subject about which there are already many books, thus saving research, and always to contradict the view of the last biographer. This, says Selina, means that she will have to portray Waugh as a sweet, gentle person, polite to everyone, and a rotten writer.

We dined on Saturday with Rupert Loewenstein, Josephine being in London. The Loewensteins have sold Biddestone and bought Petersham Lodge, Richmond. I said how much we would miss them. He said he would miss us and was miserable about leaving, but Jo was frightened and bored alone in the country. I am not surprised, but lament their departure. At dinner we discussed whether Nigel [Nicolson] had been right to publish *Portrait of a Marriage* when he did.† Selina saw no harm, seeing that both his parents were dead and his mother had been so for a decade. Rupert objected to the impiety of dishonouring one's father and mother, and opined to me, when we were alone, that the arguments reflected the difference between the Christian and the pagan point of view.

On Sunday we lunched with the Duff Hart-Davises in their farm-house at Owlpen. Excellent and enjoyable meal. She is charming and clever, and he a dear man. Their tall and good-looking son, quite unlike Duff but rather like the Augustus John drawing of Rupert, is off to Tokyo to teach English.

Thursday, 30th July

Walking with Folly in Vicarage Fields I notice how the oak trees' bark is a greeny yellow, not only on the west side facing the usual wind and rain, but all the way round. Folly adores this walk because she can run and chase imaginary foxes and hares, the former not always imaginary.

---

* Writer and journalist (b. 1950); literary editor *Spectator*, 1981–4, *Evening Standard*, 1990–7.
† Nigel Nicolson's controversial book, dealing candidly with his parents' homosexuality, first appeared in 1973, eleven years after the death of his mother and five after that of his father.

She never catches them. When I got back to the house, A. was at the gate. Look at the new moon, she said. I took off my glasses and lo, saw at least ten moons. This means not dual but decimal vision. Which reminds me that I have heard from Pat [Trevor-Roper], whom I deserted for his pupil Tom Casey, and fear from the curtness and brevity of his letter that he may be hurt.

This morning, a large party of the Attingham summer school* came to see the library, led by Geoffrey Beard.† They were polite and charming. I gave them a short talk, and they looked, admired and asked questions. One woman, American I think, looked as if she was about to make a speech. Instead she read out a paragraph from one of my books, to the effect that architectural descriptions are tedious unless they introduce a human element.

Sunday, 2nd August

Giana Blakiston‡ has just left us. She is a darling, no fuss at all, gentle, clever, right-minded, a mixture of Anne [Hill] and Billa [Harrod] without the latter's moods. Is now eighty-four and suffers from arthritis and leg trouble. Told me that her marriage to Noël was perfection. They never had a difference. She gallantly motored here from London and has now gone to stay with Noël's brother in Hampshire.

Last night we had the John Griggs to dine. They are staying at Tormarton because Joan Altrincham is very ill. Sudden collapse apparently. She will be ninety in September, if she lives. A great evening of fun and good talk, John very appreciative and humorous. He hasn't finished Lloyd George yet by a long chalk.

I telephoned Alice Witts for information about Wyck Hill [near Stow-on-the-Wold, Gloucestershire], where she lived with her parents from 1921 to 1931 and which I am to write about for the *Architectural Digest*. My memory is of a dull, ugly house, but she loved it. Remembers my father bringing Dick and me to dinner there the night before her wedding, and says she thought us the handsomest boys she had ever seen. I can't believe anyone else would have thought that.

---

* See notes to 2 July 1987.
† Writer on the English country house, and expert on plasterwork; Assistant Director (later Director) of Attingham Summer School.
‡ Rachel Georgiana Russell (1903–95); m. 1929 Noël Blakiston (1905–84), scholar, short-story writer and sometime Assistant Keeper of Public Records.

Monday, 3rd August

A. and I went to Wyck Hill House. It is ghastly. Architectually of no interest, save one thin Adamish drawing room with niched door on the curve. Now a frightfully expensive hotel catering for the wrong American rich. Derry advises me to chuck the article and he will tell editor of the *Digest* not to ask me to write about such trash.

Wednesday, 5th August

To London for the day, primarily to see exhibition at Colnaghi's of Georgian Group garden temples and follies, organised by Roger White.* Well worth while. Several drawings of Badminton Park features by Kent and Wright, and a good catalogue. M. lunched with me at Brooks's, bringing a copy of *Spycatcher*† as a present. Sweet of him, though I don't know how much I want to read it. He is off to Sweden. Returned by four o'clock train. Dined with Elspeth [Huxley] where I had hoped to see Bridget Grant, but Elspeth had mixed up the dates. Disappointing, for it would have interested me to talk of old times at Pixton. Bridget's sister Gabriel is apparently quite dotty.‡ Alone, Elspeth is relaxed and full of information and good cheer.

In the London Library this afternoon, as I waited my turn, a distinguished woman beside me was signing for at least ten books. 'Do you think anyone could help me carry them to my car outside?' she asked the assistant. 'I will, Elizabeth,' I interjected, for it was Elizabeth Longford.§ When she recognised me she threw her arms around me

---

* Architectural historian (b. 1950); Secretary of Georgian Group from 1984.

† Mrs Thatcher's Government had obtained an injunction preventing the UK publication of this book of memoirs by Peter Wright, a former MI5 officer, in which he described the methods of his service and alleged that it had tried to 'destabilise' Harold Wilson as Prime Minister. The book had however been published in America, and 'smuggled' copies were much sought-after in London.

‡ Gabriel (1911–87; m. 1943 Major Alexander Dru) and Bridget (b. 1914; m. 1935 Captain 'Eddie' Grant) were the elder daughters of Hon. Aubrey Herbert (1880–1923; see entry for 22 June 1985) and his wife Mary *née* Vesey, of Pixton Park, Somerset. J.L.-M. often visited this Catholic household in the mid 1930s, and was at one time somewhat in love with Gabriel (see entry for 21 November 1987).

§ Elizabeth Harman (1906–2002); writer; m. 1931 Hon. Frank Pakenham (later 7th Earl of Longford); romantic friend of J.L.-M. at Oxford (*c.* 1930), where she was known as 'the aesthete's moll'.

and we embraced. I see in her handsome old face not a trace of the somewhat perky, too bright, but lovable Elizabeth Harman I knew so well at Oxford.

Thursday, 6th August

My beastly [seventy-ninth] birthday. Several cards from unknown fans, all of which must be answered. Audrey lunched alone with me in Bath. Desultory talk of old times. Sweet she was, yet I could not get going. When she left me a gift of two expensive ties, I felt remorseful, and sent her an affectionate note. As she says, we are the only ones left who can remember Wickhamford and Ribbesford days.

A. organised a little dinner party for me, with the Beauforts and the Moores. Excellent dinner of quails, over which she took much trouble, and enjoyable gossip. But oh, the sadness of everything. And now Joanie Altrincham dying.

Wednesday, 12th August

On the eve of A's birthday I motor her to Heathrow, where before parting we quickly and fondly embrace. I watch her grey head bob among the crowd and disappear, and wonder if I shall ever see her again. Folly and I return home, Folly a little mystified.

Thursday, 13th August

To my amazement, A. telephones just after dinner. So we have spoken on her birthday at least. It is two o'clock with her. She says the Loewensteins' house is very pretty and comfortable but the sun is not shining in California.

Friday, 14th August

Mr and Mrs Rota turn up in Bath at eleven and stay till five looking through my papers, letters and diaries. I tremble at some of the things he may have read, but he can't have spent much time looking at anything in particular. A charming man with exquisite manners, who reminded me of Eddy Sackville before he grew a beard. Mrs Rota also charming, and read her book quietly in the library until her husband summoned her to the back room, where the papers were laid out, to take notes from his dictation.

I left them to attend Joanie Altrincham's funeral at Tormarton. Beautiful little church with truncated tower. Much to my surprise, it was packed, her relations having come in droves from London and elsewhere to say farewell to this recluse of almost ninety. Dear June [Hutchinson] came and sat beside me. As we embraced, our spectacles clashed; as I now wear mine almost permanently, I forget to remove them at such moments. We sang 'All Things Bright and Beautiful' – which makes me want to cry, as A. has decided to have this hymn at her funeral, and I already imagine myself in the role of chief mourner. Was fascinated by seventeenth-century monument opposite me commemorating in verse the virtues of the agent to the Marquess of Somebody. It was horrid outside, standing at the committal. I did not like the yellow coffin with its fancy brass cross at the foot end. Church path lined with wreaths. I caught a glimpse of ours as I left – gypsophila and white daisies.

Joanie was a stalwart woman. She grumbled too much (like me), but was very intelligent. Very direct, with high standards and principles. Not beautiful like her mother Lady Islington,[*] whom I think she rather resented, always refusing to go to concerts at Dyrham which Lady I. had once rented. The *Times* obituary, probably by John himself, was excellent on her work in the Great War, in which she served as a nurse by pretending to be older than she really was. She was not a happy woman and did not get on well with her sons.

When I got back to Bath, the Rotas had finished. He seemed to think my papers worth preserving, and said he would write and make me a proposition. I said I would like them to be kept together, for they form a sort of picture of my life.[†]

Saturday, 15th August

Today I lunched at Nether Lypiatt. In rather in a fuss lest I be late. The secretary telephoned yesterday to inform me that luncheon was to be promptly at one and I must be there at 12.30. I asked her, did 12.30 really mean 12.30 with the Princess? Answer yes, tempered by advice to be five minutes late. So armed with map of how to find this elusive

---

[*] Anne Dundas; m. 1896 Sir John Dickson-Poynder, 6th Bt (1866–1936), MP (C) for Chippenham 1892–1910, Governor of New Zealand 1910–12, cr. Baron Islington 1910 (title becoming extinct on his death).
[†] They eventually found an excellent home in the Beinecke Library at Yale.

house I arrived at 12.40. Entrance is now by north door. Escorted through house to bathing pool where crowd of children in the water. Table with drinks on the edge. Effusive greeting from Princess Marie-Christine. Prince Michael very friendly and less shy, a dear, sensitive, courteous and very stupid little man. He started mixing Pimm's and got in a fix. She soon settled things, with much advice. 'Now darling, you must first give it a stir, and then darling, when you pour you must not let the fruit splosh into the glass.'

A heavenly warm day, blue sky with a ruffle of wind. We did not sit down to eat until 1.45. All this time I stood talking to him, first about Cotswold houses and the problems of living in one, then about Mary Beaufort. The last time he saw her, lunching at Badminton, she took him for a foreign grand duke. Said his favourite relation had been Princess Alice of Athlone,* whose memory was clear to the end, and who vividly recalled Queen Victoria's *Golden* Jubilee. His nephew George St Andrews† and fiancée staying. A very nice young man, not the yob or buffoon one is led to suppose by the newspapers. Wears a fuzzy ginger beard, a pity. Intelligent and interested in current affairs. Talked of *Spycatcher*. Little fiancée *née* Apponyi, Canadian by nationality, Hungarian on father's side, Italian on mother's. A clever and well-informed girl. Princess M. appears to be very fond of them both.

We ate under a large umbrella over a long table out-of-doors on the east front. I was placed at one end opposite the Prince and on her right, with the fiancée on my right. Hostess kept jumping up a lot which interrupted conversation. Food not good – two very dry cutlets (no wonder at 2 p.m.) and a huge common sausage covered in hickory sauce. Butler a handsome young man of about twenty-three. I thought of Igor and wondered if he could do this job.

The truth is one cannot dislike the Princess. She is extremely friendly, anxious to please, does please, and makes one feel interesting. Also she enjoys conversation and has a poor opinion of the

---

* HRH Princess Alice (1883–1981); o. dau. of HRH Prince Leopold, Duke of Albany, youngest child of Queen Victoria; m. 1904 Prince Alexander of Teck (1874–1957), bro. of Queen Mary, cr. Earl of Athlone, 1917 (Governor-General of South Africa, 1923–31, of Canada, 1940–6); a much-loved figure during her widowhood, as Queen Victoria's last surviving grandchild.
† George Windsor, Earl of St Andrews (b. 1962), e.s. and heir of HRH Prince Edward, Duke of Kent. In 1988 he gave up his rights of succession to the throne to marry a Roman Catholic, Sylvana Tomaselli.

English, calling them the stupidest nation in Europe. She particularly dislikes their false modesty, which she finds hypocritical. They must always deprecate themselves. At that moment, one of the guests, Ian Bond, asked me across the table, 'Which of your books do you think the best?' I at once replied, 'They are all pretty bad.' 'There you go!' said HRH. 'What did I tell you?' She is aggrieved over the reception of her book[*] here. Said she had frankly confessed in her preface that she had done no original research and derived her opinions from other learned historians whose names she quoted. Neither Weidenfeld's nor Elizabeth Longford who read her text noticed the so-called plagiarisms. 'Anyway,' she said, rubbing her hands, 'all the beastliness has given me much publicity and I have sold 60,000 copies so far, with American sales still to come.' I congratulated her heartily, telling her that no book of mine had sold 6,000. She makes it very clear by innuendo that she dislikes the Royal Family. She mentioned her father in passing, saying that 'he was a sweet man in spite of all *they* say about him'.

Mrs Thatcher lunched here last week. I asked the Princess if she appreciated this gem of a house. Princess thought she did, but without knowing how to express her feelings. Before she came, Princess told her children the Prime Minister was coming, explaining that she was 'the headmistress of the country'. They said they thought 'Cousin Lilibet' was that, but the Princess added, 'No, the Queen is the mother of the country. She sends you to school, but it is the headmistress who makes the rules you have to obey.' Not a bad explanation.

We talked of Barbara Cartland,[†] her great friend. I said I used to meet her when I was about eighteen as I knew her younger brother Ronnie Cartland[‡] when they lived near Tewkesbury. 'Oh,' she said, 'then you must lunch with me in London on Monday. She is coming, along with Queen Geraldine[§] of Albania who is a Windischgrätz cousin of mine, etc.' Perhaps foolishly, I demurred. As we rose from the table at 3.45 for a walk round the garden, she begged me to think it over. I forgot all about it, and suppose she did too. I forgot to bow to her when we said goodbye, though I did bow deeply to him after

---

[*] *Crowned in a Far Country: Portraits of 8 Royal Brides* (Weidenfeld & Nicolson, 1986).
[†] Authoress of more than 550 novels (1901–2000); m. 1st 1927 Alexander McCorquodale (diss. 1932), 2nd 1936 his cousin Hugh McCorquodale.
[‡] A Conservative MP for Birmingham, 1935–40 (1907–40); killed in action.
[§] Countess Geraldine Apponyi (1915–2002); m. 1938 King Zog of Albania (1895–1961).

he had very courteously insisted on accompanying me to my car. Now I wonder if I should have accepted her invitation. She offered to motor me to London, saying she was a safer driver than her husband. I said that of course I would far rather accompany her than the Prince!

It is rather snobbish of me to write at such length about two people who are not out of the ordinary, but then I *am* a snob in that I am interested by people in the public eye. But though interested I don't want to be with them much. I have no wish to be taken up by royalty or move in royal circles.

Sunday, 16th August

Lunched with the Henry Robinsons at Moorwood. A sweet, happy couple, fortunate in everything they have – money, land, his farming, her decorating when it suits her, a plump and healthy little boy. She is due to have another baby next March, and they have decided to move back to the big house in 1989.

Monday, 17th August

Kind friends telephone without cease to invite me to meals. I always try to get out of luncheons, and in the evenings too would prefer to be left alone with my wireless and a book. Today I dined with Daphne [Fielding], a marvellous dinner of smoked salmon, mess of potage and sorbet. We talked of old friends and how few remain. I am absolutely at ease with her, but don't want to see much of her.

Tuesday, 18th August

Dined with Alex [Moulton] at Bradford. Dinner so disgusting that I could not finish my dry old chicken and rock-hard carrots. Alex hasn't a clue about food, the meal being prepared by a woman and left. He kept jumping up like a jack-in-the-box, washing up between mouthfuls. Much pontificating which bores me. But he always wants to get to the bottom of things, which is good. Wants to find out precisely what the heads and emblems on his plaster ceilings represent and signify. I told him to go to the library of the RIBA, which he doubtless will. Was glad to get home.

Wednesday, 19th August

Good news – the fourth of the septuplets has died. Horrid little atrocities, each weighing under 2 lbs at birth.

Thursday, 20th August

This afternoon Alexandra Allerhand,[*] who is writing about Kathleen Kennet,[†] came to tea in Bath. A nice girl who is the great-niece of K., her grandfather a brother. I liked her honest, clean, simple face. Wayland[‡] has commissioned her to write this book, her first. She is bringing up two children as a single parent. Says she has always been poor, her mother left a widow with many children until she married Paul Paget,[§] whom they all adored. Although she is (as she put it) of aristocratic descent, her sympathies are with unsophisticated people. Told me that Wayland's life has not been the predicted success. She found my letters from K. fascinating, and borrowed them to make photostats, for which I offered to pay. She has not yet met Peter Scott.[¶] Says the diaries K. kept from 1910 until her death are wonderful, well written in direct, no-nonsense way, full of keen observations and sharp pen sketches of famous people met.[**]

I dined at Tormarton with the Griggs. Very enjoyable, though the house is filthy. The Ludovic Kennedys[††] there. She greeted me with

---

[*] Alexandra Anderson (b. 1953); m. 1st 1972–89 Michael Allerhand, 2nd 1993 Gray Walker.
[†] Kathleen Bruce (1878–1947); sculptor; m. 1st 1908 Captain Robert Scott 'of the Antarctic' (d. 1912); 2nd Edward Hilton Young (1879–1960), Liberal politician, cr. Baron Kennet, 1935. In the 1930s, J.L.-M. became a protégé of this talented, tempestuous and often alarmingly direct woman, who liked young men; he wrote her obituary for *The Times*, and an essay on her in *Fourteen Friends*.
[‡] Wayland Hilton Young, 2nd Baron Kennet (b. 1923); o.c. of Kathleen by her 2nd marriage.
[§] Architect (1901–85), specialising in restoration of churches and ecclesiastical properties; m. 1971 as her 2nd husband Verily *née* Bruce (whose 1st husband Clive Anderson had d. 1957).
[¶] Sir Peter Scott (1909–89; kt 1973, CH 1987); o.c. of Kathleen by her 1st marriage to Scott of the Antarctic; sportsman, artist, naval officer, naturalist and writer; Chairman of World Wildlife Fund from 1961; m. 1st 1942–51 Elizabeth Jane Howard (J.L.-M., who never greatly liked him, acting as usher at the wedding), 2nd 1951 Philippa Talbot-Ponsonby. See entry for 12 December 1987.
[**] Alexandra's biography does not seem to have been written: six years later, J.L.-M. was visited by her cousin, Hon. Louisa Young, who had taken over the task.
[††] Ludovic Kennedy (b. 1919; kt 1994); broadcaster, politician and humanitarian campaigner; m. 1950 Moira Shearer, ballerina.

open arms, being the Moira Shearer we entertained at Roquebrune. My memory is of a pretty, red-headed, diffident, almost prim girl. Today she is extremely beautiful, full of self-confidence and affectation, not unlike Diana Menuhin.* Ludovic full of chat and charming to females, though much aged, and lame. Good conversation – about honours and their absurdity, Freddy Ashton† getting his CH and OM by making up to the Queen Mother whereas A.J.P. Taylor‡ has nothing, though would like to be a baronet just to annoy his son.

Saturday, 22nd August

I am a prey to bores. Lunched with Nancy Schuster, a dear old thing who was kind to us when she lived at 20 Lansdown Cresent. I joined her at 12.30 and did not get back until well after three, a great inroad into my working hours. Her grand flat in Great Pulteney Street resembles herself, conventional and boring. She talks about absolutely nothing. Yet she gave me a delicious luncheon, smoked trout, well-cooked meat, ice cream drenched in honey. When I got in the telephone was ringing and I had to speak to Audrey for twenty minutes, again about nothing. Folly and I dined with Desmond Briggs and Ian [Dixon]. Again smoked trout, followed by shepherd's pie and fruit salad. Desultory talk, neither highbrow nor lowbrow. Ian keeps interrupting Desmond, but is a jolly, warm-hearted creature. Now, Folly never bores me – speaks only when spoken to and then has only love to impart.

Despite these interruptions, I managed to type out the Introduction to my Cotswold book, which is now finished, in so far as a book ever is. I have enjoyed doing it and finished it in just five months, all thanks to my wonderful David Burnett. I have written a lyrical paragraph in his praise, which Alvilde will regard as too effusive.

Monday, 24th August

Last night dined at the House. David was away, and I assumed Caroline would be alone with Daphne. Not a bit of it, an enormous party of

---

* Diana Gould (1912–2003), ballerina (1930s friend of J.L.-M.); m. 1947 Yehudi Menuhin.
† Sir Frederick Ashton (1906–88); choreographer; Director of Royal Ballet until 1970.
‡ Historian (1906–90).

the young, with wives, concubines and friends. We ate in the large dining room at a table laid for at least twenty-five. I sat between two sisters, daughters of Lord Londonderry, who were idiotic in an unpretentious way which makes for ease. Cosima on my left told me that her ex-father-in-law Jeremy [Fry] once confessed to her that he had no heart at all. I said I had known that since first setting eyes on him. She thought Tony Snowdon the same. Sophia* on my right, who had on her other side the man she hopes to marry, said her generation were much more faithful than mine because they lived together before marrying. Anne Somerset† arrived in a tight mini-skirt, with a striped top of peach and green showing bare shoulders and bosom. It was not a warm evening and she must have frozen. I left early.

Today I motored to lunch with Tony Scotland‡ and Julian Berkeley§ between Newbury and Basingstoke, running into a huge traffic jam near Hungerford, I can only suppose because of morbid desire of the populus to gloat over scene of last Wednesday's massacre.¶ What a contrast to last night! At this funny little white cottage were gathered six male couples, counting Tony and Julian, I the odd man out. All very discreet, no mention of relationships which were explained to me by Tony aside. One a Chinaman. All conventionally dressed in suits, and well-off I gathered from the makes of their cars and their descriptions of their weekend cottages. We ate out-of-doors. So intelligent they were, easy and interesting. Talk of art, architecture and crime (the last prompted by Hungerford). Much hilarity and laughter. I enjoyed their company far more than the Badminton party, though it was odd to see quite so many men, wondering who belonged to whom. Perhaps the Aids threat has contributed to the fidelity of which Sophia spoke last night.

While walking Folly this morning, I ran into Don** who told me

---

* Lady Sophia Vane-Tempest-Stewart (b. 1959); dau. of 9th Marquess of Londonderry; m. 1987 John Pilkington.

† Lady Anne Somerset (b. 1955), o.d. of 11th Duke of Beaufort; m. 1988 Matthew Carr.

‡ Writer, broadcaster and journalist; on staff of BBC Radio, 1970–91 (b. 1945).

§ 2nd son of Sir Lennox Berkeley and Freda née Bernstein; musician, founder of Berkleyguard Automatic Security Systems, and defender (like his father) of the traditional liturgy of the Catholic Church (b. 1950).

¶ On Wednesday 19 August 1987, Michael Ryan, aged 27, had indiscriminately shot to death sixteen people and wounded fourteen more in the streets of Hungerford, Berkshire, finally killing himself when cornered by the police.

** Don Lane, the Beauforts' chauffeur at Badminton; his son Boris.

that Boris is beside himself because his precious motor-bike was stolen while he was at work in Bristol last Friday, and he wanted to talk to me about it. I regretted that I was going off for the day. Nevertheless Boris called this evening while I was cooking my supper, and though tired out I hadn't the heart not to ask him in. He told me that he 'worshipped' his bike, that if he ever met the thief he would murder him. Seemed so upset that I thought he would break down. I was able to sympathise with him, for I had similar feelings towards the motor-scooter Uncle Milne* gave me when I was sixteen. A substitute for a girl, I suppose. He told me he sometimes got 120 mph out of her on a deserted stretch of motorway, though the force of the wind could be frightening.

Tuesday, 25th August

Had to make a tiresome visit to London so Tom Casey could make a scan of my left eye to determine exact size of coming implant. A glorious morning when I went up at 8.30, but pouring when I arrived in London. After I had waited an hour for my scan, the business took barely twenty minutes. Mercifully got a taxi to London Library. For lack of anything better to do, I checked *Who's Who* and other works for Alfred Beit's *Independent* obituary. Then another taxi to the Savile, where I lunched with M., not too bad. I wish he would dress less scruffily and do up his top shirt button. Just like Nick, the two young I am most fond of. By tube from Bond Street to Paddington, feeling giddy as I struggled to the escalator against rushing hordes of people. I often feel like this in London, rarely in the country.

Wednesday, 26th August

Pack up Cotswold typescript, and post it. So that is out of the way for a bit. Miriam† motored her mother Eliza [Wansbrough] over to Badminton for tea. E. cheerful but could hear little in the kitchen. Miriam charming, and most handsome. Very sweet to her mother. Having disposed of her five children, she now devotes herself to her teaching at Oxford.

---

* Alec Milne Lees-Milne (1878–1931).
† Only dau. (b. 1932) of Elizabeth Wansbrough.

Thursday, 27th August

Had to rush to meet Alvilde's plane at Heathrow. Find driving at
90 mph a strain, owing to eyes. Arrive in time. Hear myself being
paged; then hear A's voice and see her sitting in a wheelchair attended
by two men, one carrying luggage. This gives me a shock. Then I see
she looks well. As soon as we reach the car she leaps to her feet, opens
car door and picks up her luggage which she deposits on back seat.
On advice of her friends in America, she pleaded incapacity to secure
a comfortable journey.

Friday, 28th August

Rupert [Hart-Davis]'s eightieth birthday. I wrote him an affectionate
letter, reminding him that he is my oldest surviving friend from Eton.

Saturday, 29th August

Birthdays thick and fast. Today we dined at the House for Caroline's.
She in high spirits, throwing her arms about, not listening to a word
I said to her at dinner. David told us that a group of squatters had
arrived in two charabancs at Swangrove. Mervyn [the gamekeeper]
was indignant and persuaded D. to confront them. They were polite
but filthy. He told them that visitors were always welcome to walk
in Swangrove but he could not allow them to camp there. If he did,
there would be no end to the numbers who might follow them.
They must go within three days. But they pleaded to remain until
Friday when they got their dole money, and he allowed this. Later,
while out riding, he stopped to see them. The grove was littered
with washing and chaos. One matriarchal woman seemed educated.
They gave him tea from a dirty mug which he did not like to wipe
in front of them. Meanwhile Mervyn tells them menacingly that if
they don't bloody well clear out they will be thrown out by the
police. Mervyn's language is colourful. When asked how he is, he
replies, 'Bugger you, I be well enough, Sir.' Which reminds me that
Haines our chauffeur used sometimes to address Dick or myself as
'you bugger you'.

Am listening to Thomas Bateman's Jacobean madrigals on Radio
Three. Of all music madrigals bore me most. I think I hate all music
written before 1680 and after 1940.

Sunday, 30th August

And today I lunched with Alice Witts at Upper Slaughter for her eighty-fifth birthday. Took her a present of a box of soap which I forgot to give her and returned with. All four surviving sisters present. The most arresting in looks is Beatrice, exactly my age, but hard to talk to because of her shyness. Edith the most appealing, intelligent and human. She is a painter but I have never seen her pictures. She said to me, 'We are the lucky ones. I go on painting, and you go on writing.' I replied that she could go on painting as long as she could hold a brush, like Titian, while a writer depended on his sanity remaining. They talked of their affection for Wyck House and I didn't like to tell them how caustic I had been about that ghastly building in my *Digest* article. They reminded me that their neighbours at Springhill, the Knoxes, had eight children, only one of which was a son. Like the Mitfords of Swinbook and Wrigleys of Wyck. Tom Mitford and Arthur Wrigley were killed in the War, and Holly Knox also died early of I don't know what – all three boys as good as gold.

Wednesday, 2nd September

To London in the morning, changing at Paddington for Ealing Broadway. From there by taxi to Old Court Hospital, Montpelier Road. Cosy Victorian suburb where the birds sing. A sort of cottage hospital, half-timber plus modernismus. Given a room overlooking garden, enormous sycamore tree visible from bed. Meet the nurse who is to sit with me throughout the first night, a dear woman from the Isle of Skye, costing me £70. A big beaming sister introduces herself. Then the anaesthetist, a genial man, who examines me and asks the usual questions. Then the accountant, a stout, genteel lady, to whom I give a cheque for £1,000. I am weighed and found to be less than the 12 stone which has been my constant weight for many years. Strange, as my belly is much larger; but I suppose my chest and limbs are wasting. Various orderlies come, one to take my valuables to put in hospital safe, another bearing a cup of tea (I am allowed to eat nothing, and am ravenous), a third to attach a bracelet to my wrist identifying me as belonging (like a dog) to Mr Casey. Finally a Filipina nurse gives me a jab in the bottom, and an enormous black man with a shining smile deftly lifts me onto a hearse and wheels me down corridors to operating theatre. I am still conscious, and greet my anaesthetist rather cheekily

with, 'Mr Deacon, I presume?' That is the last I remember. I pass comfortably into total blackness, no dreams, no flicker of the subconscious,
no sense of the world beyond. I wake in my room at 3 a.m. with the
dear lady from Skye bathing and soothing my head.

Forty-eight hours later Mr Casey rips off the bandages. When I
am first able to see with my new eye, which I keep open for only a
few seconds, everything is vivid and looks blue like those photographs of the earth from the moon. Mr C. explains how the implant
operation came about, when an American soldier got a piece of glass
inside his eye and found to his surprise that he saw better than before.
He says his profession owes much to Clementine Churchill who left
her eyes for ophthalmic research, an example which has been followed by millions.

Each morning I wake from a nightmare. In one of them, I am sightseeing in some foreign capital with John Betjeman and Feeble, Nancy
[Mitford] also being with us. We are all staying at the Embassy, which
is about to give a grand banquet to some potentate. I cannot find my
evening clothes. Time is running out. There is Nancy dressed in the
smartest conceivable dress by Lanvin and covered with jewels, saying
gaily, 'I'm going downstairs now.' There am I still in my dressing-
gown, searching desperately.

Eardley, M. and J.K.-B. all came to see me. So kind of them to slog
all this way. E. talked about the success of his latest exhibition at the
Parkin Gallery; J. about his Paxton book, half-way through; while M.
read me a chapter of his forthcoming book,* based on bitter letters
written by Duke of Windsor to his Duchess while he was attending
Queen Mary's deathbed in London.

Thursday, 10th September

Back home now, being nursed adorably by A. My new eye will, I feel
sure, be a success. Already it sees colours more vividly than the other
eye. Yesterday I worked all day, correcting my novel before submitting
it to Collins. Foolish of me to make yet another attempt after some
ten rejections. And David Burnett came to show me the edited typescript of *Cotswold Houses*. He is an excellent editor, and all his proposed changes are improvements.

---

* *The Secret File of the Duke of Windsor* (Bantam Press, 1988).

E. told me that his millionaire friend Christopher Selmes,* who has Aids, is planning to give a huge expensive party at Lyegrove† for all his friends, following which he intends to commit suicide.

Sunday, 13th September

Went to the tedious annual meeting of the local branch of CPRE in the hall at the House. Gerald Harford‡ in the chair, did it well apart from too many 'ums'. I sat at the back so I might escape, which I did after ninety minutes. A nice young man from the National Parks Commission gave a talk, but I could hardly hear him. Deaf and blind, what is the use of my attending such occasions? He wore a signet ring on his middle finger, usually a sign of bedintness among men. Looking at the audience, I noticed as usual that they were all of the middle class; none from the lower, and needless to say not one of the Somerset family. One may deride the middle classes, but it is they who really care about country things. Having looked through Simon Blow's book on hunting, I think I hate the upper classes. Their arrogance, their unquestioning superiority is, or until recently was, insufferable.

Thursday, 17th September

A nice young solicitor came yesterday morning to see A. and me about the woman we are trying to evict from our basement flat in Bath. Only last Monday, just after the expiry of the notice period, did we finally get a reply from her solicitors, merely to announce that she had no intention of quitting. Our young man says she will produce as much dirt against us as she can find, and says we should do the same with her. I am accumulating it eagerly.

Wednesday, 23rd September

Went to see poor Rosamond, upstairs in bed. She lies there all day, listening to the wireless until she is sick of it, then to her recorded books

---

* City entrepreneur (1946–88); in 1975, then aged twenty-eight, he had been accused of fraudulent practices in a Department of Trade report.

† Country house near Badminton formerly owned by J.L.-M's friend Diana, Countess of Westmorland (d. 1983).

‡ Of Little Sodbury Manor, Gloucestershire (b. 1948); m. 1985 Camilla, dau. of Alistair Horne.

until she is sick of them. No longer feels wretched, just resigned. I asked if she did not derive satisfaction from the continuing success of her books. No, she said, she was now indifferent to them and the praise they received. She feels as if they were written by someone else, someone quite different from her present self.

A. and I dined with Desmond Briggs and Ian. Also Godfrey Smith* and wife, and Simon Raven.† G. Smith a vast man, resembling old Douglas Woodruff‡ who edited the *Tablet*. White face, thick white hair, jolly countenance, as bright as a button. He said no end of brilliant and amusing things, of which I can't remember one.

Saturday, 26th September

Lunched with the Westmorlands. Jane explained the difference between shepherd's pie and cottage pie – the first containing mutton, the second beef. We ate the first today. Peter Coats was affectionate and greeted me as 'my oldest friend', literally true I suppose, as we were contemporaries at Locker's Park. So was Billy Whitaker, who Peter says is very ill with cancer. Lady Rupert Nevill there.§ I had not met her before, though we discovered many mutual friends. She is Regional Chairman of the Kent and Sussex Branch of the National Trust, but hates it because the agents are so hostile to donors. Said she would never give a property to the N.T. if she owned it.

Friday, 9th October

Got home yesterday afternoon from Munich, after a twelve-day tour of Baroque and Rococo churches and palaces with George Dix, who took infinite trouble as my chauffeur and guide. I began a diary of the tour but abandoned it, as it was becoming a catalogue of church interiors. Though enjoyable, the tour was marred for me by the condition of my eyes. I always saw things in a haze, the more decorated an interior, the more difficult to distinguish details. I fear I annoyed

---

* Journalist (b. 1926).
† Novelist (1928–2001), published by Blond & Briggs.
‡ Catholic writer and journalist (1897–1978); editor of *The Tablet*, 1936–67.
§ Lady Camilla Wallop (b. 1925), er dau. of 9th Earl of Portsmouth; m. 1944 Lord Rupert Nevill (1923–82), yr s. of 4th Marquess of Abergavenny, friend and aide of HRH The Duke of Edinburgh.

George by my inability to speak German and consequent depen-
dence on him.

George's knowledge of Austria and Bavaria is considerable.
Architects, painters, stuccoists, frescoists are at his finger-tips; so too
are the Electors of This and That, whom they married and how they
were related. George's snobbery is a necessary corollary of his great
love of history. Like Proust, he sees echoes of the great rulers of the
past in the princes of today. I have never seen anyone take so much
luggage. He brought two hats, day suits, evening suits, odd jackets, a
gold pepper-mill in case of need, a short and a long umbrella, and a
library of heavy reference books. I was glad that I had refused from
the outset to share rooms with him when I noticed his habit of spreading the contents of his six suitcases on the second bed.

Of all the churches, half of which I had seen before, that of
Weltenburg transported me most. One enters that squat little building
under the cliffs of the Danube, on the very water's edge (actually below
the bank), to be confronted by the apparition of St George on horse-
back. Nothing else is visible at first, just the silvery haze of the warrior.
Gradually other things emerge from the lightening darkness. Sad that
Weltenburg is now crowded with trippers, for one needs solitude
when encountering masterpieces, especially those of a devotional sort.

I was shocked to read in the guide books that Würzburg was almost
totally obliterated by Allied bombing on 16 March 1945. On my
return, I consulted my published diaries to see what I had written
about this. Nothing – merely frivolous gossip about Daisy Fellowes
and others. Perhaps I simply did not know of this raid at the time.

Tuesday, 13th October

On Saturday, we motored to Chatsworth in an unremitting down-
pour. The cross-country route recommended by Pam not a success.
Poor A. had to do most of the driving, owing to my eyes. Return by
motorways much easier and less exhausting. Enjoyable visit. Party
consisted of Lord and Lady Gowrie,* Jacob Rothschilds,† Tatton

---

* Alexander Hore-Ruthven, 2nd Earl of Gowrie (b. 1939); Minister for the Arts, 1983–5;
Chairman of Sotheby's, 1985–93; m. (2nd) 1974 Adelheid, Gräfin von der Schulenburg.
† Hon. N. C. J. Rothschild (b. 1936); s. father as 4th Baron Rothschild, 1990; m. 1961
Serena, er dau of Sir Philip Dunn, 2nd Bt, and Lady Mary, dau. of 5th Earl of Rosslyn
(see notes to 2 June 1986).

Sykes,* Sophie Cavendish.† Curious company for us, as all the males (including of course Andrew Devonshire) are multi-millionaires. I liked pretty Lady Gowrie, born Schulenburg. Told me her father, a friend and ally of Stauffenberg,‡ was killed by the Nazis after the failed attempt of July 1944. She was only a baby, but her family and their friends had to lie very low until the end of the war. Jacob R. very friendly, better looking than I remembered; she, Serena, daughter of Mary Erskine, has little of her mother's charm, but has inherited the looks of her grandmother, old Lady Rosslyn. Sophie still very pretty but has become highbrow in a self-conscious way, and rather embarrassed me with her intellectual jargon. Tatton, charming dilettante bachelor landowner, is beautiful, with lovely eyes.

Andrew complained to Gowrie that the present Poet Laureate§ was no good, and wanted to know who had chosen him. 'I did,' retorted Gowrie cheerfully. When asked why, he explained that it was for political reasons. He claims to be a great authority on contemporary painters and intellectuals.

I have come away with four boxes of the 6th Duke's diaries. His writing still strikes me as appalling. Before I left, I had a further word with the nice librarian Michael Pearman, who reiterated that a biography of the Bachelor Duke would never be a successful book, though it is heresy to say such a thing here where one walks daily in his footsteps. I promised I would not let him down by betraying his feelings to the Devonshires, and explained that, in my eightieth year, it mattered little to me if my book was remaindered in six months, so long as the work was interesting and I was able to do it well. I realised it was not a subject for an aspiring young biographer.

Saturday, 17th October

Anne Hill stayed with us for two nights. Unchanged mentally, but physically she has become an old woman, hobbling on two sticks. We enjoyed her visit, though she has a habit of not finishing sentences,

---

* Sir Tatton Sykes, 8th Bt (b. 1943), of Sledmere, Yorkshire.
† Yst dau. (b. 1957) of 11th Duke of Devonshire; m. 1st 1979–87 Anthony Murphy, 2nd 1988 Alastair Morrison, 3rd William Topley.
‡ Count Claus Schenk von Stauffenberg (1907–44); German staff officer responsible for the unsuccessful attempt on Hitler's life, 20 July 1944.
§ Ted Hughes (1930–98); succeeded Sir John Betjeman as Poet Laureate, 1984.

and an alarming aptitude to make jokes about the deaths and misfortunes of her friends and relations. Our betrothal has never been forgotten by her; talking of some incident which took place in the 1930s, she said 'It must have been around the time I was engaged to Jim . . .'*

The hurricane has caused damage that will not be repaired for two hundred years. Kew Gardens devastated, rare and irreplaceable trees planted by George III uprooted. M. says about 10 per cent of the trees in Hyde Park appear to be down, and the streets were deserted of traffic and people as he walked for lunch to the Savile. When he was woken at three in the morning by the appalling din, there was no electricity.

Watched Enoch Powell on television last night. A great man, too intellectual to be a successful politician. Quite unapologetic about his famous warning against coloured immigration, though he now wishes he had quoted the line from Virgil about 'the river foaming with blood' in the original Latin. He predicts civil war in the not too distant future. He has reviewed John Charmley's book on George Lloyd,† which I am currently reading. Like Powell, Lloyd was a great man who went unheeded, and a Welshman through and through. The book shows what an influence his wife Blanche was. Lloyd's fault (perhaps also Powell's) was impulse.

Sheridan and Lindy Dufferin called on us this morning before lunching at the House. Everyone says he has Aids, and makes no bones about it. I looked at him closely while talking. He certainly looks drawn, and there are some spots on the neck. Nice man, gentle and sweet. She is very different. Greets one with a gush of kissing. Her mouth is like that of her mother,‡ or Madame Cyn the Streatham brothel keeper.§

---

* The engagement was announced in May 1935 and broken off by J.L.-M. in January 1936.

† John Charmley, *Lord Lloyd and the Decline of the British Empire* (Weidenfeld & Nicolson, 1987). J.L.-M. had helped the author by introducing him to David Lloyd, son of George Lloyd and 2nd Baron (see *Holy Dread*, 29 November 1983 and 28 January 1984).

‡ Lady Isabel Manners; m. 1936 as his 2nd wife Loel Guinness, MP (C) for Bath 1931–45.

§ Cynthia Payne (b. 1932), boisterous owner of a house in Ambleside Avenue, Streatham, was charged in 1986 with running a brothel (an offence of which she had already been convicted in 1980). After a hilarious court case occupying the early weeks of 1987, she was acquitted. A film, *Personal Services*, was later made about her and her establishment; she stood for Parliament to draw attention to the absurdity of the law relating to prostitutes, and became a television personality.

Teresa and Zita [the Jungman sisters] lunched with us alone. They both talk at once and will not allow general conversation. A. and I sat back and were washed over by waves of talk. I gather they are still reading old newspapers. They visited Wilsford* the other day, for the first time in forty years.

Monday, 19th October

In Bath I found a mock-up of *Cotswold Houses* which David had sent by express mail from Southampton. Just as well I went through the illustrations, for two of them were printed back-to-front, and several captions had gone astray. No time to go through text again, for David telephoned at noon for my corrections. Much urgency, as the book is to come out a month from now.

The Bachelor's diaries are full of names of the aristocracy he dines with, enlivened by occasional tart remarks. When in Rome he is more interesting, writing about visits to the studios of the artists and sculptors who do portraits and busts of him.

While I was lunching at Hackwood, Joan Camrose drew my attention to the china off which we were eating. It was exquisite, painted with Chinese scenes. She said it was Swansea and very rare, for the Swansea works manufactured little. I said I supposed it went into the dishwashing machine, looking at the butler and footman who seemed unlikely to hand-wash. 'Never!' she said, deeply shocked. She told me that, at Knowsley, old Lady Derby† used to wash up the rarest china with her own hands. I knew this was done by ordinary ladies living in small manor houses, but was surprised to learn that patrician ladies in big houses did it too.

Thursday, 22nd October

I went to see Daphne Fielding this evening. She is wild-eyed and suffering from persecution mania. Ian Dixon called while we were talking to ask for the key of our house which A. needed to get in, and innocently remarked to D. how nice she was looking. Whereupon D., who loathes flattery, turned viciously on the poor boy and rent him. D.

---

* House near Salisbury which had belonged to the socialite The Hon. Stephen Tennant (1906–87). A sale of its contents had taken place the previous week.
† Lady Alice Montagu (1862–1957), yst dau. of 7th Duke of Manchester; m. 1889 Edward Stanley, 17th Earl of Derby (1865–1948).

told me she could trust no one, and that not only her house but her shoes were bugged. 'Look here,' she said, pointing to some loose stitches.

Friday, 23rd October

M. came down for the day from London. I wanted his advice about my papers and Rota, but the tiresome youth had little to offer and simply spent the day reading letters to me from Patrick [Kinross],[*] Harold [Nicolson], Jamesey [Pope-Hennessy], Ros, etc. I am a fool to ask for such advice. No one can give it.

Saturday, 24th October

We lunched with Nigel Nicolson who is staying at the Francis Hotel, Bath. I could see that he made A. uneasy from the fact that she asked him questions without listening to the answers. I always find him extremely companionable and full of interesting chat. He told us that his son Adam[†] is politically radical, almost on the Loony Left – though that will not stop him keeping both the Carnock title he will inherit and the fortune which is being left to him by his cousin David.[‡]

Sunday, 25th October

Billy [Henderson] and Frank [Tait] to luncheon. Billy looking better than for years, Frank rather gaunt after his operation for throat cancer. They talked of Ian McCallum who definitely has Aids, and was unable to lunch with them recently as he had been taken to St Stephen's Hospital.

Monday, 26th October

Had a struggle reviewing Girouard's country house anthology[§] for *Spectator*, and finally gave up and sent in my piece in its inadequate

[*] Patrick Balfour, 3rd Baron Kinross (1904–76); writer and journalist, on whom J.L.-M. wrote an essay in *Fourteen Friends*.

[†] Only son (b. 1957) of Nigel Nicolson; writer on walks and architecture; m. 1st 1982–92 Olivia Fane, 2nd 1993 Sarah Raven.

[‡] Nigel Nicolson was heir presumptive to the peerage of his cousin David Nicolson, 4th Baron Carnock (b. 1920).

[§] See entry for 28 January 1987.

state. I fear it is the ramblings of a lunatic, bad-tempered and contra-
dictory, and that I have simply become incapable of writing.

Wednesday, 28th October

Spectator telephoned expressing delight over my review and asking me
to do another. J.K.-B. came down from London and spent the day
reading the Bachelor Duke's diaries. He pointed out that Turner's
view of the Forum which Collins are using as the cover of their new
edition of *Roman Mornings* is in fact an evening one. I had to send him
away at five as I am frightened of driving home in the dark. It is now
clear, alas, that the new eye is not a success.

Thursday, 29th October

This morning A. heard from John Keffer,* Chairman of American
Museum, that Ian McCallum died at 4 a.m. It was double pneumonia
that killed him, brought on by Aids. He wants no funeral and no memorial of any sort. What a fearful death, the second from Aids of an intimate friend of ours. A. will be more upset than I. He was a superb
curator of the Museum, and made it what it is. I suppose he had a good
life until last year, when he began to come down with one serious illness
after another. He was probably infected by his young lover, the sinister-
looking Gerry,† who was nevertheless good to him and looked after
him. Ian was one of the handsomest young men when I met him with
John Fowler during the War. He was then a pacifist who had been in
gaol for his beliefs. I respected him for that, but always found him cold,
calculating, and filled with social ambitions which sat uneasily with his
left-wing views, hostile to authority and the police. He was a good
entertainer and loved giving parties to the élite. We were frequent guests
at Claverton where the meals were delicious, but I never much enjoyed
the company, seedy duchesses and blue-rinse American millionairesses.
He was a marvel at milking them of their money for his museum which
he adored. A pity he never trained anyone to take his place.

   Eardley, to whom I foolishly wrote that I was selling my papers, has
written back furiously to say that unless I withdraw all his letters to

---

* American engineer and lawyer (b. 1923), working in London as general counsel to oil
companies; Chairman of Trustees of American Museum from 1982.
† Gerald Theaker; manager of kitchen equipment store, Sloane Square.

me, this will be the last I receive from him. But it is too late. I am committed. I have replied that he need have no fear, as none of my papers will be seen until I am safely dead, by which time he ought to be too. And that the alternative would be to destroy them all now.

Friday, 30th October

Punctually at ten, Mr and Mrs Rota arrive with cardboard boxes. In three-quarters of an hour they have swept away all my papers, leaving dusty, empty drawers. It is a relief, like a satisfactory evacuation, yet leaves me slightly shaken and wondering. Shall I miss them? Shall I regret allowing them to be preserved in some American university library, for all to rifle through and deride? The alternative was mass destruction, which I could not bring myself to perpetrate.

Ariane has written me a letter of sympathy on the rejection of my novel by Collins. I am disappointed – it was my last throw – but not surprised.

Saturday, 31st October

Roxane the great-grandchild has been staying the week. A. has enjoyed it, while I have been bored to death. Today another child, aged five, came to tea with her. On arrival, the visiting child said, 'Is it just you? I thought I was coming to a party.' Over tea, R., aged seven, snapped at the other, 'Don't shout! You are giving me a head-ache.' Freda staying the weekend. She is desperately unhappy about Lennox, now unable to communicate in any way. She supposes he is happier at home than he would be in an institution, but the time must come when he will have to be put away.

Sunday, 1st November

Alex [Moulton] lunched and was a great success with Freda. The three of us walked to The Slates, where Alex saw the hangar door open and got into conversation with three mechanics. He talked with such interest and affability that they audibly purred. Freda whispered to one of them that he was the creator of the Moulton bicycle, at which there was much murmuring of admiration. Having inspired them with his interest and enthusiasm, he made friendly farewells and walked off with great assurance.

Having got rid of both Freda and the child, A. and I dined with the Griggs at Tormarton. They may keep on the house which would be nice for us, as our friends in the neighbourhood are thinning out. Patsy Grigg, who comes from Northern Ireland, remembers meeting M's father and uncle there when she was a girl, and being bowled over by their handsome looks.

Friday, 6th November

We dine at the House. David, just back from New York, says the latest snobbery is to boast of how many millions of dollars one has lost in the recent stock market crash.[*] All are anxious about Reagan,[†] who is now senile. After dinner, D. told me that he and Rupert Loewenstein often amuse themselves by imagining the caustic remarks I write about them in my diary.

Friday, 13th November

I have now read two of the four boxes of diaries of the Bachelor Duke. On the whole I am disappointed. He knew everyone in London and cosmopolitan society, and had hundreds of guests to stay at Chatsworth and Devonshire House, where he entertained more lavishly and exclusively than any other nobleman. Yet seldom does he give any description of these endless acquaintances and his meetings with them. I am seizing upon any straw to suggest that he is an interesting character, but so far I don't think he is one who will appeal to the readers of today, who are not interested in dukes merely because they are dukes and have left lists of encounters with their peers. He had his mistress; but what duke did and does not? That is of no interest unless scandals and domestic complications ensue, and being a bachelor he had no wife to take exception. He was highly neurotic, writes of his health on every page, was always gripped by some cold or fever, and always tired. I suspect he suffered from depression, and drank. I dare not tell Debo that I don't really think he is the material for a biography; nor do I wish to concentrate on his great works at Chatsworth and Bolton and Hardwick, about

---

[*] Amid scenes of panic, the New York Stock Market had lost almost one-quarter of its value on 19 October 1987 – 'Black Monday'.
[†] Ronald Reagan; President of USA, 1981–9.

which too much has been written already. Oh dear! Meanwhile my *Cotswold Houses* comes out next week, which will have local rather than national appeal.

I am reading Wilfred Thesiger's *The Life of my Choice*, finding it fascinating. He is two years younger than me, and was [brother] Dick's contemporary in our house at Eton, McNeile's. A curious, ascetic and admirable man, one of the last true explorers. Dislikes alcohol and tobacco. Likes hardship and goes out of his way to seek it, testing his powers of endurance. Is indifferent to architecture and even landscape, but loves savage tribesmen, and deplores western interference in their way of life. Is undoubtedly given to infatuations with handsome black boys, yet is probably chaste. Indeed his values are the old-fashioned ones of honour, decency, gentlemanly conduct, the values of the noble generation which fell in the 1914 war.

Saturday, 14th November

A Mrs Bishop,* late curator of the Holburne of Menstrie Museum, a mild little woman, came to tea to ask me about William Beckford about whom she is writing for *Bath History*. She asked several questions to which I answered, 'I must consult my notes', only to remember they were gone to Rota. This I foresee is going to be awkward in future.

Sunday, 15th November

An exasperating day of profitless entertainment. The Savorys† came for their annual luncheon visit – which means a return visit to them. Terrible boredom of parrying gush from her and polite questions from him. No sooner had they left than Ernie and Mrs Hathaway‡ appeared in the doorway, not seen for years. We asked them in to tea. They stayed interminably eating thick slices of plum cake and not

---

* Philippa Downes (b. 1929); m. 1963 Michael Bishop; Curator, 1961–5 and 1977–85, of Holburne of Menstrie Museum, Bath (founded 1882 to house art collection of Sir William Holburne of Menstrie, 5th Bt [1793–1874]). She was writing an article on 'Beckford in Bath' for the periodical *Bath History* (Vol. 2, 1988).

† John and Rachel Savory, former neighbours of L.-Ms at Alderley; in *Ancient as the Hills* (14 October 1973), J.L.-M. described her as 'the good woman of the village'.

‡ Ernest Hathaway, local builder and carpenter.

saying a word. I was so exhausted by all this that it was an effort to change and drive to Luckington, where we were to dine. But a most enjoyable evening with the Charlie Morrisons. Charlie told me that, a few days ago, Mrs Thatcher sat next to him in the House of Commons dining room and candidly confessed that she saw no solution to the Irish problem, no glimmer of light – the first time he had heard her admit defeat on any issue. Rosalind as beautiful as ever. She told me that, to her utter surprise, she had received a letter from the Madresfield Trustees offering her the house and estate on the death of Lady Beauchamp,* now aged ninety-two. She had previously understood it was all going to Lady B's Danish grandchildren. But Rosalind is, after all, the last of the Lygons, who would have succeeded to the earldom had she been a man. She and Charlie are delighted, in spite of just having completed the conversion and decoration of their present house fashioned out of three cottages, which is indeed very charming and I expect she will keep for her dowager-dom. Rosalind also told me that Robert Heber-Percy left instructions for the pigeons at Faringdon to be dyed purple and black for his funeral, which they were. The other guests the Duff Hart-Davises. A. finds him difficult, but I like him. He is uncompromising and highly intelligent. She, Phyllida, is clever too, and delightful. Dinner consisted of smoked salmon and smoked eel, the latter with a delicious strong-scented taste; then mutton, rather cold; and a pudding made of blackberries. Two kinds of white wine, and claret. I drank too much.

Monday, 16th November

Punctual to the minute as always, David Burnett arrives in Bath at ten o'clock. Having already motored to London to deliver *Cotswold Houses* to the distributors, he produces a pile of 100 copies which I sign. The book is beautifully produced, despite A's complaint of postage-stamp illustrations in margin. Extraordinary that it should be published little more than a month after my final delivery of typescript.

---

* Else 'Mona' Schiwe (1895–1989); m. 1st C. P. Doronville de la Cour of Copenhagen (d. 1924), 2nd 1936 Viscount Elmley, MP, of Madresfield Court, Malvern, Worcestershire (1903–79), who s. father 1938 as 8th and last Earl Beauchamp; her only child was a daughter by 1st marriage.

Tuesday, 17th November

London for the day, and a beastly one too. Hearing of long delays on the road to Chippenham, I set out early, but got there in no time and had to wait ages for the train, which was late owing to 'engine trouble'. To Brooks's, where I found J.K.-B. We lunched and dashed off to Winterhalter exhibition at National Portrait Gallery. A smoothness and slickness about this artist who nevertheless fascinates. Like Cecil Beaton of his day. Queen Victoria hideous with drooping lower lip and little gummy teeth; Prince Consort, even at his youngest, no cup of tea either. Had to leave for my appointment with Mrs Hammond for my eyes at three. Impossible to find a taxi, so I slogged all the way to Harley Street with my heavy bag, an effort which 'did me in', as the Bachelor Duke would say. Arrived almost an hour late. Mrs H. kindly fitted me in and tested my field of vision. Turned out lights. Produced a revolving gadget like the wing of a windmill with tiny cross in centre. I had to keep my eyes on this cross and mention when I saw a small star appear. I told her that I was not satisfied with the new eye and believed my sight was worse than before my operation three months ago.

Did find a taxi to take me to M's where he gave me tea and a madeleine. Enjoyable talk. I gave him a copy of my *Cotswold Houses*, and he gave me an expensive book on London clubs. He walked with me to Paddington, where I had to wait another half-hour for a train to come in, engine trouble again the excuse. Why the bloody hell can't they have engines that don't give trouble? Did not get to Alex Moulton for dinner until 8.30. He did not mind, as it is just heated up and there is no one to wait at table. I must say he was very sweet and solicitous about my eyes, and is getting me a special reading lamp of the most modern design.

Saturday, 21st November

Gabriel Dru has an obituary in the *Telegraph*, and quite rightly too.[*]
Of the Herberts of Pixton with whom I so often stayed, only Bridget is left. There was a time in the mid Thirties when I thought I was in love with Gabriel, and she seemed a little in love with me. She was plain, and her fingers were unkempt, but she was a dear. Had the spirit

---

[*] Written by her nephew, Auberon Waugh.

of her mother Mary, without Mary's magnificent charm. Was very gallant, and during the Spanish Civil War drove ambulances for Franco. She used to return to England full of adventure stories, which bored me rather. I should have paid attention, for she was a daredevil. In truth, I preferred her company when the rest of her family were present. She was a pious and devoted papist, as we all were then. After she married Alec Dru, some sort of professor, I hardly saw her. We faded out of each other's lives, as so often happens to great friends when one of them marries. She took to farming and was seldom off a tractor, wet or fine. Auberon,* that big, burly, ugly, clumsy idealist, was the one with the greatest charm.

And why has Jock Colville† died? He was younger than me. Extremely clever man whom I knew but slightly. The world called him a snob – but how could he be? For he was born as grand as can be, and had few intellectual equals. Why should he have bothered about stupid or common people?

Thursday, 26th November

Some interviewee on the wireless has just said that female nudes need to be painted, and male nudes sculpted. The point being that women's flesh gives rise to innumerable colours and shades, pearly white, flush pink, palest blue, even sunrise yellow, whereas men's bodies, being muscular, taut, and indeed (what women will never admit) more aesthetic and plastic, lend themselves to stone or marble rather than paint. This may be trite but I think it is true.

Collins have today sent me the first copy of *Venetian Evenings*, rather too soon on the heels of *Cotswold Houses*, and a reviewer has telephoned for a photograph of myself. I said I would not be photographed now but would send an old one if I could find it. The jacket looks pretty, but the photographs are rather muzzy, and the distressing thing is that, in my *dédicace* to Alvilde, they have spelt her name wrong, leaving out the second 'l'. Maddening. Moreover, A. is not pleased with my dedicatory remark that she is 'always in a hurry' – which exactly describes her sightseeing, and this is a sightseeing book. How one always gets into trouble. Thank goodness I changed my mind

---

* Unmarried only son of Herberts of Pixton (1922–74).
† Sir John Colville (1915–87); Private Secretary to Winston Churchill during both his wartime and post-war premierships.

about dedicating *Costwold Houses* to the Somersets. I will try to get A's page cut out, if it is not too late. Just goes to show that one should never try to be, not exactly funny in this case, but too bright I suppose, and facetious.

Friday, 27th November

At midday I installed myself in Waterstone's shop in Milsom Street at a round table piled high with *Cotswold Houses* and some of my other books, mostly paperbacks, for a signing session. A total flop. In two hours about eight women turned up, chatted, and got me to sign. Mercifully the staff were nice. Peter French, the young manager, was most friendly and gave me a book on minor classical architects brought out some years ago by their short-lived publishing firm. To show good feeling, I bought in turn the new edition of Ruskin's *Modern Painters*, which I have been trying to find for years. Finally David Burnett turned up, and we lunched around the corner. How sad I am that my association with this adorable man is coming to an end.

Saturday, 28th November

A. and I went to the party given at Claverton by the American Museum Trustees in memory of Ian McCallum. Held downstairs in the large lecture hall. Before luncheon Dallas Pratt,* that cold tied-up whiting, gave a surprisingly warm and suitable talk about Ian. Said that when he first launched the museum he telephoned the editor of the *Architectural Review* to suggest a curator. To his surprise the editor said unhesitatingly, 'I would like to apply'. When they scattered Ian's ashes this morning in the stream running through the garden, one of the friends present said, 'There goes Ian on yet another journey', while his friend Gerry read out the text of the declaration Ian made to the wartime tribunal explaining his objections to serving in the armed forces. He was certainly courageous over this, and apparently he has left £10,000 in his will to the Quakers because of their pacifist activities. 'I suppose we shall never come here again,' said A., as we drove away.

---

* American psychiatrist (1914–94), formerly of Freshford Manor near Bath; co-founder of American Museum.

Tuesday, 1st December

The dailies and weeklies are are already publishing their 'books of the year' (I have not been invited to contribute any), and Bruce Chatwin's *Songlines* seems to be top of the poll. I suppose I shall read it, and probably be irritated. I saw him last week when he came up to me in the London Library. Somewhat changed. Those fallen angel looks have withered. Poor complexion, rather spotty, though he is active and upright again after his severe illness. I said to him, 'You are having a swimgloat.' He had never heard of the expression, nor of its author, Logan Pearsall Smith.*

I have been re-reading Turgenev's *Smoke* in Mrs Garnett's superb translation. What a splendid author, so concise, poignant, easy to read. Every word a gem, and one rushes through it like a tunnel. A contrast to Shakespeare, whose *King Lear* and *Measure for Measure* I have also perused lately. One has to re-read too often, and regards it as an achievement when one manages to understand a hundred consecutive lines. Of course, the gems sparkle more than the broad, unblemished surface of Turgenev.

Wednesday, 2nd December

Abominable day in London. A. and I went by an early train, first class, but could find no seats in first class coach and eventually found two in second class. On the way back, I had to stand in first class the whole way. Went to see Casey. His verdict on my eyes not good. I need to see an oculist who may provide me with a prism. If that does not work, then another operation, because the two eyes do not synchronise, as I discovered a fortnight after the first operation.

On our return, Ian McCallum's friend Gerry Theaker arrived for the night, bringing two bottles of port. A well-informed but awkward young man, who does not look at one when speaking and has a jerky way of beginning sentences. M. tells me alarming stories about his private life – tying boys to trees, etc.

Thursday, 3rd December

John and Emma Poë came to tea in Bath. He a very *bien* and dull soldier; she has a square face like her mother Betty Batten. She really

---

* American writer and bibliophile (1865–1946), whom J.L.-M. knew in London in his last years; a coiner of words and expressions.

wished to talk to A. about Betty's past, but A. didn't want to meet them. She does not have a comfortable relationship with Mairi Bury,[*] who is her trustee. I dare say Emma, being a conventional girl, showed her disapproval of her mother's friendship with Mairi.

Saturday, 5th December

Elaine[†] brought by Simon and Tricia[‡] to luncheon here. They all looked miserable. After luncheon Simon took me aside in the kitchen and announced that the firm of which he was a director had made him redundant. It is dreadful for him and for them all. Fortunately Elaine is quite well-off, and will now stay on in Cyprus so he will eventually inherit her property without death duties. I had imagined Simon was doing well, as he splashed about a good deal, big vulgar cars and the new house. O Lord!

At dinner with the Loewensteins, Josephine talked of the eccentricity of her mother, Miss.[§] Lives entirely alone in a London house, no daily cleaner even. Every evening before going to bed she cleans one room. This tires her and ensures sound sleep. House spotlessly clean, though tumbling down. She will have nothing to do with what she calls 'machines'. Has no television, no radio, no frigidaire, nothing which can go wrong and oblige her to call repairers. Can't bear having plumbers, workmen, carpenters, menders in her house. Won't wear spectacles, reads with magnifying glass. Sees no one. When she tearfully lamented the death of her old friend Lady de Ramsey, Josephine asked when she had last seen her. 'Not for forty-four years,' Miss replied, 'but I live in the past and it is unsympathetic of you not to understand my deep sorrow.'

Sunday, 6th December

A very dark day. We lunched with Nicky and Susanna Johnston, large party. Little Rosie came in after our arrival, and begged to talk to me

---

[*] Lady Mairi Vane-Tempest-Stewart (b. 1921), dau. of 7th Marquess of Londonderry; m. 1940–58 Viscount Bury (1911–68), e.s. of 9th Earl of Albemarle; châtelaine (under auspices of N.T. for Northern Ireland) of Mount Stewart, Co. Down.

[†] J.L.-M's sister-in-law, widow of his brother Dick (see notes to 29 May 1985).

[‡] J.L.-M's nephew Simon Lees-Milne (b. 1939); m. (2nd) 1976 Patricia Derrick.

[§] Hon. Mary Biddulph (1906–91); m. 1929–38 Montagu Lowry-Corry.

alone. She dragged me into the hall, where a woman was suckling her young, so we sat on the stairs, where she described her nine months in prison. She went to three, the first, Holloway, the worst. The wardresses peddled drugs to the prisoners and were mostly lesbian. If you did not respond to their advances – and R. did not – they took it out on you. R. made up her mind early on to write a book about her experiences. It was this which kept her going. The worse the experiences, the better copy for the book. That is how she consoled herself.

Wednesday, 9th December

To London for the night at Brooks's. M. called on me at six, rather pale and breathless, having come from the Lister Hospital where he is being treated for some tormenting allergy. The woman who examined him told him he was 'a wreck' and she would have to sort him out. This sort of treatment always delights M. Then the dinner in the subscription room given by the Devonshires for Pam Jackson's eightieth. Woman looking splendid in shimmering gold. I didn't enjoy it much, being placed between Sophie Cavendish and Mrs Richard Bailey.* Opposite me were E. Winn and Jonathan Guinness† who were enjoying animated conversation and fun. I tried to join in without causing offence to my neighbours. But I was feeling happy, for earlier, at Moorfield Hospital, a charming Mrs Macleod had provided a prism for my left eye, a mere plastic lens which she stuck on the back of the glass lens as a temporary measure. But it has stopped, or at least substantially reduced, my double vision. Such a relief.

Thursday, 10th December

Nick, looking splendid in dark suit, breakfasted with me at Brooks's. So charming, sweet and interested. I really love this boy. He 'made' such a good breakfast too, which I always like – bacon, sausages and eggs, plenty of brown toast and coffee.

---

* Rosemary Mitford (b. 1911); m. 1932 J.L.-M's school contemporary Dick Bailey (1908–67). (See notes to 29 June 1985, 26 March 1986, 28 July 1986. Both Rosemary and Dick were first cousins of the Mitford sisters; Rosemary was the elder sister of Clementine Beit.)

† Hon. Jonathan Guinness (b. 1930); eldest son of Diana Mosley by her 1st marriage to Brian Guinness, later 2nd Baron Moyne (to which title he succeeded as 3rd Baron, 1992).

At midday to visit Ros in bed. Calm and resigned, beautiful in her way, yet longing for death. We talked tenderly, and I felt a deep affection. On leaving we embraced warmly and both wept a little. Each time I see her I wonder if it is the last. She told me to read Laurens van der Post,* whom she considers an excellent mentor for the Prince of Wales – though others think him a dangerously other-worldly influence on the heir to the throne.

Walked from Clareville Grove to the Boltons for luncheon with the Beits. Six of us, with Garrett Drogheda and Pamela Egremont. Agreeable, for we all talked together at a round table, mostly reminisc-ing about Emerald [Cunard].† Clementine getting forgetful and repet-itive. She offered to send me a new book on Bonnie Prince Charlie's affair with his Sobieska cousin, and I offered to send her *Venetian Evenings*. Lady E. a real beauty, only a little faded in her sixties; extremely elegant, tall and upright, her hair dressed like a great Edwardian lady. Wearing lovely white satin blouse with diamond brooch at neck. I was surprised to notice a little down on her lip and chin, strange for someone so self-consciously chic. Though friendly and communicative today, I suspect she is an arm-lengthener. I can't but be fascinated.

Saturday, 12th December

This was an event. When Peter Scott‡ thanked me for my congratu-lations on his CH (oh coveted honour!), he invited us to visit him one day at Slimbridge. So I let four months elapse and wrote again, goaded by A. He replied asking us to come this morning 'for a sherry'. His little house what one would expect, modern, modest, commonplace, without taste good or bad. Received at door by wife, no-nonsense woman in jeans. Peter bustled forward to greet us, a little gnome, bent

---

* South African-born writer (1906–96) interested in mysticism and the Jungian concept of the collective unconscious.

† Maud Burke of San Francisco (1872–1948); m. 1895 Sir Bache Cunard; London hostess.

‡ J.L.-M. had often met Peter Scott with his mother in the 1930s and 1940s. In *Fourteen Friends* (published seven years after Scott's death in 1989), he wrote: 'He was always jolly with me, while knowing full well that I was not his sort. Nor was he mine . . . There was nothing cosy about his extraverted wardroom bonhomie . . . He was a high-minded, con-ventional, successful leader of men; and as a conservationist of wild life, without an equal. But he was a self-centred philistine without a glimmer of humour, and with a heart as cold as stone.'

and small, white face, dewlaps. Never an Adonis, he was once attractive, sturdy and vivacious. Now an elder of great distinction. Very welcoming, hands outstretched, how delightful to see you at last, etc. Affability itself. Led us to their large studio room, walls of books, unfinished paintings of birds on easels. Untidy and cosy, the working man's den. The entire west wall is a huge picture window looking out onto a large pond, on which are swarms of birds, some of great rarity, two mud islands covered with squatting ducks, geese, swans. An astonishing and wonderful sight. Then a *huroch* – and a flotilla of Bewick swans descend like aeroplanes. Indeed, some geese have to take off from a sort of airstrip, and descend like Concorde. At times the sky almost black with birds.

Peter produced the actual telescope which had belonged to Thomas Bewick,* through which we looked at the Bewick swans. Or rather, A. managed to – the vision was too narrow for me to see much, but it was nevertheless an experience. He says Slimbridge costs £3 million a year to run, largely owing to the huge quantities of grain needed for feeding. While we watched, a boy appeared with a barrow, slinging a shower of grain. Those birds which knew their turn had not arrived waited, while others surged forward. What a wonderful and praiseworthy enterprise. Each migratory bird is ringed. Most are known individually and given nicknames, Big Brother, the Little One, etc. One of the girls who keeps the records in the office visited Russia, where in a bay on the Baltic she instantly recognised Big Brother and wife, paddling on the shore.

A fascinating hour and Peter most affable. He got on splendidly with A., a fellow ornithologist, and asked her what I did. I asked Peter if the swans had been affected by the Chernobyl fall-out.† He said no, not at all; it was a coincidence that the disaster occurred just at the time they were moulting.

Thursday, 17th December

I thought I should tell Dr King about the swelling on the right side of my face. He took it seriously and said he would find a specialist to

---

* Ornithologist and printmaker (1753–1828), illustrator of *A History of British Birds*.

† The world's worst nuclear power accident had occurred on 25/6 April 1986 when a reactor exploded at the Chernobyl plant in the Ukraine. It was later believed that the accident had affected the physical environment of the whole northern hemisphere for some three years.

look at it. After consulting Charlton, the surgeon who cured me of prostate cancer three years ago, he is sending me to a Mr Young in the Circus. Odd thing is that I feel no pain and am not conscious of any growth inside the cheek, though Dr K. seems to have detected one. Poor little Audrey who lunched with us on Tuesday has a large growth like a corn beside her nose. I told her of my trouble to cheer her up. Strange that we should both sprout facial growths, hers on the outside and mine on the inside.

The 'Age of Chivalry' exhibition at Burlington House is stupendous. During the hour I spent there I saw three rooms, galloping around the remainder to see what lay in store for me next time. What exhibits! Whole fifteenth-century windows transported from Canterbury Cathedral; a recumbent effigy of a thirteenth-century Duke of Normandy, painted crimson and gold; figures from the West front of Wells Cathedral; twelfth-century illuminations; little sculpted heads . . . it was all so stirring, so deeply moving, so devotional, that I came away feeling that these early Gothic centuries had produced the greatest works of art the world has ever known. They belong to some seraphic universe, even when depicting depravities and mental cruelties. I want to see them again and again.

Selina Hastings came here yesterday after calling on Daphne Fielding to talk about Evelyn Waugh. She was so exhausted, having just returned from France, where she had seen Diana [Mosley] in Paris and Graham Greene[*] in the South, that A. put her to bed in the afternoon. By the time I returned from Bath she was up, and as bright as the proverbial button. As A. says, the little kitten face is an illusion. She told us that Caroline Blackwood[†] had written a strange sort of book about Maître Blum[‡] and submitted it to *Harper's* for serialisation. It is vicious, not only about the Maître but also poor M., and in S's view unpublishable. Blackwood is not just a demon but a fantasist. She was recently sent by *Harper's* to interview Mrs Kinnock,[§] and was so

---

[*] Novelist (1904–91).

[†] Lady Caroline Blackwood (1931–96); novelist; dau. of 4th Marquess of Dufferin & Ava.

[‡] The formidable Paris lawyer of the Duchess of Windsor, for whom Michael Bloch had been working since 1979, and whom Caroline Blackwood had interviewed in 1980. C.B's book *The Last of the Duchess* – effectively a novel in which she omitted to change the names of the real people upon whom her story was based – only appeared in 1995, soon after Maître Blum's death and not long before her own.

[§] Glenys Roberts (b. 1944); m. 1967 Neil Kinnock (b. 1942), Leader of Labour Party 1983–92; MEP (Lab.) Wales.

drunk that she passed out on arrival. When she came to, Mrs K. could only talk to her for a few minutes before her next appointment. Next day B. delivered a brilliantly written piece, which was duly submitted to Mrs K., a condition of the interview. It transpired that Mrs K. had uttered not a single word which had been attributed to her, and B. had simply made the whole thing up. I must warn M.

Saturday, 19th December

We motored to Tisbury for the luncheon given by Humphrey and Solveig* to Janet Stone on her seventy-fifth birthday. Held in a restaurant in this small village. Excellent it was too – fresh smoked salmon, chicken in delicious sauce, *crème brûlée*. Humphrey an adorable man, saintly and sympathetic like his father Reynolds. Solveig charming too. A lovely family party, in which we felt honoured to be included. I was put between Janet and her very pretty and intelligent daughter Emma.† Emma's sister Phyllida also beautiful. After the pudding we all changed places, and I found myself talking to Janet's sister Gabriel Pike,‡ formerly head of the Women's Institute. She talked of her grief over the deaths of her beloved dogs, killed when they chased sheep over a cliff near her Pembrokeshire cottage. A couple of Dutch teenagers were hiking past at the time and offered to retrieve the bodies. They then dug a grave for them, leaving it to Mrs P. to shovel in the last sods. What sensibility. Janet looked chic in a black dress and hat with a small feather. She hasn't a wrinkle and has the figure of a girl. Has just given all her papers to the Bodleian. How sad that the party could not be attended by her brothers, the late Bishop of Worcester, Archbishop of Melbourne and Archdeacon of New Zealand.

Tuesday, 22nd December

My appointment with Mr Young at 20 The Circus. Nice middle-aged man with close-cropped grey hair. In very little time he examined the inside of my mouth and the glands of my throat and neck, and pronounced that he would have to do a biopsy, for which he fixed another

---

* Humphrey Stone (b. 1942); typographical designer; m. 1968 Solveig Atcheson.
† Emma Stone (b. 1952); m. 1977 Ian Beck, illustrator.
‡ Gabrielle Woods (1916–99); Chairman of W.I., 1961–6; m. 1942 Major George Pike.

appointment Wednesday next. It would only take half an hour and I could go home immediately afterwards. When I asked what I might be in for, he replied cautiously that once he knew what it was, he would know how to treat it. I returned to Badminton feeling low and apprehensive. Darling A. made light and refused to show any anxiety. Together we watched telly – first Elisabeth Welch,* who must be eighty, singing delicious pre-war songs by Gershwin, then Horowitz playing Mozart's Piano Concerto 23. We lay on her bed, our heads touching and hands clasped. I try not to fear the worst, but wonder if anything is now worthwhile. Do I continue struggling with the Bachelor Duke's boring diaries?

Friday, 25th December

We have Burnet [Pavitt] staying, a perfect guest. He is happy doing anything or nothing, and full of chat and entertainment. A. overwhelmed me with presents. I wish she would not give me quite so many things that I do not need, like a small wireless set. The more such gadgets one has, the more they have to be replenished. In addition she gave me a large red pullover, a pair of woolly-lined gloves, two pairs of pyjamas, and an ivory-backed hairbrush to replace the one I lost in a train. How good and kind she is; yet I feel sick at heart. We lunched at the House – more exchange of little gifts. Ate in the big dining room, David at head of table, double doors left open so he could look straight through the lesser dining room and the windows into the Park and East Avenue. David looking bored, that look that freezes me up. I sat next to Caroline, great fun, and that loony girl Tracy [Worcester], talking of Friends of the Earth. Eddie† in another world. Beautiful table, long white cloth covered in shining silver, some twenty seated. Marvellous banquet, turkey melting in mouth, best plum pudding ever. A sauceboat of flaming brandy was brought in, terrifying the girl who carried and also me as I ladled it onto my plate. Crackers, and paper hats. I managed to acquit myself with reasonable cheer. Burnet enchanted by the beauty and lavishness of the scene, wondering that it did not engender revolutionary feelings. It is certainly civilised living – or is it? Such empty heads, the children.

---

* Legendary *chanteuse* whose career spanned eight decades; she also starred in many British films of the 1930s, appearing alongside Paul Robeson and Rex Harrison.
† See entry for 13 March 1985.

Sunday, 27th December

We lunched with the Jacob Rothschilds at Stowell Park, a house full of nice things. Most of these inherited, but I coveted a collection of ravishing framed drawings of sheep by Henry Moore.* Serena very friendly. Jacob has extremely good manners and draws one out. But the focus of attention his mother, Barbara Ghika.† Now very frail, she maintains an extraordinary dignity and presence, though absolutely natural and uncontrived. Looks like porcelain. I can never forget her irresistible appeal when I first met her in Rome in the days when she was living with Rex Warner. I see her now – in the back of a horse-drawn carriage sailing down the Corso; in churches, gazing languidly and intelligently at ceilings without expressing an opinion; in the Campagna, sitting on the grass with a wide-spread skirt around her, amongst wild flowers and butterflies, waiting, as if time meant nothing, for Rex and me to return from some wayside church we were examining.

Wednesday, 30th December

To Bath Clinic this morning for my biopsy. A. insisted on accompanying me, the greatest solace having her there. I felt nothing. There was no interval between local anaesthetic and operation, which took about twenty minutes. I await the verdict next Tuesday. If it is malignancy, I dare say I shall be upset. Yet I am reaching a condition of resignation owing to my advanced age, brought home to me when I am shown a photograph of my red, haggard face. After all, my life is almost done, cancer or no cancer, and my working life finishing. I wish, oh how I wish it had been more successful.

The tumour on J.L.-M's cheek was found to be malignant; but the treatment, though painful and protracted, proved successful. He was to live for another ten years, during which he wrote his biography of the Bachelor Duke (the first of his books to be published by John Murray), finally found a publisher for his novel, and brought out two volumes of reminiscences and two more of diaries. Almost to the end, he remained lucid and active – and kept up his journal.

---

* Artist and sculptor (1898–1986).
† Barbara Hutchinson (sister of Jeremy, Baron Hutchinson); m. 1st (1933–46) 3rd Baron Rothschild, 2nd 1949 Rex Warner, 3rd 1961 Nico Hadjikyriakou-Ghika, painter (she d. 1989).

APPENDIX

AMERICAN VISIT, OCTOBER–NOVEMBER 1985

These are J.L.-M's 'disjointed notes' of his only trip across the Atlantic, from 30 October to 15 November 1985, to be read in conjunction with the brief account in his main diary. (Lists of paintings which he saw at various galleries are omitted.)

'Welcome to Washington! Welcome to Washington!' a voice calls from a tape as we wait one and a half hours queueing behind a barrier to have our passports inspected.

Air of opulence in Washington. No litter; a clean city. Many noble classical buildings, particularly in Capitol area.

Eighty per cent of citizens are black. We are told that many blacks have raised themselves to middle-class status and are rich. The Mayor a black. All taxi-drivers, servants and waiters black. Friendly and civilised nevertheless. Why cannot this be the case in England? Blacks seem content, though most of their jobs menial.

In lecture room of National Gallery the chairs are of steel – handsome, not vulgar like our stack-a-by chairs.

Airport central building very handsome with Chinese flavour. The modern buildings far better than ours and even the dreary tower blocks not shoddy.

Taxi-drivers both here and in New York exceedingly stupid. Don't know the most famous landmarks like National Gallery in Washington or Metropolitan Museum in New York.

We drove in funny old double-decker London buses from hotel to White House. Escorted by two outriders on motor-bicycles waving aside traffic, sirens blaring. Faces of people standing on pavements aghast with surprise. Received by Mrs Reagan, supported on both sides by uniformed attendants. Manner very sweet. Handsome face, but head too big for body, of which scarcely anything left. A cavity in place of diaphragm. Anorexic? When asked how she kept so slim, she answered, 'Worry'. Our names announced one by one as we filed past her. Then allowed to roam. Rooms very pretty indeed. Decorated work – what we call Regency style.

Given luncheon in Capitol. The English MPs and peers separated and allowed into Chamber. We herded into Rotunda. Given buffet lunch-eon. A. told not to sit on window sill.

Tony Mitchell and I took Metro. A black lady in a glass box came out to show us how to buy a ticket from a slot machine. Metro vaulting like that of Pantheon, Rome, huge grey square panels. Impressive, but the grey of cement always dreary.

Lunch Margeries* at French Embassy, Edwardian Tudor mansion with large garden. Sat next to a Dupont lady of eighty. Enormously rich. She drove off in a Rolls-Royce the size of a lorry and equipped with tables and chairs and cocktail bars. On my other side a very young man who helped Gervase [Jackson-Stops] with arrangement of pictures [at 'Treasure Houses' exhibition]. Called Russell,† works at Christie's, immense self-confidence like David Carritt‡ of old days. Always amazes me how they can be so self-assured. I envy them.

---

* Emmanuel Jaquin ('Bobbie') de Margerie (1924–91); French Ambassador to London, 1981–4, and Washington, 1984–7; m. 1953 Hélène Hottinguer.
† Francis Russell (b. 1949); Director of Christie's.
‡ Art expert (1927–82), renowned for the 'discovery' of lost or unrecognised master-pieces. J.L.-M. recounted his first meeting with him (5 November 1946) in *Caves of Ice*: 'A perky youth dashed into the room [at Upton] with abounding self-confidence . . . I must say his knowledge of pictures and everything else touched upon was astounding . . . Though polite he is too sure of himself.'

Beauty of highways through miles and miles of woods. Trees in full autumn colour, brighter than to be seen in England. Deep red of dogwood. Miles of forests.

Mount Vernon. George Washington's* house. Grand in miniature. Really covetable. Connected to balancing wings by open corridor colonnades thro' which glimpses of wide Potomac River, absolutely unchanged site and view since W's day. Preserved not without expenditure of much money and effort by the Ladies of Mount Vernon who look after it beautifully. Nice furniture, generous staircase hall. Bedroom in which he lived upstairs. An intimate house with appurtenances.

Stratford, where we stayed in a log cabin. Cold night, slept badly. This house of General Lee† v. beautiful red brick. Vanbrughian chimney stacks, conjoined and arched at either end – not unlike those at Frampton. Said to be miniature version of Haddo, Archie Aberdeen's‡ house (where Archie promised to take me, but his death intervened). You mount exterior steps to *piano nobile*. Bedrooms all below in basement. First floor one unlit attic. Evening reception by candlelight. In every room a ghost-like figure advances, dressed as a nineteenth- (or is it eighteenth?) century maid in mob-cap, who curtseys and chats about the room. Rather maddening. Extreme gentility and politeness.

Camden, early Victorian, owner Mr Pratt, 100 years old. His baby brother was killed in Civil War in year 1862 by cannon fired from battleship in river which destroyed the tower. Rooms unaltered since decorated by his mother in 1857. Astonishing link. Shook hands with Mr Pratt seated in armchair. Not gaga. Pratt a descendant of Lord Camden. Something touching in the links with England. Desire to build houses like those the early settlers remembered at home. Architect's elevation drawings of Camden signed N. G. Starkwether of Baltimore. Lady in short speech of welcome said she started motoring to Washington to meet the [exhibition] lenders at the dinner given, then funked meeting the dukes and lords. 'But now looking at you all you don't seem so terrifying as I thought.'

---

* George Washington (1732–99), 1st President of United States, who lived the life of a gentleman farmer at Mount Vernon, 1759–74.
† Robert E. Lee (1807–70); commander-in-chief of Confederate armies in American Civil War. Stratford, in Westmoreland County, Virginia, had originally been acquired by his English-born ancestor Richard Lee (d. 1664).
‡ Lord Archibald Gordon (1913–84); s. brother 1974 as 5th Marquess of Aberdeen.

Sabine Mount, circa 1730, still owned by ninth generation of family which built it. Nice, simple country people. House *un peu délabrée*. Portraits of ancestors very indifferent by local American artists on canvases now undulating from frames.

Along the roadsides of Virginia and at corners of highways are tatty little tin boxes with 'The Daily Progress' painted thereon into which newspapers for each residence are shoved by the newspaper boy.

Pouring rain spoilt our too-short stop for night at *Williamsburg*. Town so charming, each house such a perfect fake of Queen Anne that I thought how happy one would be to live there. Governor's Palace a marvel of fakery. Brickwork with blue headers. Entrance hall decoration of armour; circle of rifles on ceiling and walls. Brass door furniture. No detail overlooked. Contemporary garden layout.

Bremo. A Palladian villa. Seldom seen. Never open to public. Large estate. The son and friend had been shooting wild turkeys. A very important house built 1819 by General Cocke[*] (whose descendants received us). Brown columns to portico. Style in England would be *c.* 1720. Opens on hall with Doric entablature. Large pedimented doors, the inner broken for a bust. Wainscot grained concealing goodness knows what woods underneath. Sash-bars not thick but thin. So too are other features, late Georgian like the staircase. Far front overlooking James River like Inigo Jones's Queen's House. Recessed portico 'in antis'. Balustrade round roof. Pair of wings, pilastered & pedimented, now joined to main block by colonnades (not good). A lived-in house. Very high on my list.

Charlottesville. University planned, built and organised by Jefferson,[†] more or less on plan of Marly.[‡] Unlike Marly the facing pavilions are linked by long roofed colonnades. Drenching rain & lightning while there. Professor Frederick Nicholls, well-known authority on Jefferson, gave us a talk while we ate picnic luncheon.

---

[*] John Hartwell Cocke (1780–1866); co-founder with Jefferson of University of Virginia; opponent of slavery.

[†] Thomas Jefferson (1743–1826); author of American Declaration of Independence, 1776; US Minister to France, 1785–9; Secretary of State, 1790–3; Vice-President, 1797–1801; 3rd President of United States, 1801–9; founded University of Virginia, 1819.

[‡] French royal demesne near Orsay where Louis XIV constructed a château and created a park; the château was destroyed after the Revolution, but the park and its pavilions remain.

My review of Ann Fleming's* letters apparently published in Thursday's *Times*.

Monticello. All the quirks of that strange mind. Like Leonardo, like Goethe, Jefferson a great experimenter. The finished building inside – for we only saw that and by candlelight – most unsatisfactory as a home. An architectural masterpiece in accordance with the rules, making little allowance for the practical. Again the pivotal door between dining room and serving room, an improvement on the hatch: door between hall and saloon. You open one valve and the other follows suit; an odd contraption beside the fireplaces (these more neo-classical than Palladian with oval Adamesque plaques) which brings bottles of wine on a sort of elevator from the basement. seven-day clock over front door on long pulleys either side of door hanging, four weights to each rope which as they descend are measured against Mon., Tues., Wed. marked on wall. Jefferson miscalculated and had to make holes in floorboards so that weights could descend to basement. Face like a kitchen clock.

No fine staircase. He disapproved of the waste of space they entailed. So provided two very mean, narrow, twisted stairs with high treads to bedroom floor. There, window levels uncomfortably on the floor level. Several unsightly skylights in ceilings sloping. Jefferson's bedroom ingenious. Bed within recess so that by getting out of bed on one side he stepped into bedroom: from other side into his library or working room, his quills, geometrical instruments, globes, architectural desk, long reclining leather chairs with book-rest still in place.

Candlelight though agreeable does not enable one to study detail. On arrival by bus we pitched into a deluge of rain. Tail-end of Hurricane Wong. Never experienced the like. Within fifty yards my trousers drenched in spite of waterproof and umbrella. Made tremendous mistake in leaving my galoshes in Washington. Consequence wet feet all these days.

Ghastly cocktail party at Monticello, followed by another at Farmington Country Club where we staying, followed by ghastly dinner party with music. Inaudible. Sat between Virginian matron in red plush called Sacher and Jack Wheeler-Bennett's widow, Lady

---

* This volume, edited by her literary executor Mark Amory, had just been published by Collins.

W.-B.,* who is Virginian and has retired here. Voice like a mosquito. Heard not a word, but a jolly, frail little old lady.

Next morning, Prof. Nicholls offered to take us back to Monticello before departure at 8.30. A. and I both up and packed by 7.45, but decided through sheer weakness to put it off. I shall regret this folly all my remaining days.

Oatlands, near Leesburg, very boring house and garden belonging to National Trust. And a mile away *Oakhill*, very different kettle of fish where we were all given delicious luncheon on ground floor in sort of crypt. This a large house in red brick. Austere outside, luxurious within. Plan of central hall, two large rooms flanking and others behind. Rich owners called Prendergast; probably weekenders, different from the real, slightly impoverished landed gentry such as still live in Virginia.

'I like your suit', said the doorman this morning as I left Washington hotel. And one of the guards at the Smithsonian asked me, 'Are you a prince?' I answered 'Yes' so as not to disappoint him.

1914, Rittenhouse Square, Philadelphia. We stay with Henry McIlhenny who has three Victorian houses knocked into one. Consequently with three staircases one is constantly confused. Rest of square, once grandest residential area in the city, to be compared with Berkeley Square, and has changed since A. last stayed here in 1954.

House filled with choicest furniture, silver and pictures, all of which Henry will bequeath to the Art Gallery of which he was Chairman and has been and still is a munificent benefactor. He is a sort of Medician prince – in old age very stout with enormous head and ears and paunch. His grandfather was an Irish peasant. He is now a figure of great stature in this city. Loves gossip; has extraordinary affected voice like a corncrake; very kind and generous. Without being an intellectual he is very knowledgeable about the arts and music.

11 November called here Veterans' Day. Were motored in the morning to Andalusia property on Delaware River, residence since

---

* Ruth Harrison Risher of Charlottesville, Virginia; m. 1945 Sir John Wheeler-Bennett (1902–75), historian and secret service agent, British Editor-in-Chief of captured German Foreign Ministry archives, official biographer of King George VI.

seventeenth century of extremely rich Biddle family.* Our host, Jimmy Biddle, attractive man in fifties. Lives in a Gothic cottage the size of a very large rectory. Main house eighteenth-century with neo-Greek front added after Temple of Theseus, Athens – reminding me of The Grange, Alresford. Contains Joseph Bonaparte's bed, for he came to live across the river in exile.

Two Italian countesses to lunch with Henry, charming women from Florence. A. and I took train to New York, club class, free drinks and good service. In N. York stay at Knickerbocker Club, mid-Victorian, comfortable and stuffy.

At six to Mr and Mrs David Rockefeller,† large house in 65th St. Large upstairs drawing room of fine panelling. Again pictures of highest quality – Picasso (naked girl), Seurat, Cézanne, Monet – the lot. Chelsea china and very grand service of Derby of 200 pieces, Mr R. said. A few people assembled. Usual gushing ladies asking about my books. Distinguished ex-ambassador to Russia – Kenyon? – told me that as a young man in the Foreign Office he learned how to draft despatches from Harold N[icolson]. H. taught him that history could also be literature.

We had a good dinner in Knickerbocker, empty and stuffy.

Something very exciting about these towering skyscrapers, forming deep canyons. Their tops lost in clouds. We went after dinner to Empire State Building. Took lift to lookout belvedere at very top, 150th floor, a thousand feet above sea level. Clouds swirling around us. Building slightly swaying, vertiginous and alarming. No view whatsoever. A disagreeable experience.

Although the weather is incredibly warm for mid November in New York, steam issues from holes and grids in the streets.

World Trade Center. Observation deck on 107th floor. Gothic arch, ogee at summit; vertical windows quarter-mile high. Lunched on 44th floor. Absolutely wonderful building. The vertical lines of outside walls. Improvement would be a spire or something to alleviate the square sky-line. Architecture within very acceptable – groined roofs.

---

* The house was begun in 1797 by Nicholas Biddle, banker, poet, experimental farmer, and political adversary of President Andrew Jackson, and expanded in the Greek revival style 1806–35 by the architects Benjamin H. Latrobe and Thomas U. Walter.
† American banker, philanthropist and art collector (b. 1915); yst s. of John D. Rockefeller Jr; Chairman, Chase Manhattan Bank, 1969–81; m. 1940 Margaret McGrath (she d. 1996).

We failed either to see skyscrapers from the harbour or to view the city from above at twilight. Pity. But we only had three days in N.Y. of which one [only] was fairly fine.

Letters from J.L.-M. to the editor add a few further impressions.

Williamsburg, Sunday, 3rd November 1985: I write to you from a sumptuous double room here, exhausted by the schedule of our tour through Virginia. Immensely enjoy visiting the old colonial houses, some museums, others still owned by families who built them *circa* 1720, long before the colony broke away. But the entertainment is ghastly. Wherever we go there are cocktail parties, and meals at which speeches of gush from both sides are customary. Tonight, having seen three houses and a museum here, I struck. Refused to attend another reception and dinner and have ordered a sandwich and glass of wine in our room. A., who won't miss anything and has gone off with the others, will be furious . . .

Washington, Wednesday, 6th November: I like Washington. Some noble buildings, and Georgetown is just like Chelsea. And I like the materialistic side of America. Things work. I spent the whole of today in the National Gallery and have seen half of it. We also went to the Space Museum and saw the film taken by the astronauts which was so thrilling I felt sick. I also walked to the Lincoln Memorial . . . America is not conducive to correspondence. So I merely tell you that I am very well and interested in all I see, but not in all I do. I abominate the entertaining and being polite, the most wearisome practice . . . Did you see me on the TV news, among the dukes and duchesses of the exhibition group?

1914 Rittenhouse Square, Philadelphia, Monday, 11th November: This is like staying with Lord Rosebery in Berkeley Square. Our host is not entirely dissimilar in character, riches and possessions – and tastes, being more overtly artistic than the Victorian PM. He is a millionaire and a sort of king here. Has donated a great share of works of art to the Museum, largely built by his father, a huge neo-Grecian building of honey-coloured stone on a natural acropolis . . . Here he lives in three conjoined houses like Mr Beckford. Every picture is a masterpiece by Ingres, El Greco or Renoir, every piece of furniture by Boulle, Jacob or Chippendale. He's a nice, big, burly gossipy cultivated

Yankee whose grandfather was an Irish peasant who made a fortune out of gas meters. The entertainment has been a strain. Dinners of 16, more often 20. Deaf and dense I strain to catch the drawling gush of elderly matrons who make brave efforts to interest me with accounts of their apartments in Los Angeles and Palladian villas in Honolulu, in a temperature, artificially induced, of 100° Fahrenheit. Every person I have met has been kind and friendly. But oh, I could not live here.

Tuesday, 19th November: I write this listening to the strains of a Beethoven Concerto 35,000 ft above Newfoundland (where my mother, in the 1920s, used to stay for months on end with her adulterous baronet lover). We are travelling in utmost comfort, super-club class, owing to A's brilliance and efficiency. She learnt yesterday that her first cousin was Chairman of BA . . . My word, the expense of North America. Am ruined. Can't say I care for New York, except for the skyscrapers . . . Otherwise the only pleasures I derived from N.Y. were the spoils of Europe in the Museums. Rather disturbing to come upon whole rooms torn from Parisian *hôtels* and English country houses, not to mention the loot of paintings and *objets d'art* . . . Knickerbocker Club very '*bien*' and old-fashioned. One is not allowed to pay for anything, so a bill for every drink and telephone call will be sent to Brooks's and paid by me in dollars. Seems a ridiculous arrangement but the idea behind it, I guess, is that true American gentlemen do not deign to handle filthy lucre . . .

Index

Note: Published works of JL-M are given as separate entries; other works are given under authors. Current properties of the National Trust are given in small capitals.